GREAT LAKES

8 8   G R E A T
V A C A T I O N S

GREAT LAKES

88 GREAT VACATIONS

Doris Scharfenberg

COUNTRY ROADS PRESS
Oaks, Pennsylvania

3 9082 06307874 8

88 Great Vacations: Great Lakes
© 1996 by Doris Scharfenberg. All rights reserved.

Published by Country Roads Press
P.O. Box 838, 2170 West Drive
Oaks, PA 19456

Illustrations by Dale Ingrid Swensson.
Text design & Typesetting by Allen Crider.
Cover Photograph: Satellite image provided by Terra NOVA's
    MapFactory, Los Altos, CA (415)948-1256 or www.mapfactory.com.

ISBN 1-56626-135-X

Library of Congress Cataloging-in-Publication Data

Scharfenberg, Doris.
    88 great vacations, Great Lakes / Doris Scharfenberg.
        p.   cm.
    Includes index.
    ISBN 1-56626-135-X (alk. paper)
    1. Great Lakes Region—Guidebooks.   I. Title.
    F551.S33   1996
    916.704'33—dc20   96-3589
                                                 CIP

Printed in the United States of America.
10 9 8 7 6 5 4 3 2 1

Contents

Introduction

How GREAT these lakes!

Five wide, shimmering seas reaching into America's heartland with more than 10,000 miles of coast, almost 100,000 square miles of surface; the largest fresh-water reservoir on the planet, a wonder of the world.

If these bodies had been called "seas" instead of lakes perhaps there would be fewer yawns from the uninformed when visiting the Great Lakes was recommended. It is news to many, for example, that you cannot see across them. It takes a ferry six hours to go from Houghton (western upper Michigan) to Isle Royale (western Lake Superior), and well over three hours for the Michigan-Wisconsin ferry to cross Lake Michigan.

Their amazing size influences the weather; their international commerce touches the world. These big-picture facts aside, for the you-me-and-the-kids vacationer the Great Lakes is a getaway region with incredible advantages. Easy-reach destinations, four complete seasons, accommodations and eateries for every budget or no budget at all, variety of landscape, and space—free, open and recreative space. Broad beaches stretch to far horizons, glassy-towered megacities contrasting with the lakes' garland of small towns. Fishing, golfing, camping, winter sports, hiking, boating, lighthouses, old forts, wineries, ethnic fests, and history told in hundreds of painless lessons. From great museums to roadside fruit stands—your pick.

Circling the lakes, Michigan, Superior, Huron, Erie, and Ontario (plus Lake Saint Claire, not considered one of the biggies), here are eighty-eight vacation starting points, a list that uses the coast as a base line but doesn't hang around the beach.

There are a few accommodations mentioned, such as restaurants, but limited space did not permit detailed coverage. We have long passed the days when the weary traveler stumbles into town and needs someone to show the way to the inn. Instead, we are greeted by billboards before exit ramps and motel or fast-food-chain logos in bright neon against the night sky. (This writer deplores the sameness franchises have inflicted on our towns, but that's another matter.) If the village of your choice is too small, ask at the gas pump or ma-and-pa diner. The best way to find overnight stops with a difference is in advance planning, although committing yourself to a specific spot at a specific hour may rob you of chances to browse and linger around the places that intrigue you. Plan in general terms, scan the racks at any visitors center, or call travel bureaus (see chapter endings) for maps and folders. The personnel at state border welcome centers are trained to help, even while they can't promote one resort, bed and breakfast, etc., over another. To see an attraction late in the day, it's smart to call ahead for hours.

Spelling note: The Canadians spell in the British manner and some Americans like it better that way. For example, "theater" is becoming "theatre" more and more often. "Center" as in "Center For the Arts" is quite apt to be "Centre". My guide was to spell it the way it was being spelled by the local folks using the word. Mileage and kilometers may have crossed paths, but I usually tried to figure out both.

Eighty-eight suggestions are a beginning. You'll discover a thousand more as the Great Lakes flow into your life.

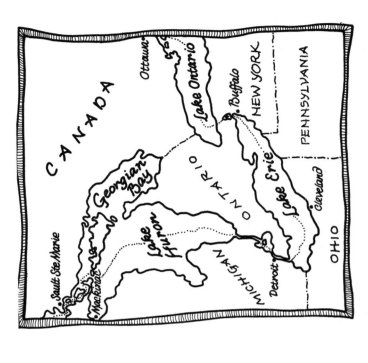

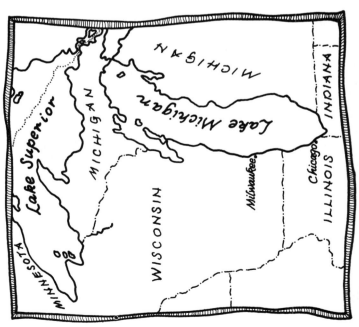

Lake Michigan

1.

An Adventure Called Chicago

An Oz-like skyline stretches along a wide blue inland sea. A Peruvian quartet with native flutes may be playing jazz on Michigan Avenue. There's a barnyard with chickens in a midtown zoo, and the Chicago River runs green on St. Patrick's Day. Expected or surprising, Chicago vibrates with its own sales pitches.

Take the view from the north steps of the Field Museum of Natural History. You look directly up a segment of Lake Shore Drive, across Grant Park, with the Shedd Aquarium and Chicago Marina on the right, massed skyscrapers (this city pioneered them) left and ahead. The gleaming Standard Oil Building, its contours as relentless as an elevator shaft, rises to eighty floors in front of you; the Sears Tower is easy to spot.

On a bright warm afternoon the scene exhilarates like won money.

Start exploring with a "Loop" (blocks served by the elevated train) walk on State Street, through the lofty atriums of Marshall Field's Department Store, out under its clock and past the lacey (like the trimming on a bishop's sleeve) iron entrance to Carson Pirie Scott. The Daly Civic Center has Picasso's giant brooding sculpture; the First National Bank Plaza has a mosaic wall by Marc Chagall. Watch river boats, peer into lobbies, then beam up to the Sears Tower Skydeck for a view from the top.

A few blocks uptown in the elegant precincts of Water Tower Place (high rise mall), Neiman Marcus, and the Terra Museum of American Art on North

Michigan Avenue, you can again see the wide world of Chicago from atop the Hancock Center. Or take in the "Here's Chicago" show, Visitors Center, 163 East Pearson Street. The little castle in the center of the road disguises a Victorian water tower, the only building to survive the infamous fire of 1871, started when Mrs. O'Leary's cranky cow kicked over a lantern.

Innovative Chicago is a sampler of changing design experiments: high-rise brick, set-backs, glass for outside walls, and prairie influences. Architectural walking tours start hourly from the Archicenter, 310 South Michigan. Other tours specialize in Frank Lloyd Wright, the Historic Pullman District, Chicago From the Lake, name-your-era and/or special interest. Tour by boat, double-deck bus, limo, or plane. Chicago even has tours of sites haunted by long-dead gangsters. A ride on the El (not during rush hours) can be a great adventure for youngsters who live far from such trips. Then on to a museum.

Museum of Broadcast Communication, in the Chicago Cultural Center (a beautiful Italianate palace once housing the Chicago Public Library), Michigan Avenue at Washington Street. There are thousands of radio and television programs, and commercials fill their archives; re-visit Howdy Doody, Lucy, and the California Raisins, or see Jack Benny's vault. 312-629-6000.

Art Institute of Chicago, South Michigan at Adams Street. See forty centuries of painting and sculpture and a there-it-is! collection of instantly recognizable modern works such as Grant Wood's "American Gothic" or Seurat's "Sunday Afternoon on the Isle of La Grande Jatte." Visit the Thorne Miniature Rooms before heading to the Museum's large shop and cafeteria. 312-443-3600.

Field Museum of Natural History, Roosevelt Road at Lake Shore Drive. One of world's great museums, this has an Albertosaurus (Tyrannosaurous Rex-like) watching two huge elephants fight in the cavernous front hall. Encircling exhibits act as short cuts to Egypt, China, the South Seas, the ice age, and even the world of bats. It should not be done in a day. 312-922-9410. 9:00 A.M. to 5:00 P.M. Admission.

Shedd Aquarium, 1200 Lake Shore Drive. The world's largest set of fishbowls includes a 90,000-gallon tank holding living coral and tropical fish, sharks, sea turtles and other specimens. Watch divers enter to feed fish and talk to viewers. In a glass-walled amphitheater that seems to merge with Lake Michigan, whales and dolphins cavort in midwest waters. 312-939-2426. Lower fee on Thursdays.

Adler Planetarium (behind Aquarium). Stars, planets, and plain talk about space, telescopes, and time travel are featured. Three floors of exhibits and a zinger of a Sky Show. 312-322-0300.

Academy of Science, 2001 North Clark Street (next to Lincoln Park Zoo), Chicago's first natural-history museum and, delightfully, a manageable size. A prehistoric forest, an Ice Age cave, and Chicago before people are among the dioramas. 312-871-2668.

Museum of Science and Industry, 57th Street at Lake Shore Drive. Gigantic. The MSI tries to explain how things work: communication systems, sciences, agriculture, etc., using a realistic coal mine, submarine, space center (moon rock, too), and Omnimax Theater. All ages and hands-on. 312-684-1414.

Dusable Museum, 740 East 56th Place, not far from the above. You'll find stories of Americans of African descent, arts, crafts, and accomplishments; the guides here are among the museum's treasures. 312-947-0600.

Mexican Fine Arts Center Museum, 1852 West 19th Street. Three galleries host changing exhibits of the best Mexican painters and muralists. One gallery has an auditorium for music and dance recitals by emerging talents. 312-738-1503.

Museum of Contemporary Art, 237 East Ontario. Neon twists, computer art, and experimental photography are on display. If it's the latest, it could be here. 312-280-2600.

Museums for everyone—Poles, Greeks, Lithuanians, Ukrainians, Swedes, and their kin; a Surgical Museum for future MDs; holography, photography, Oriental history, the Jewish experience; Kohl Children's Museum; Expressway Children's Museum, American Police Center/ Museum. Complete lists are available from the visitors center.

Browse "museums" of living humanity, people who share ancestors and who like living near the cooking they grew up with. Discover neighborhoods, such as Chinatown (Wentworth south of Cemak Road.), Little Italy (south of the University of Illinois near the Dan Ryan Expressway), or Greektown (north of the same university). Or explore neighborhoods of economic choice and common interests such as the glitzy Gold Coast (a drive-by eyeful), Old Town (restored chic and nightlife), Hyde Park (University of Chicago area), or the arty Near North (antiques, galleries, "new" Navy Pier).

Mid-Eastern, Mexican, or Japanese—seventy-seven defined neighborhoods in Chicago have unique bakeries, restaurants, and shops. The Halsted Street /Clybourn Avenue crossing boasts (on Halsted) a hot entertainment and dining area. There are rows of atmospheric diners also on the Clybourn Avenue "corridor" near DePaul University. About ten theaters in a ten-by-twenty block on the north side spread from Lincoln Park/Old Town to Wrigleyville.

Theater Tix (312-902-1919) fine tunes the information on Chicago Theaters (over fifty of them). Best bet for the sheer fun of it is Second City in Old Town

Chicago's fanciful watertower was completed in 1869.

at 1616 Wells Street. Contemporary sass that launched the careers of Mike Nichols and Elaine May, Joan Rivers, Shelly Berman, John Belushi, and others of that crowd. Or go to Zanies for top stand-up routines. Warning: Those sitting in front get joked about.

Two animal neighborhoods, the Brookfield Zoo (8400 West 31st Street, Brookfield) and the Lincoln Park Zoo (only five minutes from midtown) offer unrehearsed fun all year, and performance events are constants. Spend a summer evening with the Chicago Symphony under the stars in Grant Park or a concert at Ravina Park. The next day make it a White Sox or Cubs game.

Annually, Chicago Blues and Gospel Fest are in June; the Taste of Chicago Festival and Chi Country Music Festival, July; Jazz and Latin Music, September. Chicago's main nourishment probably comes from deep-dish pizza, thick and meaty, such as Uno's makes on Ohio Street. Visitors looking for a classic meal, however, can hardly top the dining rooms of the big "old money" hotels. Also in the major leagues: Bella Vista, Italian (1001 West Belmont); Old Prague, Bohemian (5928 West Cermak); or the Chestnut Street Grill, (Water Tower Place, 845 North Michigan). Free spirits go to Ed Debevic's for meatloaf, wise-cracks, and wonderfully zany decor. Jammed at meal-times (640 North Wells).

Four thousand dollars a night will get you the top suite at the Hilton Towers. Real people might go to the Midland—great breakfast and less royal price (127 West Adams). The rest of us can find our own luxury on the hotel lists tucked in Chicago area infor-mation: Chicago Convention and Tourism Bureau, 312-567-8500.

2.

Windy City Neighbors:
Northeastern Illinois

In the mega-environs of Chicago, communities merge like watercolors on wet paper; you may go through several towns thinking you are still in Big Windy.

To the southwest, Joliet flourished when construction of the Illinois & Michigan Canal made a connection between Chicago and the Illinois River at La Salle/Peru, eliminating the last barrier to water-borne freight from the Atlantic coast to the Mississippi River. Today's barges use the Chicago Shipping and Sanitation Canal, often leaving sections of the old canal waterless. The old trench has found new life as a ninety-seven-mile-long Heritage Corridor nurturing eleven state parks, thirty-seven nature preserves, and over two hundred historic districts. A real winner among these scenic state parks, Starved Rock near Utica, has high cliffs, several waterfalls, and a park lodge along with modern campsites. 815-667-4726. For more about the Corridor and the towns or parks it touches, drop in at 30 North Bluff Street, Joliet, or call 815-727-2323 or 800-926-2262.

An entrance to the Corridor at Channahon (follow US 6 west from Joliet) gives you more places to hike or bike along the waterway, canoe in it and ice skate or cross-country ski upon it when the ice is declared safe. Trivia note: Billy the Kid and Jesse James were among the diggers on this project and Channahon is the Illinois altitude champ at 1,235 feet above sea level at Charles Mound.

Back in Joliet, the premier showplace is the restored, glittering 1926 Rialto Square Theater in the heart of downtown. Details and programs are available at the Joliet Visitors Center, 81 North Chicago Street. 815-727-2323.

Chicago gardeners like to drive to Momence, about sixty miles south of the city on I-57 to exit 315 and then east for ten miles. If you come in mid-August, they will be having the Gladiolus Festival; but any time from July to September it is delightful to wander roads south of town to see fields of bright colors, from oranges to pastels. 815-472-4620.

Immediately west of Chicago, the Brookfield Zoo was one of the first to take animals out of cages and successfully put them behind moats. Other zoos aped the idea. Brookfield has a new Tropic World addition, a steamy rain forest that makes a great midwinter minibreak. 8400 West 31st Street and First Avenue. 708-242-2630. Also west of Chicago via Washington Avenue, Oak Park was home to Ernest Hemingway, Edgar Rice Burroughs, and Richard Bach, and is a goal for devotees of Frank Lloyd Wright. A treasury of Victoriana is here, too. For tours, call 708-8448-1976.

In Elgin (home of the watch), architecture goes from Flemish Renaissance to Egyptian Revival throughout a big Historic District. Their Elgin Public Museum at 225 Grand Boulevard specializes in natural history and anthropology (708-741-6655), and a neat place for kids is the Elgin Children's Discovery Museum at 38 South Grove. 708-742-4236.

Evanston, Chicago's closest northern neighbor and where Northwestern University is a tour by itself, blooms as a kind of cultural activity supermarket and antique shop milieu with lakefront beaches and super garage sales. For ideas, call the Northern Illinois Tourist Council, 815-964-6482, and ask about the Evanston Art Center, the Mitchell Indian Museum, Northlight Theatre, Mary and Leigh Block Gallery (African, European Impressionists, American Realists), or have them point the way to the windsurf rentals.

Wilmette's Baha'i House of Worship, Linden at
Sheridan Road, is open to all faiths. Forty years of
craftsmanship went into building the nine-sided
domed structure, a gleaming white and lacy artwork.
The Kohl Children's Museum of Wilmette charms the
under-ten-years set—very interactive and creative. 165
Green Bay Road. 708-251-7781.

Up a notch in Glencoe (Lake Cook Road near
Edens Expressway), the Chicago Botanic Garden
blooms with three-hundred acres of demo gardens,
bulb gardens, fruit and vegetable plots, and a charming Japanese retreat. At Lake Cook and Green Bay
Road. 708-835-5440. In Highland Park, Ravina
Park's pavilion serves a summertime feast of the
Chicago Symphony, jazz, dance, and headline soloists.
312-RAVINIA.

Gurnee Mills, world's largest outlet mall, will
elate the binge shopper. Also at Gurnee Village is
the large and popular theme park, Six Flags Great
America. Rides, shows, fun. 708-249-1776. A Gurnee
item you may have doubts about, visible from US
41, is the "Gold Pyramid House". One-ninth the size
of Tut's tomb and plated with 24-karat gold, it is a
real residence open to the public by appointment.
708-662-6666.

The far northern corner of Lincoln's state is an
unlikely place to find Lipizzan Stallions, a long-time
attraction in Europe, but the stately steeds prance
in their famed formations in Wadsworth twice a week
during July and August. 17000 Wadsworth Road.
708-623-7272.

East a tad, you'll find Illinois Beach State Park
and Lodge in Zion—big water, full services, conference
center, and fishing. Look in on the handsome Power
House in Zion for a hands-on energy show. Winthrop
Harbor's North Point Marina, also giving the State
Park as its address, is clearly one of the largest floating

dock marinas of the Great Lakes with fifteen hundred slips, two hundred for boats of two hundred feet or longer, and all the services. Swimming is nearby. 708-662-4811 or 312-662-4828.

This surface-scratching survey barely peeks into the Illinois north country catalogue. How about a Cookie Jar Museum in Lemont, near the Mother Theresa Museum; the McDonald's (Golden Arches and Happy Meals) Museum on Lee Street in Des Plaines; ornate Victorian houses in Geneva; flea markets or riverboat excursions in St. Charles. Farther west, the Illinois Railway Museum has rolling stock of more than two hundred and fifty cars and locomotives, including the Burlington Zephyr Streamliner. Olsen Road, Union (that's the town). Exit Tollway 1-90 at US 20 toward Rockford, then follow museum signs.

Rockford takes its time seriously, starting with a Time Museum and the devices for measuring the stuff of our lives. On North Main, close to the Rockford Art Museum, the Burpee Museum of Natural History focuses on creature life, rocks, rills, and planetary matters. Ask for details on the Tinker Swiss Cottage, Coronado Theater, Midway Village, and Rockford Museum Center. The Rockford Area Visitors Center can give you a full roster of galleries and other attractions. 815-963-8111 or 800-521-0849.

For more information:
Illinois Tourist Information Center,
310 South Michigan, Suite 108,
Chicago, IL 60604, 312-793-2094.
Lake County Illinois Visitors Center,
800-LAKE NOW.

3.

Southeastern Wisconsin: Look Again

Take a child by the hand and come back to Wisconsin. Once a playground with rich credentials, Lake Geneva will never again be the super-elite "Newport of the West," but in new-age Wisconsin luxury is still alive and well. "Old World Wisconsin" in Eagle joins the great outdoor museum list with original farm buildings straight out of Wisconsin's past, and Kenosha's upscale shopping malls rate among the nation's top ten.

Close to the Illinois state line and Wisconsin Information Center on I-94, Kenosha's Kemper Center on Lake Michigan is a prime place to begin. This complex of mid-1800s historic structures on the shore encompasses the Anderson Arts Center, a fine regional gallery, and a large handicap-aware fishing pier for all comers. Grounds are open all year, dawn to dusk, but most of the buildings are shown by appointment. Harmony Hall, on the lake front, rings quite naturally with four-part vocalizing as home of the Society of Barbershop Singing in America. Visit its museum before dropping in on the Kenosha County Historic Museum or Kenosha Public Museum (an eclectic collection of wildlife, Indian lore, and ivory). Complete Kenosha information: 414-654-7307 or 800-654-7309.

Malted milkshakes were dreamed up in Racine, proud locale of a Frank Lloyd Wright breakthrough, the Johnson Wax Building. Here, Wright abandoned regular pillars and used golf-tee-shaped tapered columns to open up interior floor space. The building did not cave in as some predicted, but changed commercial design. Racine's Historic Museum occupies a former Carnegie Library; its Wustum Museum of Fine Arts can be found in the city's northwest side.

11

Big Racine draws are the films shown at the Gilden Rondell Theater on the grounds of the Johnson Company and also a newly renovated Racine Zoological Gardens on the lake front. It's a good town in which to find a charter boat for deep-lake fishing. Complete Racine, theater, zoo, and museum information: 800-C-Racine.

For an inland loop, take Route 20 to Waterford and Green Meadows Farm (where junior can actually milk a cow), then on to East Troy's Electric Railroad Museum, a piece of cake for trolley lovers remembering the lines that used to exist between area towns. Tour includes a ten-mile ride to a rail yard. 414-548-3837.

Take US 43 to Route 83, exit north to Route 99 and go west to Eagle. Signs to "Old World Wisconsin," an outdoor museum, will bring you to the huge round barn/visitors center and a place in the country as it was in the days of your great-grandparents. Ten authentic farmsteads, each echoing a different ethnic heritage, are far enough away from each other to give the feel of an empty territory ready to be settled. An 1870s cross-roads village adds its message. Costumed interpreters are everywhere. Call 414-594-2116.

Drive south to Delavan on the north shore of a lake with the same name for a ringside view of circus history at the Clown Hall of Fame. Believe it or not (as Ripley once said), twenty-six different circuses used to make Delavan their winter quarters, and a jolly host of old-timers from the big tents are buried here. 414-728-9075.

Lake Geneva history includes the rich, richer, and extremely rich. Once, it was lined with beyond-cost houses, including a mansion with a wing duplicating a Buddhist temple made of nineteen kinds of ornately carved wood from Ceylon. Razed, burned, and their lawns subdivided, very few of these palaces remain.

Now guests can stay in wonderfully restored Victorian bed and breakfasts, rustic log cabins, or slick new resort/convention centers. Take informative "steamboat " tours on the five-thousand-acre lake, golf, fish and bike. At Big Foot Beach State Park, 1,900 feet of sandy waterside fun. The park number is 414-248-2528.

As befitting "America's Dairyland" where more than thirty-five percent of all U.S. cheese is made, Wisconsin leads in the number of cheese factories offering tours. Mornings are the best time to go. Try Merkt's Cheese, 19241 83rd Street, Bristol, west of Kenosha and just south of Highway 50. 800-558-3298. The town of Brodhead, west of Beloit near US 81, has two cheese mills: Decatur Dairy, 608-897-8661, and the Spring Creek Cheese Co-op, 608-897-2555.

The land of the semisacred cow also leads in the mileage of old railroad beds that have been turned into bike/hike trails. "The Dells" of south-central Wisconsin and a blitz of natural and show-biz attractions, from scenic cliffs to sky acrobats, are easy to reach. So is the steam train ride at North Freedom and the Circus Museum at Baraboo complete with big top, animal acts, and amazing high-wire feats. A beats-all dwelling/fantastic miscellany museum called the House on the Rock is a place where oddities go to extremes, as in its "Infinity Room," which juts out into space—seemingly forever. Near Spring Green. Call Wisconsin Information Center, 414-279-6856.

For more information:
House on the Rock, 608-935-3639.
Wisconsin Dells, 608-254-4636 or 800-22-DELLS.
Dells Scenic Boat Tours, 608-254-8555.
Tommy Bartlett's Ski, Sky, and Stage Show, 608-254-2525.
Circus World Museum at Baraboo, 608-356-0800.
Mid-Continent Railway Museum (and train ride), North Freedom, 608-522-4261.

4.

It's Cheer That Makes Milwaukee Famous

C heer, as in "Gemütlichkeit" (good feelings), is
Milwaukee talk for "have more bratwurst, chocolate, another beer, cheese...." Words of warmth in this
town are ninety percent food-speak, although not
always in German. A score of nationalities tout their
heritage—and Milwaukee—with cheerful zest.

Site of America's first Polish Basilica, home plate
for the Brewers, folk dance capital of the U.S., Milwaukee hosts the world's longest circus parade in July
and the world's largest multi-ethnic party each fall.
It is a conservative enclave where neighborhoods go
through generations unchanged. Lake-shore mansions
and sleek suburbs haven't dented Milwaukee's blue-
collar pride in large areas of neat frame houses, closer
than walls in a phone booth, with identical roofs and
tidy yards.

A solidly built Flemish Renaissance city hall
straight from an old world stands mirrored in the
glass towers of downtown Grant Avenue in the walka-
bly compact city center. Skywalks link the Boston
Store, Marshall Field, and Bank One Plaza with other
shops, hotels, and the Milwaukee Exposition Convention Center and Arena (MECCA). One block beyond
the skywalks' west end sits the user-friendly Milwaukee County Museum where a model village shows
back-home rooms of Swedes, Mexicans, and other
city citizens. Costumed guides chat about the rooms
while doing ethnic craftwork. Upstairs, dioramas with
sound tracks put viewers into buffalo hunts, dinosaur
battles, and bird habitats. A great rain-forest exhibit
and outstanding museum shop. 800 West Wells
Street. 414-278-2700.

In walking "der brewer's" streets, you expect a
sniff of the hops, but it is more often chocolate from

the Ambrosia factory or the aromas of Usinger's famed sausages. The meat store, with Bavarian murals outside and classic Deutche meats inside, is on Third Street near West State. Across Third Street spreads Maders, quintessential Milwaukee German restaurant. 414-271-3377 or 800-558-7171. The bright new paint in this old neighborhood covers buildings made of locally fired pale yellow bricks. Pale brick won Milwaukee the nickname of "Cream City".

"Clock tower town" would not be out of line. City hall's 350-foot clock tower doubles as a bulletin board reading "Tennis, July 18" or "Welcome Shriners." The four-faced Allen Bradley Clock can be seen from I-794. A clock tower tops the Mackie Building on East Michigan Street where the restored Grain Exchange Room is a Victorian artwork.

Or "Theater Town" would be apt. The splendidly plush old Pabst Theater (where Pavlova danced and Casals played his cello), the Performing Arts Center, Riverside Theater, and Repertory Theater are here, and the Milwaukee Symphony, the ballet, and opera all get rare amounts of citizen support. Ticket outlet: 510 West Kilbourn. 414-271-3335.

Still to go are the museums and other public attractions. The lake-front Milwaukee Art Museum on North Lincoln gives visitors an exciting feeling of floating over Lake Michigan while viewing a wide-ranging collection. 414-271-9508. The Milwaukee Public Library on West Wisconsin Avenue is a 1898 landmark housing the Marine Historical Society, Audubon bird collections, and the Milwaukee Road railroad. 414-278-3000. Mitchell Park Horticultural Conservatory (the Domes) at 524 South Laydon, features a desert and the tropics plus a five-season flower show under separate soaring glass canopies. 414-649-9800. Boerner Botanical Gardens has annuals, perennials, wildflowers, paintings, and primrose paths, plus a huge rose display. 414-529-1870. Milwaukee County Zoo, fifteen minutes from downtown at 10001 Blue Mound Road, has animals to talk to (four thousand species) behind their moats and glass barriers. There's also the Zoo train, Heritage Farm, and fun. 414-771-3040. The house that suds built—ornate woodwork and fancy iron trims the Flemish Renaissance Pabst (beer) Mansion. 414-931-0808.

Miller Brewery offers tours of its facilities. (Only about two percent of the citizens of Milwaukee work in the beer trade). 4251 West State Street. 414-931-0808. Ask the Visitors Bureau about the possibilities of seeing Harley-Davidsons assembled.

The new Bradley Center in the heart of town is home to the Milwaukee Bucks, the Milwaukee Wave soccer team, the Admirals hockey team, and the Marquette Warriors. The Milwaukee Brewers use the Milwaukee County Stadium. 414-933-1818, for information; 414-933-9000, for credit-card ticket purchases. NASCAR-sanctioned races at State Fair Park.

"City of Festivals" events include the People Parade (ethnic floats, marching bands, dancers) in June; Summerfest, world's largest (that phrase again) outdoor music event, for eleven days on the lake front, in July. Also in July, the big Circus Parade, another all-out blow-out starring the circus collections of Baraboo, Wisconsin (one thousand animals, seventy hand-carved wagons, hundreds of performers).

Dine in a different country every week, from John Ernst (German) to the Brothers Three (Serbian) and Bits of Britain. For information on accommodations, restaurants, night life, suburban attractions, game schedules, boat rides (on the Milwaukee River via water taxi or the whole port area and river on a small cruiser), events, and insider tips, ask at your hotel desk or contact the numbers listed below.

For more information:
Greater Milwaukee Convention and
Visitors Bureau, 510 Kilbourn Avenue,
414-273-3950 or 800-231-0903.
Events Fun Line, 414-799-1177. Taped message
updated daily.
Wisconsin Tourism, 608-266-2161. WI and neigh-
boring states, 800-432-TRIP.

5.

Wisconsin/Michigan Link: Ferryland

For two hours there is no hint of land. Passengers
hike around the long deck, settle into staterooms, or play cards in the lounge. They are crossing
Lake Michigan at full speed ahead—if they pay attention, they can feel the faint throb of a hard-working
engine or the rock of a wave, but they can't ignore
the size of the lake beneath them. It is a minor sea,
and they are on a special voyage.

Only one plucky survivor is left from a fleet of
auto/train/passenger ferries that once rolled like trolleys across Lake Michigan, linking Chicago, Muskegon, Gary, Milwaukee, and cities of the lake. Not
easily confused with cruise ships, these working vessels owned by the railroads were large enough to carry
boxcars and autos, while passengers had their own
deck, dining service, and a few amenities. Décor rarely
soared above early bus station.

Ferries were to the lakes what steamboats were to
the Mississippi. However, times changed, interstate-
highway trucking bit deeply into rail-freight revenue,
and the ferries had to go—almost. Determined folks
on both sides of the lake struggled to keep the last
boat afloat until an industrialist who worked on ferries as a young man brought new funds. The refitted

Badger now runs between Manitowoc, Wisconsin, and Ludington, Michigan—the nearest thing to ocean travel many Americans will ever experience.

And it's fun. The 410-foot *Badger* sails twice every twenty-four hours in midsummer, with a slower schedule in spring and fall. There are movies, a cafeteria, video games, spruced-up staterooms (small but private), a gift shop, TV, card tables, and more fresh air than you've had all year. Best of all, both anchor towns are destinations by themselves, and you save twelve hours of driving around the lake.

Manitowoc. Very close to the town of Two Rivers, whose name means "Home of the Good Spirit," Manitowoc also claims to be home of that dietary challenge, the ice-cream sundae, and (until recently) America's oldest department store.

With a history anchored in the workings and legends of the lakes, Manitowoc houses an in-depth collection of Great Lakes ship memorabilia, models and mock-ups, research files, and artifacts. The city once boasted ten shipbuilders and had almost seven thousand vessels at its wharves every year. To tour the Manitowoc Maritime Museum is to float into a smooth sea of freshwater history lessons.

In World War II, Manitowoc marine construction focused on mine sweepers and submarines. In memory of its subs and the local folks who riveted them together, a World War II sub, SS *Cobia*, is shown to Museum visitors who have no claustrophobic problems on a forty-five-minute tour. 414-684-0218.

Post-war freighters needed a deeper port, and Manitowoc's ship-building days drifted away.

Other kinds of collections fill the Rahr-West Museum, housed in a slightly somber Victorian mansion that grew modern wings. Inside, a bright cache of nineteenth-century American furniture and paintings, Chinese carvings, dolls, art glass, and Indian artifacts are found, plus Georgia O'Keefe. Changing contemporary shows are crowned with the museum's permanent ownership of Wisconsin-born O'Keefe's *Birch and Pine Tree No. 2*. Museum: 414-683-4501.

Theater, music groups, and touring symphonies perform in the Capitol Civic Center; forty glistening antique cars are displayed at Zunker's Museum on McArthur Drive. Pinecrest Historical Village, three miles west of I-43 (exit 152), offers sixty acres of gardens, restored buildings, exhibits, picnic space, and special down-home events from May to Labor Day and weekends into October. 414-755-2291. Magnus Aviation has rides from the County Airport by appointment. 414-682-0043. Or find a table at the Breakwater Restaurant (Inn on the Bay) on the lake shore and watch the car-ferry come into port.

Ludington is a smaller port with "Our Town" ambience, glorious sunsets, a long pier for fishing, and plenty of hospitality. James Ludington, who owned a lumber mill, planned it almost this way. Because of its halfway-up position on the lake and a ready supply of wood for steamships, the city of Ludington enjoyed boom years as a port and is now a prime destination for boaters or anyone with an eye on the $50,000-top-prize American Salmon Derby, held in late August and early September.

As Mason County's seat, Ludington is graced by a county courthouse, built in 1893, complete with clock tower and lawn benches. Step inside and enjoy, then gaze at the gingerbreaded Victorian house on the corner of Court and Lavinia Streets.

The Mason County Historical Society has gathered smaller, irreplaceable buildings for preservation at White Pine Village and Rose Hawley Museum. The county's first jailhouse, a one-room school, blacksmith's shops, and other structures removed from earlier sites are arranged to look as though they'd always been together. Visitors may find themselves acting as jurors at a trial or helping with the cooking. The Village sponsors great special events for summer, from vintage-car shows to bluegrass fests. Follow the signs on the south side of town to Lake Shore Drive. 616-843-4808.

The favorite non-event in town is an evening stroll to Lakefront Park to maybe catch a band concert, watch the sunset, fish from the pier, or just give the kids one last romp before bedtime—wide sandy beach, glorious spot.

For the ferry trip, be ready to rise early—the trip to Manitowoc requires lining up at 7:00 A.M. Or for further adventure, head up the coast to the spectacular Sleeping Bear National Lakeshore.

For more information:

Manitowoc Visitor Information, 800-MARITYM or 414-793-2490.

Ludington Information, 800-542-4600.

Lake Michigan Car-ferry Reservations, Information, 800-841-4243.

(Ludington Office, 616-845-555; Manitowoc Office, 414-684-3537)

6.

Up To The Open Door

North from Milwaukee, beyond the drum-roll beat of the Chicago area, into change-of-life pace. Mega-traffic vanishes.

Scaled-down Port Washington is where busy Milwaukeans head for a day of deep-lake sport fishing or strolling the breakwater to an art-deco lighthouse. Walk by the Ozaukee County Courthouse (that's real gold-plate on the dome) and the Pebble House on Grand Avenue built of stones from Lake Michigan beaches.

There are two state parks off US 43 before you reach Sheboygan, a bratwurst meal, and Jaycee Park (beach, waterslide, the wet works). The Sheboygan County Museum is in a former mansion housing a different history collection in every room, at 3110 Erie Avenue. 414-458-1103. The Kohler Arts Center complex, another mansion with additions for theater, music, and graphic arts, is at 608 New York Avenue (at Sixth). 414-458-6144.

Sheboygan's Indian Mound Park contains eighteen effigy burial mounds among self-guided trails in an exceedingly pleasant preserve. It's a good place to take a breather. There are more trails in Maywood Environmental Park, north in Maywood.

Ask about ethnic festivals (bratwurst should be a clue) and cross-country skiing or hiking. Wisconsin has been a leader in turning old railroad beds into biking trails, a great way to explore the state.

Manitowoc, the link to Michigan, was visited in the previous chapter, but again, don't miss the Marine Museum there.

On your way north, stop at the Two Rivers (Berners for an ice-cream sundae fix) and another maritime collection, the Great Lakes Coast Guard Museum. There's also a fishing village with an old wooden lighthouse and shipwreck display. There are golf courses, resorts, and plenty of reasons not to hurry.

Then drive on to Kewauwee (where the world's tallest grandfather clock stands in front of the factory that makes them), Algoma (a fishing center with a winery hosting taste tests), and finally to Sturgeon Bay, official gateway to scenic and legendary Door County.

This slim finger of land pointing out into Lake Michigan has more than two hundred and fifty miles of shoreline, three dozen off-shore islands (some public, some private), eight golf courses, and an artist's sampler of landscapes—rugged limestone cliffs, tropic sand beaches, farms from picture books, woods, quiet lanes, plus a world of wildflowers.

Twelve lighthouses stand guard in an area that has seen its share of shipwrecks. Eagle Bluff Light, built in 1868 between Ephriam and Fish Creek, is open to the public in summer; or visit the 1851 Cana Island Light, northeast of Baileys harbor.

Part of the Door legend comes from having the best "fish boils" in Wisconsin, where fresh whitefish is cooked with onions and potatoes, with a great flash of flame and cameras clicking. Beyond dining on fish, Sturgeon Bay builds boats from freighters to yachts to rowboats. Self-guided tour directions to Sturgeon Bay's historic districts are available at most business counters. There is more marine history in the Door County Maritime Museum, next to a shipyard with the largest gantry crane on the Great Lakes. Include the Door County Museum's variety of historic exhibits on your circuit.

In a region of boats, an old-car museum stands out. Three miles north of the Sturgeon Bay Bridge on Highway 42/57, antique autos are parked on yesterday's streets amid displays of other memorabilia. Then follow your map to Whitefish Dunes State Park or just zig-zag around the peninsula's back roads to nearly hidden bays, craft shops, homey eateries, and off-road resorts.

Ephiam, Fish Creek (take a little theater break here), Egg Harbor, fresh fruit stands (or pick your own), and golf are here. The Birch Music Center in Egg Harbor swirls in light classical and big bands, with featured artists going for a full season.

The ferry to Washington Island off the tip of the peninsula leaves from the Northport Pier. 414-854-2972.

A stronghold of Icelandic heritage, you'll find small museums, an Art and Nature Center, and places to buy weavings from the local looms. The Cherry Train or Viking Tour Train will transport those without cars or bikes, although the island could inspire a statue to get up and hike.

Door County calls winter its secret season, a time when Belgian draft horses draw a sleigh through the streets of Fish Creek and towns are linked not just by roads but by snowmobile trails. The peninsula is also a wonderland of modest-to-luxury resorts, bed and breakfasts, and small inns, so go any time. The Door, you might say, stands open.

For more information:
Door County Chamber of Commerce,
 414-743-4456 or 800-52-RELAX.

7.

Home Of The Packers, Cities Of The Fox

Yes, Virginia, there really is an Oshkosh, and the Green Bay Packers really began as a packing company's football team.

Green Bay fits tightly around the base of a long Lake Michigan inlet, a natural gateway to the upper Great Lakes, cities along the Fox River, and Door County. The river, flowing north, runs through the center of town. Fastest-growing area in the state, if not the Midwest, Green Bay's population hovers now at about 100,000.

There may be ten or twelve persons from that number who aren't Packer football fans, but they are an unusually silent minority. As soon as you settle in your hotel, head to Lambeau Field (Stadium) and the Packers' Hall of Fame. (It's an interesting walk-around, even if you thought Lambeau was a Wisconsin cheese.) Tickets to home games are literally sold years in advance, so don't plan your vacation around seeing one. The state-of-the-art Hall of Fame shares space with a sports arena and the Exposition Hall, close enough to the stadium to walk, but there's a shuttle bus. Call 414-499-4281 for a list of events.

Green Bay's handsome old courthouse is center-piece of the downtown area. Nearby in the Neville Public Museum, a clear plastic manikin teaches anatomy, and geologic history is traced by a 7,500-square-foot showpiece, "The Edge of the Inland Sea." Art, history, and science. 414-448-4450.

The world's largest steam locomotive, the train used by Eisenhower in Europe during World War II, has eighty railroad cars of varying vintage. For train buffs, the National Railroad Museum is more than a whistle stop. There's a one-mile ride in elderly passenger cars and a twenty-minute multimedia show called *Rails to America*. In the reception center and Hood Junction Depot, dioramas, HO layouts, plus dozens of books to buy on rail subjects fill a very large museum shop. It's enough to make a train buff out of a Martian. Take exit 172 to Ashland north, then east at Cormier. 2285 South Broadway. 414-435-7245 or 414-437-7623.

Another Green Bay touchdown point should be the Heritage Hill Living History Museum, where talk is set back at least one hundred years. Forty acres of historic and reconstructed buildings (twenty-five in all) are pleasantly set about, with costumed guides giving lessons in the one-room school or sharing recipes from a farm kitchen. Life in four time periods (pioneer, military life on the frontier, small town, and agri/ethnic) are laced together with demonstrations and re-enactments. It's at the intersection of Highway 172 and Webster Avenue. 414-448-5150.

Ask about the Barkhausen Waterfowl Preserve Interpretive Center, Brown County New Zoo, Children's Museum, and Oneida Nation Museum, or consult the schedule of the Weidner Center for Performing Arts. Neither snow nor night nor New Years Day in the morning stops the action at the Oneida Bingo and Casino complex, with its mall, restaurants, hotel, and free shuttle service.

US 41 links cities of the Fox River Valley and the wide waters of Lake Winnebago. Close to the highway, Little Chute, Kaukauna, Neenah, Menasha, and Appleton were flour-mill towns that eventually converted to paper production (from Huggies diapers to the box your refrigerator came in) as their biggest business. Some delightful Victorian—and rich—neighborhoods in Neenah, Dutch heritage in Little Chute, lovely river vistas in Kaukauna (where the restored 1800s Grignon Mansion invites daytime guests), and Menasha are among the area's attractions. Neemah's Bergstom-Mahler Museum was a private house given to the city along with the owner's art collection. It's famous for an extravagant assemblage of paperweights and a new look at art glass.

Twenty-two feet high, spirited, and flowing with childhood delights, the sculpture entitled *Children Playing in the Rain* by local artist Dallas Anderson has made a popular splash. Take time out in Neemah's Riverside Park and see why. Another hit is the Children's Museum in Appleton, off in one corner of Avenue Mall at 10 College Avenue. Very new (as of this writing), it has been acclaimed as one of the nation's best. Among the reasons is "Grandma's Attic" where kids can dress in period costumes or football helmets, a pint-size minimarket, and a mural of parading mamas with doors in their tummies so kids can see how baby brother looks in his various stages. 414-734-3226.

Appleton was home to the diverse talents of writer Edna Ferber and escape-artist Harry Houdini, the man who made great escapes his middle name. A vivid exhibit at the Houdini Historical Center on East College Avenue has the stuff nightmares are made of—handcuffs, leg irons, lock picks, and restraints, all items from which he escaped. Video footage, more than a hundred and fifty photographs, and tricks you must not try at home are included. The fascination of this man's life has drawn visitors to the center from around the world. Downstairs (same building) is a paper-making exhibit. Watch the basics and make a sheet for yourself. 414-733-8445.

Appleton is home to the Little Sandwich Theater in Valley Fair Mall and the Attic Theater, while Neenah hosts the Riverside Players; all have summer shows. More theater can be found at Lawrence University, Appleton, and the University of Wisconsin, Menasha.

Oshkosh, the man, was an Indian chief made famous by the buttons on millions of sturdy overalls. There's an Oshkosh factory outlet store at 3001 South Washburn, Highways 41 and 44. Oshkosh, the city, spreads out on the west side of Lake Winnebago, largest freshwater lake in the U.S. outside of the Great Lakes. It's big enough for lighthouses at Fond Du Lac, Neenah, and Oshkosh, but only twenty-one feet at its deepest point. There are perch, walleye, bass, and carp in abundance, plus a unique population of sturgeon. The latter, however, can only be caught legally by spearing one through an ice hole in February—which does a lot to protect the dream-size species. To learn more lake lore, the narration aboard the cruise boat *Pioneer Princess* is a super-pleasant education. It's at the Pioneer Inn and Marina, where dining is rather special too. 1000 Pioneer Drive. 414-233-1980 or 800-683-1980. Or sup in the halls of an old mill at the

Granary, a National Historic Site now noted for steaks. 50 West Sixth Avenue, across the river from the Oshkosh Convention Center.

The big BIG show in Oshkosh is the Experimental Aircraft Association's Air Adventure Museum, a premier collection of rare and significant aircraft. Antiques, military fighters, gliders, and an astonishing number of planes built in home garages are here. A replica of the Wright brothers plane, of Lindberg's *Spirit of St. Louis*, a Messer-schmidt, and Sikorsky S-38 are among the aircraft. Five theaters, World War ll hanger, photo galleries, and gift shops are included. It's next door to the world's largest annual aviation event, the EAA Fly-in Convention. 3000 Pobereezny Road. 414-426-4818.

The Oshkosh Public Museum and Paine Art Center and Arboretum (1331 and 1410 Algoma Roads, respectively) are both mansions given over to the public interests. At the Public Museum, the subjects leap from Indian artifacts to Tiffany glass to dolls and a replica train depot on the grounds. At Paine's, finely appointed rooms in a baronial Tudor house are graced with a five-acre formal garden.

The 1883 Grand Opera House, restored and lustrous, adds drama to its concerts, plays, and dance performances. 100 High Avenue. Call for tours: 414-424-2355.

At this point, you can easily reach the Wisconsin Dells, the House on the Rock in Spring Green, and the lakes of the north. Take the time to visit these.

For more information:

Oshkosh Convention & Visitors Bureau,
414-236-5250 or 800-876-5250.

Green Bay Visitors & Convention Bureau,
414-494-9507 or 800-236-3976.

Fox Cities Convention & Visitors Bureau,
414-734-3358.

8.

Northern Exposure, Wis-Mich Style

We've reached a different part of the planet—same lake, same coast, but as removed from the high-intensity life of Chicago as a camp lantern is from a strobe light.

This was once a major logging center (more than five million logs came down the Menominee River in 1893), but never the gateway to China. When the geography of the American continent was unknown to Europeans, it was hoped a shortcut to the riches of the Orient would be found in these regions. Jean Nicolet, first French voyaguer to paddle into Lake Michigan, packed a silk robe in his canoe to be properly dressed when he reached the emperor's court.

Traveling north on US 41, visit the little white church in Peshtigo to learn about the horrendous fire that broke out on the same day as the Chicago and Manistee (Michigan) fires. More than eight hundred lives were lost in that under-played disaster. Farther along, Marinette (perhaps a contraction of "Marie Antoinette) and Menominee (meaning "wild rice") are intertwined so tightly one has to remember a state line, plus city limits, runs between them. History is a shared tale. The Marinette County Historical Museum (off US 41 as you cross the river, on Stephenson Island) tells much with scale models of schooners and a large diorama of a logging camp, plus a wealth of lumber-biz data.

In the Marinette County courthouse Upper Wisconsin Exchange (UWEX) office, pick up a map showing the county's many waterfalls, found on a refreshing little circle tour, spectacular amid autumn colors.

Menominee's County Historical Museum on 2nd Street has more of the area's logging story in a hand-carved miniature camp. At the Michigan highway visitors center, a stone reputed by Indian legend to grant wishes to those who touch it waits for you.

Try to catch the spunky July Waterfront Festival-Sport Fishing Tournament and the county fair in August.

Pull away from US 41 to take M 36 to Escanaba, a coastal route past J.M.Wells State Park and forest recreation areas. Two miles south of the reddish Cedar River, Wells Park gives vacationers two miles of beach on Green Bay. Outdoor center, boat launch, hiking trails, and 178 campsites are on 695 acres. 906-863-9747. Canoeing, boat rentals, more camping, and supplies are in Cedar River (the town) plus info on the cross-country skiing and snowmobiling for which the area gets high marks. Big jump hills are not far away in Vulcan and Iron Mountain, scenes of great ski competitions.

Citizens of Escanaba like to refer to their city as "the Riviera of the North" (hear that, mon ami?), combining small-town homeyness, big-town options, and a long sunny beach. On a one-and-a-half-mile curving waterfront across from big, comfortable old houses, citizens soak up sun, swim, and peek through the Delta County Historical Museum or lighthouse. On summer Wednesday evenings, there's a concert in the bandshell.

The town is justifiably proud of the William Bonifas Fine Arts Center, home of a 365-seat theater, art gallery, and craft classes. There are dozens of places to shop and good big-meal restaurants. Of special historic interest is the House of Ludington Hotel, the place on Ludington Street with the outside elevator and green awnings. Henry Ford, J.P. Sousa, and Swedish royalty have dined here. Classy, delicious dining.

The Upper Peninsula State Fair takes over as Escanaba's biggest August wing-ding on a calendar that includes a Steam and Gas Engine Show. Before leaving, try some back roads (G 38) for ghostly relics from past villages and nostalgic photo opportunities.

Towns around Little Bay De Noc, like Gladstone and Rapid River, dote on their waterside parks, marinas, and pleasant walks. You may have trouble getting the kids out of Gladstone's imaginative park play structure. On the peninsula separating Big from Little Bay De Noc are a few picnic places and an old lighthouse at Peninsula Point.

Fayette, at Fayette State Park on the Garden Peninsula (east shore of Big Bay De Noc, named for De Noc Indians), is not to be missed. The prettiest ghost town anywhere and tenderly preserved in its own post-Civil War time warp, Fayette occupies a tiny sub-peninsula and harbor facing high white cliffs. Close to the cliffs stood the smelter, source of Fayette's income. There's a doctor's home/office, opera house, and hotel (that once had hot running water and a privy attached by a bridge). Life here had pleasantries, especially at boss-level. There were visiting theatricals, a small band, and even a debating team. In the visitors center, a large scale model with narration tells the story of Fayette until 1891 when new iron methods forced a shut-down. Today, however, the ghost town has more spirit than any time since the fires went out, offering interpretive programs, a minimarina, campgrounds, and hiking trails in and around the park. 906-644-2603.

For more information:

Michigan Department of Tourism, 800-YES-MICH.

Wisconsin Tourism, 608-226-2161; neighboring states, 800-372-2737; national, 800-432-TRIP.

9.

Top Of The Lake; A Long Swim To Chicago

From the Bays Du Noc eastward, from the Mackinac Bridge westward, the green-blue world of Michigan's Upper Peninsula changes slowly...with care. Although US 2 is a vital passage to northern U.S./mid-Canada borderlands, it isn't a four-lane expressway yet. That's the glory of it.

With two wide lanes and room for bikers, the highway skims the Hiawatha National and Lake Superior State Forests, a region of waterfalls hidden in deep woods, fishing streams, waves against a world of sand, and the undulating patterns of low dunes. Plus, there are tasty meat pies called "pasties" (rhymes with nasty) for lunch.

Detour at Cook to Indian Lake and Palms Book (not brook) State Parks. The latter wins fame for Kitchiti-ki-pi, a natural deep tureen with water as clear as Irish crystal gushing in at ten thousand gallons a minute. On a raft moved by passengers and a pulley, visitors gaze into thirty to forty feet of water, watch the trout, and see tossed coins go down, down, down. Camping can be found at nearby Indian Lake State Park, with three hundred sites and an Indian museum reminding us of who camped here first. 906-341-2355.

Manistique, one of many French names on Michigan's coasts, once buzzed with twenty logging mills. Today, this largest community on the north shore has excellent motels and hearty dining rooms, plus some of the best steelhead and salmon fishing in Michigan and a wide beach facing lengthwise down three hundred miles of Lake Michigan.

Gulliver's limestone quarries aren't any place to climb around, but take the road to the park at Seul Shoix Point (pronounced SISHwah) and a sturdy old

The Mackinac Bridge:
A Highway In the Sky

It has been called "an iron wedding band joining the Upper and Lower Peninsulas" and an "engineering feat equal to the pyramids."

It is always called beautiful.

Just a few feet shorter than the Golden Gate or Verrazano Narrows Bridges, from cable anchorage to cable anchorage, the bridge across the Straits of Mackinac is the longest suspension bridge in the Western Hemisphere. Like the others, there were skeptics who said it couldn't be done and years of debate before the project began. Yet here it is, a ten-minute slice of your trip.

Designer David B. Steinman insisted on the colors: ivory for the towers, green for the cables and rails. In a realm of blue sky and water, the harmony is perfection, while the plain facts are fun.

Height of towers above water, 552 feet

Length, 17,918 feet

Weight, over a million tons (more than twelve Washington Monuments)

Miles of wire in supporting cables, 42,000

Tons of concrete, 931,000

Tons of steel, 71,000

Open-grill lanes (next to concrete lanes) allow the wind to go through the bridge instead of pushing the road upward. It is one of the safest bridges in the world. $1.50 for cars to cross; $2.50 if you are pulling a one-axle trailer; $3.50 for two axles or bus; $1.00 for motorcycles.

On Labor Day morning, the bridge is open to pedestrians in a marvelous folk-march event that draws over forty thousand people. (P. S. If you "freeze" on bridges, the Mackinac Bridge Authority will help you across. They assist about eight hundred people a year.) 800-666-0160.

lighthouse that likes to have its picture taken. There are few facilities, but the tables make it a nice picnic site.

About fifteen miles north of Blaney Park on M 77, the Seney National Wildlife Refuge gives creatures who need it a wide safe space. Visitors hike boardwalks and paths around small lakes near the entrance to watch masses of Canada geese or single red-wing blackbirds, but they can't go roaming the back trails alone. However, guided tours near the end of the day may have you within camera distance of a black bear, beaver, or fox. A main reward is tapping into the ranger's knowledge of our northwoods ecosystem. Excellent visitors center. 906-586-9801.

Naubinway marks the northernmost point on Lake Michigan; hereafter, you slant toward the south. If the weather is good, get out of the car at the east end of the Cut River Bridge, a surprisingly high and sturdy span, and walk down the lakeside stairs to the beach. It's a lovely, refreshing spot, but not if steps are a problem for you.

A grandly scenic stretch of road, right next to the water's edge, runs between Cut River and St. Ignace. There are no facilities, but it's another place to squander time happily.

Adjacent to the west side of the Mackinac Bridge, the Father Marquette National Memorial, Museum, and State Park (all in one) has lessons of its own. The Memorial is a simple, nondenominational tribute to the extraordinary pioneer priest who traveled by foot and canoe into a cold, hostile territory. His story contrasts sharply with the scene the memorial faces: Luxury vans, cars, and supply-loaded trucks come over a highway through the winds to friendly, thermostated motels. 906-643-8620.

(Note: This chapter concentrates on the top of Lake Michigan—Mackinaw City, Mackinac Island, St.

Ignace—and the world east of the bridge are taken up
as Lake Huron destinations.)

Tucked under the south side of the bridge, Fort
Michilimackinac (one syllable at a time and "ac" is
pronounced "aw") is a remarkable 1712 construction.
Built by the French when France expected Britain,
and perhaps the Spanish, to try muscling in on their
lucrative fur trade. However, the fort became British
in 1760, as France lost its power in North America.
An Indian massacre of the British took place here. For
this and other reasons, the British decided to move to
the safer ground of Mackinac Island. Fort Michilamac,
with high stockade walls, is one of the oldest archeological digs in the country. Sight and sound shows
in the chapel, quarters, and workhouses are worth volumes. There are demonstrations, bright events. 906-
847-3328.

Wilderness State Park, on the south shore's turning point, has no traffic, no crowds, no noise except
the raucous sea gulls. It's an oasis of solitude just a
short drive from the big drawing cards at Mackinaw
City or Petoskey. You'll find lighthouses (some abandoned), trails, wetlands, forests, and thirty miles of
coast. Also, there's cross-country skiing and trails for
snowmobiles—all on 7,500 acres—a destination by
itself. 616-436-5381.

Wind up at a local landmark, the Legs Inn, a tav-
ern/restaurant made from Lake Michigan stones and
lacquered tree roots or gnarls, set on a scenic bluff.
There's authentic Polish cuisine in addition to an
American menu. 616-526-2281.

For more information:
**Upper Peninsula Travel and Recreation
 Association, 906-774-5480.**
West Michigan Tourist Association, 616-456-8557.

10.

Charmed Circle: Harbor Springs, Petoskey, Charlevoix

These are three personality towns, all part of an area predestined for the sounds of swishing golf clubs and flapping sails. In past generations, trains, steamers, and private yachts from Chicago brought well-heeled escapists and their household staffs to summer homes with wide lawns and pleasant verandas. Ernest Hemingway's folks, Sara Teasdale, the Reynold's family (of aluminum fame) were drawn to this pleasant milieu of water and hills. Harbor Springs and Petoskey are both on Little Traverse Bay; Charlevoix is around the bend to the south.

As pretty as the proverbial picture, Harbor Springs is clearly an elite enclave of settled-in money, yet meals in the dining rooms are reasonable and the natives friendly. For a better view, go up East Bluff Drive to look down on rooftops and bay and maybe an incoming yacht.

The Andrew Blackbird Museum on East Main gives insights on Harbor Springs' very earliest history. Postmaster and blacksmith, Blackbird compiled books on Indian lore. Browse the upscale shops then drive north on 119 for a ride on one of the prettiest roads in the state to a meal or drink at Legs Inn, Cross Village, a Michigan legend (see chapter 9). Top Polish-American cuisine is featured, and building fixings are made from twisted trees. 616-436-5381.

Very close by, Nub's Nob and Boyne Highlands are all-year luxury resorts with multiple ski facilities, golf, and a variety of housing. (Nub's: 616-526-2131. Boyne: 616-526-2171.) Go south to 119 and Petoskey, which has been the workhorse anchor of the area, with discount stores, a hospital, and most of the motels. The town's pride and joy is the northside refurbished "Gaslight" district of ultra-smart shops and boutiques. The Petoskey Area Visitors Center at 401 East Mitchell occupies a corner near the vintage Perry Hotel, where such groups as the Hemingway Society like to meet. Snuggled tight against this stylish corner, tiny Bay View has a panache all its own. Bay View started as a Methodist summer retreat; today, its shady streets and Victorian houses are listed among America's largest historic neighborhoods. Ask about their summer concert programs—and don't forget the nineteenth-century hotels, Stafford's Bay View Inn, 800-456-1917, and the Terrace Hotel.

At the bayside, near the pier and park, the old railroad depot has been turned into The Little Traverse Bay Historical Society Museum. Exhibits include Hemingway data, Bruce Catton (famed Civil War historian) memorabilia, Indian artworks, and a stuffed passenger pigeon, now extinct, but once the most plentiful bird in North America. Logging stole the birds' habitat, while gourmet appetites slaughtered millions. 516-347-2620. Beneath the waters of the bay, too deep to be disturbed, stands a rare tribute: a simple monument to the sailors who died on the Great Lakes.

Charlevoix's flower-lined streets (perhaps too crowded in late summer) and neat old houses (and new condos) are positioned between Lake Michigan and Round Lake, the entry to Lake Charlevoix, where the boat population is a reminder that Michigan has more registered boats than any other state. Sailboats, a Coast Guard cutter, yachts, and fishing charters go in and out, taking turns with motorists who patiently wait for the drawbridge to go down. At Grant and Park Avenues are the famous stone "gnome" houses designed in the 1920s by Earl Young. Rounded roofs and recessed doors give them a seven-dwarfs look. The venerable John Cross Fishery still sells its smoked and fresh catches to area dining rooms. Take a scenic cruise on the *Miss Charlevoix*, 616-547-2371, or ride the Beaver Island ferry, a two-hour trip to a Lake Michigan isle where a zealot at odds with the Mormon Church once made himself king. It's a small village, with an odd history, few motels, biking, golf, a lighthouse, and peace. 616-547-2311. Another happy way to go is on the schooner *Appledore* with all sheets to the wind, three times daily around Lake Charlevoix. 616-547-0024.

Charlevoix's Art Fair, Venetian Festival, and Antique/Classic Boat Show bring huge crowds. South of town, Fisherman's Island State Park is special—a natural, unspoiled jewel. There are rustic campsites (no electricity or running water) and a wealth of unmarked trails and beauty. On US 31. 616-547-6641.

Michigan's northwest Lower Peninsula has been dubbed the golf coast, as it's hard to be a long drive from a course. The same goes for downhill and cross-country skiers. The list of resorts with designer fairways and ski runs is too long for these pages, but the resorts cover all pocketbooks and housing needs. There are charter boats and canoes, too.

For more information:
West Michigan Tourist Association, 616-456-8557.
Boyne Country Visitors Bureau (Petoskey), 616-348-2755 or 800-845-2828.
Charlevoix Visitors Bureau, 616-547-2101 or 800-367-8557.

11.

A Sleeping Bear In A Bowl Of Cherries: The Traverse City Regions

In Indian lore, a mother bear and two cubs tried swimming across Lake Michigan to escape a forest fire. The mother reached land safely but fell asleep as she waited, while her exhausted cubs sank not far from shore. The Great Spirit Manitou took pity and turned her into a giant sand dune, then brought her cubs to the surface as islands to be with their mother forever. These are now North and South Manitou.

The "Sleeping Bear" dunes, cliffs of sand rising to three to four hundred feet above the water's edge, form a spectacular crown on a scenic region. Fruit trees (most of the world's tart cherries grow here) bloom in the springtime, vineyards put a rich green corduroy on the hills; bays sparkle; towns are neat and bright. Grand Traverse and Leelanau Counties have growing populations, but undiminishing all-season appeal.

Exploring north to south along US 31, pause at Amon Orchards for fruit and a tour, then go on to the Music House (both near Acme and the high-rising Grand Traverse Resort). The Music House's superb collection of mechanical instruments runs from music boxes to a thirty-foot Belgian dance hall organ and a player piano turning out "Rhapsody in Blue" via a roll cut by Gershwin himself. 616-938-9300.

Rounding the bend into Traverse City, it is clear by the number of motels that you are in popular territory. They edge the two-part Grand Traverse Bay shoulder-to-shoulder until the break at Traverse City State Park.

The sapphire-blue bay was an added gift from the glaciers that shaped the Great Lakes. Glacial action left a ridge down the center, the ultra-scenic Mission Peninsula, splitting the bay into east and west arms. Early French traders called these wide waters "le Grand Traverse," or "the "great crossing." The name held on.

City browsing starts at the waterfront Cinch Park Marina, Beach, and Zoo. Along with elk, deer, lynx, waterfowl, and other born-in-Michigan creatures, a mini steam train gives fun minirides. A tunnel will let you avoid traffic on your walk to Front Street, heart of downtown. Visit the hundred-year-old restored Opera House, history with a busy future. After golden years and dilapidated times, the auditorium is now used for a variety of public and private events. It's on the National Register. 616-938-9300.

Front Street glows with antiques, bookstores, places to eat cherry pie, and schedules of events, biggest of which is the National Cherry Festival in July, an all-out eight-day extravaganza. Any time of year, however, you can fill up on live theater, mainline malls, historic homes, symphony, night life, and boats, boats, and more boats. Two local eye-catchers, the tall ships *Malabar* (two cruises daily) and *Manitou* (three- and six-day cruises), turn into dream boats under full sail. South West Shore Drive, 616-941-2000. Marinas wait all around the bay for boaters and charter boats.

Don't miss a drive up Center Road on the Mission Peninsula to wineries, scenic views, and a lighthouse at the far end—sensational when the trees are in flower.

South of town, the famed National Music Camp and Interlochen Arts Academy, a year-round school, bustle with talented youngsters. Walk among tall pines and hear kids from all over the U.S. and dozens of foreign countries practicing their flutes or cellos. Recitals, concerts, and art exhibits. 616-276-9511. (Interlochen State Park, with camping, is across the road.)

The Leelanau Peninsula (the little finger of Michigan's lower peninsula mitten) lies quilted with vineyards and fruit farms, sewn together with hilly country roads. On the Traverse Bay side, Suttons Bay (place all bets on the Leelanau Sands Casino, just north of Suttons) and Northport are little art-filled treasure towns. At the far north point, the Leelanau State Park is a good place to search for Petoskey stones (wet them to better spot coral formations) and to visit a lighthouse with a museum. 616-386-5422.

The ferry (reservations needed) to Manitou Island departs from Leland, near the prettied-up remnants of old commercial fishing docks, with enough fish nets and gray siding left to give authenticity. A dam with continuing spill-off gives you a chance to see the coho salmon jumping before you go shopping in crafty places. Mexican imports, mostly glass and jewelry, are of very high quality and quite a few are bargains. The Leelanau Historical Museum has a realistic ice-fishing display among its worth-seeing area memorabilia.

More than one and a quarter million people visit Sleeping Bear Dunes National Lakeshore annually, but the glory is that it never seems crowded. Pierce Stocking Scenic Drive turns and climbs through the park for seven miles, with places to get out and see high over the surrounding countryside or along a breath-taking shore. Tramping around freely is not allowed, but there's one giant dune with a parking lot for little and big kids to scramble up—a real challenge—and tumble happily down. There are marked trails for hiking up to scenic overlooks. Books, data, and movie presentation are at the Visitors Center Headquarters in Empire. 616-326-5134.

Canoe rentals are available for those who'd like an easy paddle on waterways that flow through the hardwoods and in the dune-side wetlands. Try the Riverside Canoe Rentals by the Platt River Bridge between Empire and Frankfort. 616-325-5622.

The Traverse City/Leelanau area is famed for great restaurants, some of them tucked away in homey farmhouses or waterside resorts. Try the Bowers Harbor Inn on the Mission Peninsula (elegant), the adjacent Bowery (informal), LaBecasse (French country cuisine), Rowe Inn (Michigan menu specials), Trillium (top of the G.Traverse Resort tower), Top of the Park (downtown excellence), Mabels, Cousin Jenny's, or the Cove, to name a few. Get a real list with numbers from the phone book or visitors centers, along with events schedules and accommodations, then ask the lady at the counter for her favorite. Over twenty-five first-class golf courses are here, as well as a dozen ski centers (with cross-country trails everywhere). There's snowmobiling, ballooning, dog sleds, and VASA (world-class cross-country ski meet) races. ("VASA" is short for Vasaloppet, a Swedish race that inspired the Traverse City event.) Fishing derbies. Boat races. Sunning out on the beach.

That's life in a bowl of cherries.

For more information:
Traverse City Convention and Visitors Bureau, 616-947-1120 or 800-TRAVERS.

12.
Michigan's Wide-Awake Sunset Towns

By rare geologic luck, Michigan has a long chain of lakes immediately behind its western coast. Lake Macatawa (Holland), Muskegon Lake (Muskegon), Pere Marquette Lake (Ludington), and Manistee Lake are among the many lakes providing safe, ready-made harbors for commerce and pleasure. Neither the Wisconsin coast nor any Lake Huron shore has this advantage.

With so many places to pull in out of storms, an endless (or so they thought) supply of lumber for commerce, splendid beaches, and the "sunset advantage," this side of the Wolverine State turned into a travel destination before motor cars were invented. Trains, steamships, and even inter-urban trolleys came up from Chicago and cities of the Midwest to be met by buggies and family wagons.

Follow M 22 south from Empire (but don't skip a walk-around in this little hamlet). It's a pretty road curling along the edge of the lake, past hilly farms, through tree-covered passages, going from one appealing town to another. Near Crystal Lake, the Point Betsie road (watch for the small sign) is a very short stretch to a favorite photo opportunity at the Betsie lighthouse. No trespassing, however.

With scenic bluffs and a great beach, Frankfort was another trans-lake port when the Ann Arbor Railroad Ferry docked here. Lest anyone forget, the east-side road (M 115) into town still has a "gateway" arch with a steamship on it. Near the Coast Guard station, lighthouse, and breakwater, a simple cross marks the spot where Father Marquette may have died. (There's another cross, with the same story in Ludington; not even historians know for sure.) Honeymoon cozy with dining room, that's the Hotel Frankfort on Main Street. 616-352-9671.

Big time in Frankfort is the fall glider Fly-In when the sky fills up with humans who would rather be birds. There are great fall colors everywhere, and it's a beautiful time to take up canoeing on the Benzie River. Detour east on the Benzie River Road to the studio of an area legend, Gwen Frostic, a white-haired determined naturalist and artist who is still going strong as of this writing. She single-handedly established a 280-acre nature preserve while building her business with ancient presses from Heidelberg, turning out prints of flora and fauna etchings and woodcuts. The building (Gwen's own project) and setting are now at near-shrine status. 616-882 5505.

We shudder today at the very idea, but there were over a thousand sawmills in Michigan by 1860, with hundreds of them along the Lake Michigan coast.

Manistee ("Spirit of the Woods") was one more lumber town, but with a difference. When forest fires and total lack of resource management took the forests (now largely regrown), Manistee had enough salt and gypsum to survive nicely in the chemical business. They also shared the coast's ideal fruit-growing conditions, plus one of those helpful lake harbors.

Take a flight over the area or stroll on recently refurbished downtown streets, one nostalgic block at a time. The Lyman Drug Company is a neat branch of the Manistee County Historical Museum; the main branch is in the Holly Water Works plant at First near Cedar. 616-723-5531. The National Register of Historic Places lists Manistee's 1903 Ramsdell Theater, where the summer-play season is extra long. 616-723-9948. Four-Forty West (that's the name) lets you gaze at traffic on the Manistee River while dining. 616-723-7902.

Spend a while in the Ludington State Park, where four thousand splendid acres would make an outdoor fan out of any hothouse plant. There's a lighthouse to hike to, bass to fish for, and 398 campsites. 616-843-8671. For noncampers, this region has no shortage of motels, bed and breakfasts, and family resorts. (See "Ferryland" chapter for Ludington, the town.)

Pentwater's port holds pleasure boats only. It's a scrubbed and wickered early resort town where concerts in the park on summer Thursday evenings have been a steady tradition.

White Lake, Whitehall, and Montague share special attractions, including Montague's Lighthouse Museum, plus the world's largest weathervane. Another is the Blue Lake Fine Arts Camp, a top-ranking music-school facility. Victor Borge, Count Basie, and others have appeared here in summer programs. 616-894-9026. There are lots of bed and breakfasts and family resort opportunities along this coast, as well as calendars full of community events. There's great canoeing along the White and other rivers that feel remote but aren't.

For more information:
West Michigan Tourist Association, 616-456-8557.
Frankfort Chamber of Commerce, 616-352-7251.
Manistee County Information, 616-723-2575.
Ludington Area Convention & Visitors Bureau, 616-845-0324.

13.

Lakeside Bonanzas In Muskegon

T he largest city on the east coast of Lake Michigan sprawls loosely over a wide area, ties in with a great state park, and would like some things in its past to be forgotten. In 1887, forty-seven Muskegon sawmills were consuming forests like locusts on a binge, leaving years of depression when the trees ran out. Eventually new industries arrived, but visitors grew used to smokestacks and a dull town.

Forget that. In today's Muskegon, manufacturing has moved to tidier industrial parks, with old work-a-day structures turned into shops and restaurants. There's sparkle. Waterfront Centre, a former eyesore, is now filled with offices, shops, and places to dine. The multi-shop Muskegon Mall was one of the first anywhere to enclose existing buildings. The Frauenthal Center for Performing Arts (encompassing the old Michigan Theater) and Gallery Row shops are right in the thick of it. That barometer of civic activity, the hotel and convention center, is rarely empty.

One lumberman who didn't desert his town in the bad old days was Charles Hackley, a name you keep meeting (Hackley Avenue, Hackley Hospital, Hackley Park). His house with seven fireplaces and fantasy woodwork, and the Hume family house next door on Business Route 31, are textbook studies of the bric-a-brac era. Open for tours. 616-722-7578.

In the Muskegon County Museum's Lumber Queen gallery, dioramas and paintings are a swift course in area history. It's one block west of Hackley Park on West Clay at Fourth. 616-722-0278. Generating much pride, the Muskegon Museum of Art has been called the finest in western Michigan. John Curry's *Tornado Over Kansas*, portraits of Martin Luther and his wife by their friend Cranach, *St. Jerome in Penitence* by Van Cleve, Hopper, N.C. Wyeth, Homer, and many more are here. There are changing exhibits and a fine gift shop. 616-722-2600.

Wander through the Hackley Public Library, a Romanesque they-don't-build-'em-anymore mansion with incredible leaded glass and stone fireplaces. Or walk in a tight, straight line through the submarine USS *Silversides*, permanently moored in Muskegon after sinking twenty-three ships during World War II. Space inside was so tight bunks had to be put in the torpedo room. 616-755-1230. A fascinating tour.

Change pace at Pleasure Island Water Park. There are high and scary ways to be spilled through tubes and skipped across water; and there's minigolf, pedal boats, and a kiddie area. Michigan Adventure Park includes two rollercoasters and a wave pool.

Don't miss the Great Lumbertown Music Festival, the Miss Michigan Pageant, the Blue Grass Fest, parades, and live music on the lawn. Laser shows may be watched from Heritage Park; there are concerts with old movies by the Michigan Theater Organ Club, the Muskegon Symphony, and fishing derbies. Grab a calendar.

Winter has a rare special. One of only four luge runs in the country (as of this writing) belongs to Muskegon State Park and is generally available to those who want to try it or for Olympic team practice. It has six hundred meters of carefully calibrated curves and a luge clinic. It's $10.00 for the first visit, $5.00 for additional times, plus park-entry fee. There are miles of cross-county ski trails, camp sites, beach, and space. 616-744-3480.

In Hoffmaster State Park on the south side, with more trees, beach, and dunes, the Gillette Visitors Center has sharp lessons in dune dynamics, natural history, and a 180-foot overlook of the shoreline world. It's worth a major detour. 616-798-3711.

Forget dull; remember bright, new Muskegon. It's been around a while now.

For more information:
Muskegon Visitors Bureau, 349 West Webster, Muskegon, MI 49443, 616-722-3751.

14.

Town Of The Dancing Waters: Grand Haven

Two shouts below Muskegon, a trio of towns shares a watery access to Michigan's southern heartland: Grand Haven, Ferrysburg, and Spring Lake. Grand Haven is largest and the only one with water on three sides, but the three are close enough to share the same big events.

The Coast Guard Festival, in late July, is when a stately white cutter wearing a crest on its stack and a painted ribbon across its bow comes into the Grand River from Lake Michigan, flags fluttering and crew standing at attention. The cutter is star and chief honoree of the Festival, followed by a wake of sails, outboards, rafts, tugs, and odd put-togethers that float. A tragedy is also remembered in all this fun: In World War II, the Coast Guard escort *Escanaba* was torpedoed, and it sank with all on board. The whole crew was from Grand Haven. Respects paid, there follows a week of merriment, parades, fishing derbies, and watching the fountain. The fountain is the planet's largest musical spray piece; its jets whirl, twirl, grow tall or shrink, change color, and keep time with everybody's favorite music. Audiences watch from across the river, at the end of Washington, Grand Haven's main business street.

A two-and-a-half-mile waterside boardwalk passes places to shop, have an ice-cream cone, or to go out and see waves trying to wash away the lighthouse. The walk also goes past the old railroad station, recycled into the Tri-Cities Historical Museum. A "puffer belly" and three rail cars sit next to it, permanently out of steam.

Docked just a few feet away, an old-fashioned stern-wheeler makes daily trips around the waterfront and into Spring Lake. Every Wednesday and Saturday morning, a farmer's market is also set up here to vend the wares of a fabulous fruit-growing region.

An historic Story & Clark Piano Company factory has been converted into a boutique mall with eateries. Harbourfront Place on Washington Street. Walk over to the Grand Haven Community Center at Columbus and Fourth to see what art shows, plays, or musical events are due to open. If walking gets tough, ride the trolley, really a perky bus tooling around (with narration) between beach and downtown, connecting (on request) to transports going to the other two towns. 616-842-3200.

Parks and piers are everywhere; beach-combing and pier-fishing merge into major occupations. The Grand Haven State Park is one of the most-visited parks in the state system—short on trees, but with a glorious spread of sand.

Here's the place to try an as-yet-unmentioned transport, a hot-air balloon. The Michigan Balloon

Corporation will happily lift you up, up, and away for an unequaled view of Lake Michigan and Grand Haven. Harbourfront Place. 616-846-8660.

There's marvelous fall color, ice-fishing, and cross-country skiing, as well as area winterfests.

For more information:

Grand Haven Area Visitors Bureau, 616-842-4910 or 616-842-4499.

15.

New Furnishings For Grand Rapids

Stand at the door of the Oval Office, then fish for salmon in a business suit one block away—you can do it in Grand Rapids, Michigan's second largest city. Planted as a seedling village on a curve of the Grand River where water bubbled down over a stretch of rocks, the city's fame and fortune came from lumbering, manufacturing, cleansers (Amway Products), publishing, and in some measure from being the boyhood home of President Gerald Ford. The biggest claim to fame, however, has been as a furniture maker without peer. Through mail-order catalogs and the best stores, if the new rocker or bed came from Grand Rapids, it had to be good.

Recently, Grand Rapids has been acquiring new furnishings for itself faster than an eager bride. Expensive additions to the zoo, a lavish botanical greenhouse, new public museum, refurbished civic theater, two new sports facilities (one incomplete as of this writing), and other projects have 1990 dates on them.

Two major museums (one a sedate fifteen years old) are only yards apart on the west bank of the river, downtown. In the 1981 Gerald R. Ford Museum, mementos include letters of outrage Ford received when he pardoned Nixon, an eerily meticulous life-size reproduction of the Oval Office as it was in Ford's time, gifts from world leaders, reflections on Betty Ford's battles and courage, and documentary films. A sobering new display acts as a Vietnam War Memorial. 616-456-2674.

Next door and also riverside, the Van Andel Public Museum opened in 1995, centering on area history, natural science, and technology. A seventy-six-foot whale skeleton soars over a three-story gallery where the massive wheel of a 1905 Corliss engine turns steadily and the tower clock from the old Grand Rapids city hall is mounted so that visitors see the inside works. Down an enclosed breezeway, a jaunty 1928 carousel prances around in its own housing to the tunes of a Wurlitzer band organ.

When local furniture makers took their best samples to the 1876 Centennial Exhibition in Philadelphia, Grand Rapids became the Paris of home outfitting. The story is in the Van Andel, along with streets of old shops, a rich display of Anishinabe Indian ware, a planetarium, and dioramas of eye-fooling realism showing Michigan habitats. There's an excellent cafeteria and bookstore. 616-456-3966.

A block upstream, spectators can watch salmon leap over a fish ladder at the Sixth Street dam or join businessmen who pack rod, reel, and waders as well as briefcases for a fishing lunch break.

More new city expansions can be found at the John Ball Park Zoo. Among the exhibits are an ultra-modern Living Shores Aquarium, octopus tanks, and tidal pool; a Southern Patagonian display (the southern hemisphere's equivalent to a Michigan climate), and Pacific Northwest coast showcase. Siberian tigers, snow leopards, bald eagles, and zoo regulars are here, too. The entrance is at Fulton Street and Valley Road, just east of downtown. 616-336-4300.

Opened to the public in 1995, the monumental Frederik Meijer Gardens and Sculpture Garden offers the largest jungle conservatory in the state. A towering glass shelter houses seven hundred varieties of tropical foliage, while outside, visitors hike on four-season nature trails and admire fifty bronze treasures by famous artists. North of 1-96 off East Beltline on Bradford. 616-459-8287.

Back in the easily reached heart of the city, a bright red forty-two-ton stabile by Alexander Calder marks the city/county buildings complex. Two blocks south, the Monroe Center Mall ties together variety shopping, restaurants, one of the country's largest artfestival (in the spring) sites, a place for concerts, and people events. All of this is near the Grand Rapids Art Museum where twelve galleries show off six centuries of fine art. Pearl and Division Streets. 616-459-4676.

Slightly east, at the top of an obvious rise, the Heritage Hill historic district claims nearly five dozen different styles of period architecture. Variations on Italianate Victorian, Spanish Revival, Prairie, and even (at 264 College SE) a Queen Anne log house. The Meyer May House is the most completely furnished and restored Frank Lloyd Wright house anywhere. The ornate Voigt House, at 115 College SE, has touring hours and lots of neighborhood information. 616-456-3977. For a list, locations, and free walking map, go to the Heritage Hill Association office, 126 College (in rear). 616-459-8950.

Accommodations and restaurants (over seven hundred, a rare per capita average) encompass bed-and-breakfast rooms (the Peach House on Heritage Hill) or the classy Cygnus Lounge atop the four-star Amway Grand Plaza Hotel Tower. Follow a different drummer at the Rhythm Kitchen (Monroe Mall), Charley's Crab (on the river), or the German ethnic-steeped Schnitzelbank Restaurant on the near south side.

Grand Rapids is a little-suspected cultural mecca with a symphony in top form and Michigan's only ballet company, plus Opera Grand Rapids and Grand Rapids Civic Theatre. The Council For Performing Arts for Children has hands-on work shops and productions just for the kids. Call 616-459-2787 to hear what's being presented.

Also coming as of this writing is a state-of-the-art arena for hockey and big entertainments; here today is the new facility for the Whitecaps (Oakland A's affiliates).

Meanwhile, the Amway Corporation invites you to a one-hour tour of their high-tech facilities in nearby Ada. 616-676-6701.

In Grand Rapids, you are not only close to the Lake Michigan shore and in prime fruit farm country, but to the attractions of Kalamazoo (Aviation History Museum or Air Zoo, a collection of World War II aircraft), Grand Ledge riverboat cruises, and to Lansing.

For more information:

West Michigan Tourist Association, (free vacation information and travel guides), 136 East Fulton near downtown mall, 616-456-8557.

Grand Rapids/Kent County Convention & Visitors Bureau, 800-678-9859.

16.

Saucy Holland Days

Minutes from Lake Michigan, the sweet city of Holland hugs the east end of Lake Macatawa, quiet, scrubbed, and as lively as a tulip in the breeze. Founded by Netherlands' immigrants, its population today is a diverse mix, yet the Dutch heritage remains in charge. You can see it in a phone book full of names like Van der Hoven or in stair-step roof lines. (The stair-step design is said to have been used by the practical Dutch to help chimney sweeps get to work quickly.)

First stop should be Windmill Island, midtown site of a 230-year old Dutch mill straight off the pages of the National Geographic. Reaching nearly ten stories into the wind, "De Swaan" was the last mill allowed to leave Holland after World War II (when it was a sniper's target. Bullet holes are still visible). Buy flour ground by costumed workers, then tour the minivillage shops. An old-world draaimolen (carousel) and summer schedule of wooden-shoe (klompen) dancing can be found, along with Dutch gardens—camera time, for sure.

The Big Read Lighthouse, Holland Harbor, Michigan

The handsome Ninth Street Christian Reformed Church was the only building in Holland to survive a disastrous fire in 1871, the same year as the Chicago fire. Once a year, services are in Dutch. Nearby at Twelfth Street and Central Avenue, a Netherlands Museum fills the former house of a prosperous Hollander with details of Dutch home life, including a cook stove, Delft tiles, and pewterware. There's even a dollhouse from great-great-grandma's times, an import shop, and klompen dancers out back on summer days.

Rough and finished furniture pieces and parts will tantalize home craftsmen and decorators alike in the Baker Furniture Museum, a warehouse-like display on Sixth Street and Columbia Avenue.

Tulip bulbs are clearly the number-one Holland souvenir. However, after the fields of two million tulips in every possible variation have faded, iris, gladioli, and other bulbs take over. If the bulbs you want aren't available, growers will mail them at planting time. (Try Veldheers Tulip Farm, US 31 and Quincy Road.)

DeKlomp's artists (next to Veldheers) work on Delftware, the familiar blue- and-white ceramic pottery. Watch the whole process as they make lamps, vases, and tiles. Or see log chunks turned into the wooden shoes that were so practical for working in soggy Dutch fields. With four pairs of socks, they can be quite comfy and won't fly off when you kick.

More klompen dancing girls might be seen at Dutch Village, at St. James and US 31. Amid the three-quarter scale buildings, canal, and huge street organ, there's a cheese house where they will weigh you to determine whether or not you're a witch. (Witches are said to weigh almost nothing, so put stones in your pocket!). Dine in the very Dutch Queen's Restaurant (you will weigh something more when you leave) on solidly delicious fare, then shop in Manufacturer's Marketplace (discount mall) right behind the Village. A Wooden Shoe Factory, also on

US 31, has pine footwear, made on the spot, along with souvenirs and general supplies.

Among the nation's top community flings, up there with Mardi Gras and the Rose Bowl parade, is the annual May Tulip Festival. Curb-side tulip beds are in full bloom; events are all over town. The biggest is the twice-daily blocks-long line of costumed dancers scrubbing the streets and kicking up their heels. (Hint: those Dutch "boys" are girls, more available for dance rehearsals). A wonderful, squeaky-clean show.

To grandparents in the party who can't cope with all this energy, suggest the nationally acclaimed Evergreen Commons Senior Center, large and exciting. They'll enjoy the woodshop, sewing room, easy chairs, lunch, and friends. 480 State Street, 616-396-7100.

U-Pick orchards, beaches (try Holland State Park), boats to rent, canoes to paddle, fish to fry—all are here. Holland is close to Muskegon, Grand Rapids, Saugatuck, state forests, and quiet towns. And there's excellent "antiquing" in and near Allegan, the appealing county seat.

For more information:
Holland Convention and Visitors Bureau,
   616-396-4221.
West Michigan Tourist Association, 616-456-8557.

17.

Artful Saugatuck

Searchers for the perfect bed and breakfast do considerable pausing around Saugatuck, sometimes called the Martha's Vineyard of the Midwest. It is a village that manages to be famous, chic, historic, quaint, and unspoiled all at once. An even smaller hamlet, Douglas, shares the same wide spot on the Kalamazoo River (called Lake Kalamazoo) just inside the coast of Lake Michigan and a few miles south of Holland.

Hidden from big-lake boaters behind a row of tall dunes and trees, Saugatuck's Victorian roots are clearly visible in its well-preserved roof lines and porches, echoed by a gazebo bandstand in the park and a long boardwalk. Tiny white lights on Butler Street are a modern evening touch, but they certainly look quaint.

The east side of the shore is the commercial heart of Saugatuck, linked to west-side houses by a regular road bridge, but also by an old chain ferry during the summer. Sturdy visitors can pull themselves across and then climb 282 steps to the summit of Mount Baldhead (a high stable dune) for a scenic view, or they can follow the road to Oval Beach, a beautiful spread of sand open to the public on Lake Michigan.

You will notice a high count of historic markers. Digging into the past is part of the local fun. Logging, boat-building, and shipping fruit were the main industries for many years; arts, crafts, and summer visitors are today's focus. Note the comfort station in the waterfront park, a humble structure muraled in a French pointillist style. Four art schools flourished in Saugatuck at one time, and the Chicago Art Institute still runs the Ox Bow Workshop. Arts-and-craft shows are the town's biggest events.

It's a community made for slow browsing, with more than four dozen galleries, gift, jewelry, and antique shops, and boutiques. Shop names (True Glitz, Cats Fifth Avenue) make fun reading. Nearby, the Red Barn Theater, third oldest professional summer-stock company in Michigan, has a sprightly assortment of plays, musicals, and excellent notices. Wednesday-evening concerts in the park are a July/August treat. There's a chamber-music festival every summer. Scenic excitement comes with dune

buggy rides on local sand hills—rides to high overlooks by experienced drivers. 616-857-2253.

There's no fast food, but plenty of good meals in
a couple of fine dining rooms and lounges, with old-
fashioned ice cream and fudge. Stop in the Tabor Hill
Wine Port for a tasting session or make a reservation
for high tea (not every day) at the Maplewood Hotel
bed and breakfast on Butler Street. 616-857-1771.

Breakfast is a meal you can count on. Some of
the cozy and quilted retreats of Saugatuck's bed-and-
breakfast houses have been nationally acclaimed.
Wickwood Inn won raves in *Glamour* and *Adventure
Road Magazine* (among others), and the Maplewood
would please royalty.

The most visible item on the water is the SS *Kee-
watin*, a 350-foot luxury Great Lakes cruise ship
retired in 1965 to become a museum. In the heyday
of Great Lakes cruising, these vessels connected big
cities to tiny ports like Saugatuck, and passengers were
as happy as Mediterranean sightseers. Docked in Douglas, tours include its dining room, staterooms, and
captain's cabin.

Close at hand are dune buggy rides, golf courses,
or sightseeing cruises along the river and out into the
big lake on a breezy stern-wheeler, the *Queen of
Saugatuck* (616-857-4261) or the *City of Douglas* (616-
857-2151). Ask about renting canoes or fishing for
coho salmon from a charter boat on Lake Michigan.
Those who love Saugatuck will enjoy Allegan, the
county seat with a high population of antique shops
and a bent for flea markets. There are U-Pick farms and
golf just down the road apiece—anywhere in the area.

For more information:
Saugatuck Chamber of Commerce, 616-857-1701.

18.
Michigan's Sunny Southwest Corner

The number of brochures declaring this or that vacation spot as an "all-season paradise" could fill the hold of a large freighter. However, the southwest corner of Michigan has a hefty list of year-round getaway goals, from scenic to gastronomic, with U-Pick farms, wineries, wonderful beaches, pretty towns, great fishing, winter sports, fall color, and quick access. Two hours from Chicago, three from Detroit, five from Cleveland—easy drives.

We come from the north on I-196 toward South Haven where eighty-five percent of Michigan's blueberry crop is grown within a fifteen-mile radius. The National Blueberry Festival in August hits the top-favorite list. In the past, South Haven has been a spot for grand hotels, cruise ships, and high-society life. You couldn't guess that now, although it is the longest established resort center on Lake Michigan. Attention today focuses on festivals, fruit picking, or catching fish. Three town beaches are open to the public.

The 1850 Liberty Hyde Bailey Museum/house was the boyhood home of the famed Michigan horticulturist. For the ardent grower, Bailey's gardens are open by appointment. 616-637-3251. On the water, the Lake Michigan Maritime Museum has made its home in a renovated houseboat, a showcase for freshwater marine memorabilia with a research library and boardwalk to view the current boat parade. 616-637-8078. A Heritage Boat Gathering and Championship Hobie Regatta are other major summer events. Meanwhile, you can slip into something comfortable and rent a canoe at one of many outfitters for a day on the tranquil Black River.

Inland on M-43, Bangor's old depot is now a toy-train layout and manufacturing operation. Twenty-five miles farther lies Kalamazoo, the K'zoo Nature Center (six hundred acres, nature trails, barnyard, homestead, and programs), and the Kalamazoo Aviation History Museum, an Air Zoo of fighter planes with names like Cobra and Tiger. Follow the Red Arrow Highway west to Paw Paw, where you can taste the products of the St. Julian or Warner wine companies.

More wineries are in the rolling hills south of Paw Paw (and hence south of I-94), in Taber Hill and Lemon Creek, closely connected with fruit farms and roadside produce sheds. The Tree-Mendus Fruit Farm near Eau Claire, Wick's Apple House close to Dowagiac, and Stover's U-Pick at Berrien Springs are listed in easily obtained brochures. The Herb Barn and Farmhouse Inn (reservations are a must) near Benton Harbor for back-to-Mom food or Schmidts Blueberries at Bridgman are recommended–they all bring you near antique shops, flea markets, historic sites, and garden getaways. Row after row of lush green vineyards and orchards will slow down everyone but a drag racer.

Ramble eastward a bit to visit the magic store in Colon where magicians from around the world shop for the latest in hat tricks and disappearing birds. See the unique city hall and depot (used in movies) in Niles, and visit Fernwood Gardens near Berrien Springs, a place to bedazzle any budding botanist. You'll find lunch, trails, and more.

Back on the coast, the St. Joseph River divides the twin cities of St. Joseph and Benton Harbor, double hosts to the Blossomtime Festival (late April to early May). It's a time when back-country roads are photographers' dreams, with fruit trees in full glory. St. Joseph, on a bluff overlooking Lake Michigan, offers a bright, revamped downtown with outdoor sculpture, parks, an art center, and imaginative kids' museum.

The red-and-white lighthouse on one of the piers protecting the harbor entrance can be seen on a series of U.S.postage stamps. Lake Bluff Park marks the spot where explorer LaSalle waited in vain for his ship *Griffon* to show up (it vanished, the first recorded loss on the Great Lakes) and where he built the first lower-peninsula fort in 1679. It's a lovely place to watch boats, picnic, or hear a summer band concert right across from the lively Krasl Art Center on Lake Boulevard. Local artists are featured along with touring art collections. 616-983-0271. Two minutes down the boulevard, the Curious Kid's Museum is brightly geared to a child's inquiring mind. Interactive science and medical exhibits (they do not practice surgery on each other), face painting, hand puppets, and other fun stuff. 616-983-2543.

South of this point, the communities are small, the parks spacious. Grand Mere State Park (too new to be listed on many maps) lets you escape from everything. Exit I-94 and follow Thornton Drive south. There's a picnic shelter, but that's all except for paths over dunes and through trees around South Lake to Lake Michigan.

At Warren Dunes State Park, a two-and-a-half-mile stretch of public beach, is the kind of lofty sand piles that hang-gliders and high-energy children dearly love. You'll find two hundred acres of carefully guarded woods, a bathhouse, a food stand, and nearly two hundred campsites (get there early). 616-426-4013. Between these park attractions, at Bridgman, the handsome quarters of the Cook Energy Center (Michigan and Indiana Electric Company) puts on a vivid show. The case for nuclear energy is not the whole pitch, however; information on solar heat and fossil fuels is part of it. A snack bar and patio face Lake Michigan.

For motels, bed and breakfasts, and the best of dining, check visitors center brochure racks at the state line and drop in wherever travel information is indicated.

For more information:
Southwestern Michigan Tourist Council,
   616-925-6301.

19.
Indiana Calling

The south curve of Lake Michigan belongs to Indiana, a bend of boggling variety. The hulking silhouettes of steel mills, nuclear cooling towers, miles of national lakeshore and state park beaches, marinas, shopping, history, and even a zoo are here. The old cliche, "something for everyone," fits.

Michigan City edges close to the Michigan State line, only sixty miles from midtown Chicago. Once, shipping and building Pullman cars were the big industries; today, it's compact kitchens, gauges, cookies, hospitality, and charter-boat fishing.

Start sightseeing at the 135-year-old lighthouse (now a museum) near the marina and Washington Park. (Trivia note: A woman, Miss Harriet Colfax, was light keeper for forty-three nineteenth-century years, a duty not lightly handed to females.) In the same park, watch boats, picnic, or talk to animals in a surprisingly fine zoo, one of the oldest in the state. Walking atop wooded sand dunes, you see dozens of animals, reptiles in a children's castle, and a petting barn. Admission is charged.

At the John Blank Center for the Arts, three galleries have changing exhibits in a variety of media. Neat gift shop. 219-874-4900. Or swirl through the "house that freight cars built," the early 1900s Barker mansion, where the original furniture stands near hand-carved fireplaces. 219-873-1520. The Festival

Players Guild (Canterbury Theater) does summer and winter musicals, comedies, and classics. 219-874-4269.

For shopping addicts, the Lighthouse Place Outlet Center includes restaurants and a Visitors Information Center. 219-879-6506. Marquette Mall (Carson, Pirie, Scott) has additional options; the location is spelled out on billboards.

A very short drive south on US 35, the LaPorte County Museum has among its twenty thousand heirlooms one of the best collections of antique firearms in the U.S. 219-326-6808. In another direction (east) from Michigan City on County Road 1000 North (two and a half miles east of State Road 39), the Hesston Steam Museum's outdoor collection of steam equipment, from traction engines and sawmills to steam train rides, is open all summer. Admission is charged. 219-872-7405.

Manufacturers wanted to mine the sand; developers want to turn it into a midwestern Riviera. Luckily for the rest of us, the area of dunes and shoreline comprising the National Lakeshore and Indiana Dunes State Park (the park within the Lakeshore) are still in the hands of we-the-people. The eighteen-hundred-acre State Park at Chesterson has three large and tempting dunes, but dunes are unexpectedly fragile objects. Climb only in designated spots. For maps and camping information, to see films, pick up books, or find the way to the bathhouse, stop at the Visitors Center, US 12 at Kemil, about three miles east of Indiana 49. 219-926-4520.

Drop by the Burns International Waterway at Portage, Indiana's only deep-water port. Plenty of charter boats are here, too. 800-231-6857. In Hammond, H. and J. Wood's Old Mill was the first industrial site on the shore. There's a visitors center, a grist mill still grinding corn, a blacksmith shop, and other early traces. 800-ALL LAKE.

Other enticements include area fruit farms, a multitude of antique shops (big flea market in Cedar Lake), the Meyer Scottish Castle in Dyer, top-name shows in Merrillville's Star Plaza Theatre, and Valparaiso's fortress jail, now a cell-filled museum. Valparaiso University has the nation's largest university chapel. This is not too far from South Bend/Notre Dame territory and a Studebaker Museum or from Amish Country, Nappanee, and real Amish farm cooking. Big area motel or bed-and-breakfast list.

For more information:

Michigan City Visitors Center, 219-879-6506.

LaPort County Convention and Visitors Bureau, 219-872-5055 or toll free in IL, KY, MI, OH, 800-634-2650.

Lake Superior

20.

Wisconsin's Lake Superior World

Northern Wisconsin is as solidly rooted in out-door life as a pine tree. INdoors is for when it rains or for having a beer or hunkering down until morning, but outdoors is for living. And yet...there are touches of luxury in heavy use, like motels with indoor pools and great dining rooms.

Exploring the lands of Lake Superior in clockwise fashion, we use northern Wisconsin and the town of Hurley for a starting gate.

A hundred years ago when iron ore and lumber were the coin of life, Hurley had a hell-bent boom-town beginning. Today, the law-abiding community on the state line and US 2 pitches groceries, bait, and motel space to tourists, skiers, bikers, and fishermen. Art/fair folks fill up the summers, but you'll get a feel-ing that winter is Hurley's favorite season. There are well-equipped ski resorts, plus miles and miles of snowmobile and cross-country ski trails cut through the Wisconsin forests.

Hurley's old Iron County Courthouse has switched to the role of Historical Museum, an open door to the lumber-mining past of the region. On the National Register of Historic Places, its tall clock tower once tried (often vainly) to remind a boisterous popu-lation to get back to work. The same brown stone, used in fashionable New York City mansions, comes from nearby quarries.

Take a waterfalls break south on Highway 169 to Gurney (Potato Falls) or to Copper Falls State Park. Driving west on US 2, the first glimpse of Lake Superior comes at Ashland. The wide white and refurbished Chequamegon Hotel, as inviting as grandma's porch, sits squarely at the water's edge, the better to watch long ships passing or a ferry head up to Bayfield.

A Soo Line Railroad Ore Dock looms over the highway and out into Chequamegon Bay. Eighteen hundred feet of heavy-duty shipping facility, it was built between 1916 and 1925. This is the largest concrete structure of its kind in the world. More leftovers of an earlier port are in the collections of the Ashland Historical Society Museum, inhabiting a nineteenth-century mansion. There are dolls, farm tools, railroading photos, and bits of a world that was. On Chapple Avenue, 715-862-7185. The Romanesque Ashland City Hall is also on the National Register of Historic Places and still filling its assigned duties.

For what-where information, stop on Third Avenue at the former Soo Line Railroad Depot, now the Northern Wisconsin Interpretive Center. A thirty-six-foot-square map lights up with routes, area museums, parks, waterfalls, and whatever. 800-284-9484 or 715-682-6600. Turn north from US 2 onto Highway 13 to such prospects as Washburn, Bayfield, Madeline Island, and the Apostle Islands National Lakeshore. Washburn, seat of Bayfield County (with a brownstone courthouse), was a quarry and fishing town; it now shelters a modest enclave of potters, weavers, carvers, painters, and other folks in the art scene. Inspiring views are along the Lakeshore Walking Trail, which begins at the West End Boat Landing. The performing arts get their break in Big Top Chautauqua, north of town. In a large blue-and-white-striped tent, musicals, plays, concerts, and personal appearances are regular features.

Bayfield may overdose on comparisons to a New England fishing town, but those who know both see the resemblance. The road curves past old shops and new condos to a large marina. The Rittenburg House bed and breakfast and other structures perched on the hillsides seem classic Victoriana. Check the Old Firehouse & Police Museum and the Booth Cooperage, Wisconsin's only working barrel factory/museum.

Madeline Island, largest of the Apostle group and reached by ferry, calls its one village La Pointe. Shops, restaurants, accommodations (even a small airport) are here plus modern roads and a little bus to take you around. Woods Hall Craft Shop and the Madeline Island Historical Museum deal in local insights. Ferry: 715-747-2051.

Sailing on Superior

The Apostle Island National Lakeshore encompasses twenty scattered wilderness isles and a narrow edge of Bayfield County coast. There's limited rough camping, but for day trips, it's total pure escape. 715-779-3397.

Back on the mainland, head west through the villages of Cornucopia and Herbster, past boat launching sites and ma-pa hospitality businesses. Stay on Highway H until it becomes 27 and takes you south to Hayward and the Fresh Water Fishing Hall of Fame's four-story muskelunge. Believe me, folks, it is a new thrill to stand behind muskie teeth and see far away. The cantilevered steel and fiber-glass structure hides a long stairway portrait gallery going up to the mouth-porch. Out-sized fish, gardens, and a real building for a showcase, the National Freshwater Fishing Hall of Fame keeps tabs on record catches (regulations discourage fakery) and photos of beaming fishermen. Outboard motors and famous tackle boxes are here. Not to miss! 715-634-4440.

Traveling back up to the BIG lake, stop at the Wisconsin Information Center next to Superior's (the city) Barker's Island on US 53 for things to see on the way back to Milwaukee—or wherever. Barker's Island acts as a municipal recreation hub. From here, Duluth Superior Excursions will take you on a two-hour tour of the giant Duluth-Superior harbor layout on the *Vista Queen* (or *King*). Same locale: the last remaining whaleback freighter (bulges like a fat whale) is now the SS *Meteor* Maritime Museum. On the other side of the highway and looking over the whole scene, the Fairlawn Mansion and Museum has exhibits supplemented with lawn socials and other special events. 715-394-5712.

For more information:
Wisconsin Information Center, 715-392-1662.

Superior Visitor Information Center, 715-392-2773
or 800-942-5313.

21.

Duluth...On Purpose

Going to Duluth used to be almost incidental. As
the continent's farthest inland port, Duluth life
revolved around the shipping of ore and grain and
coping in stoic style with long winters. A beautiful
locale, there's a long steep hillside (a San Francisco
touch) before you reach flat high ground. It used to
be a tad short on fun.

No more. People love Duluth, a bright destination by itself. It's full of lively arts, outlets and malls,
sports, and lumberjack helpings of food. Winter loses
its bite under enclosed skywalks linking much of
downtown and a warm calendar of city events.

The undisputed symbol of Duluth has been the
high squarish aerial bridge that lifts a road out of the
way when freighters (many from overseas) enter the
harbor. You can see it, looking like a giant handle,
from most parts of town—an image for coffee mugs,
T-shirts, and neckties. Next to the bridge, one becomes
a part of the steadiest spectator crowd in town, all
watching ships come and go, the bridge lift and lower.
A waterside boardwalk lets you stroll, bike, and gaze.
Next to the walk, there's a Veterans Memorial and
mosaic tile wall with Duluth seaport images.

Steps from the bridge, the Marine Museum shows
films and has model ships and exhibits on the navigational aspects of running a major port. Walk the pier
to the lighthouse and hope a ship passes while you
are just yards away. (Twenty-four-hour boat-watcher's
hotline operates in season: 218-722-6489.)

Two blocks up: Grand Slam Adventure World is an all-year indoor playground with minigolf, basketball, baseball, billiards, bumper cars, a restaurant, and more. Free admission. 396 Lake Avenue, Canal Park. The *William A. Irvin*, a cargo carrier docked nearby, opens for summer tours. See the whole intriguing works. 800-628-8385.

Duluth proves its entertainment-worth in the waterfront Arena Auditorium (there's a skywalk to this also) with concerts, summer arts, and winter sports, plus Arena ice hockey (watch a curling game from a skywalk window). Brightest spot of all is the Depot, the St. Louis County Heritage and Arts Center. It's a grand old French chateau-style train station housing eight different cultural organizations. There's a terrific collection of trains, engines, and streetcars under the wing of the Lake Superior Museum of Transportation. The Chisholm Museum focuses on world cultures with an emphasis on children. The St. Louis County Historical Society works on the Minnesota heritage. Still in the Depot, Duluth's Art Institute has an extensive schedule of changing exhibits in its galleries. Four performing groups, Duluth Ballet, Superior/Duluth Symphony, Duluth Playhouse, and Matinee Musicale, can be enjoyed here. All museums are covered by one admission fee. 218-727-8025. (Performances are specially ticketed.)

On the campus of the University of Minnesota-Duluth, the Tweed Museum of Art displays nine galleries of American and European paintings. A scholarly place, the Karples Manuscript Library Museum has original drafts of great documents, from the U.S. Bill of Rights to Handel's *Messiah*. The Constitution of the Confederate States of America is in Duluth! 218-728-0630.

Think rich at Glensheen Mansion on the shores of Lake Superior—carriage house, landscaped gardens, and thirty-nine rooms. Or talk natural at the Lake Superior Zoological Gardens, home to over five hundred species. Picnic area and campgrounds are nearby. 218-624-1502.

Rare in-city downhill skiing can be found at Spirit Mountain on the west side of town. The city has snowmobile and cross-country trails, as well as ice hockey, dog sled races, and ice carving. Winter is clearly Duluth's piece of cake.

About a ninety-minute drive north on US 53 and US 169 to Chisholm (note the U.S. Hockey Hall of Fame on the west side of the road at Eveleth), home of Ironworld, a different kind of theme park that tells the story of the Mesabi Range and the thousands of immigrants who came to work the mines in the late 1880s. The grounds include a stunning museum cantilevered over a former open pit, a train ride around the pit's edge, and living-history tapes (find a chair, put on earphones, and listen to old-timers casually tell their own stories of hardships endured on the bitter Minnesota frontier). In summer, big-name entertainers come to the handsome amphitheater; ethnic booths serve their specialties. Forget mileage and go. There's a restaurant and a shop. 800-777-8497.

This is also the way up to the Boundary Waters Canoe Area on the Canadian border, a fabulous canoeing, fishing, adventure region, with beautifully marked snowmobile trails and great hiking. And then there's Virginia, another city to explore.

For more information:
Duluth Convention and Visitors Bureau,
    218-722-4011 or 800-4-DULUTH.
Minnesota Office of Tourism, St. Paul, MN
    800-657-3700 (U.S.), 800-766-8687 (from Canada).

22.

Exploring The Arrowhead

S quint at a map of Minnesota to see why the sharply pointed upper northeastern corner is nicknamed Arrowhead Country. It fits. The corner penetrates the memory and sticks there with misty rugged shores, snug lodges, and the view from the top of the next hill.

Coming from Duluth to reach Two Harbors, pass up the divided highway and take a lake-hugging low road, County 61. It's narrower and slower, but who cares with all those chances to turn out, all those patches of yellow marigold, pink lupine, wild berries, and a pebbly shore. The North Shore Scenic Railroad also goes to Two Harbors. Ask at Duluth's Depot.

Settlers came to Two Harbors in 1850, hopefully in springtime. Their clustered cabins grew up to be a major taconite (little pellets of iron) shipping port where part of today's fun is watching long freighters ease in and out to load. Antique hunters love the shops on 7th Avenue or browsing through the old Duluth and Iron Range Railroad Depot, home of the Lake County Historical Museum. Visit the 3M (as in Scotch Tape) /Dwan Museum, the Two Harbors light station, and a coal-fired tugboat. There are band concerts on summer Thursday evenings and treat yourself to a piece of pie (other items too) at the Blueberry House, also on 7th (which turns back into 61).

There's happy agate hunting for rock hounds at Flood Bay and a big stuffed moose to stare at in the lobby of the Superior Shores resort. 800-242-1988. More pie, more meals of renown can be had at Betty's Pies, a north-shore tradition with scrumptious reasons.

Find an old-timer and ask about scenic spots, like the gazebo at Silver Cliff, a gem to photograph. There are a number of places along 61 with access to the

Superior Hiking Trail, a path which will be three hundred miles long in due time; it's part of a lodge-to-lodge hiking route parallel to the shore.

The most commemorated image on the lake has to be the Split Rock lighthouse (now on a postage stamp). The stalwart, reliable beacon atop a slab of ancient rock has the impact of a great sermon without words. When builders went to work on the project in 1910, there were no roads to haul materials; everything was pulled up from cargo ships by derricks. Now, with roads and footpaths aplenty, no spot on the lake gets more attention. Visitors can climb to the top of the light eleven months a year. There's an interpretive center, camping, and more. 218-226-4372.

Space does not permit a total listing of scenic sights or worthy stops. Goosebury Falls, Caribou Falls, Cascade Falls are three dramatic spills on the Baptism River. Beaver Bay (the J. Beargrease Dogsled Race from Duluth to Portage was named for a legendary Native American who is buried here) has its rock shops, seven state parks, and half of the wayside parks in all of Minnesota. Near Tettegouche State Park, M-1 begins its curving path up to Ely, the only highway connecting the coast with US 53 and cities of the Mesabi Iron Range. Drive this route at sunrise, and you might spot a moose. Best to stay back and watch, as they are temperamental creatures.

Other roads meander northward, best known as the Sawbill, Caribou, Arrowhead, or Gunflint Trails, all leading to inland lodges and fish-filled lakes. Some of the best, least-crowded, longest-drop (over one thousand feet) skiing in the Midwest can be found at Lutzen where a chain of ancient mountains is twice as high as any close rival. Lutzen offers mid-America's only gondola, five double chairs, one T-bar, thirty-four runs (soon to be forty-nine), and slopes of up to one and a quarter miles. Luxury lodge or modest digs, motel prices are earth-bound compared to more famous regions. Central reservations: 800-360-ROOM or 218-663-7284. Rave notices from ski publications. Summer comers can try the Alpine slide down Eagle Mountain, ride the gondola, play golf on a new eighteen-hole championship course (with Lake Superior as a wow of a backdrop), or head off on one of the endless mountain biking paths. (Isn't two thousand miles of trail in the Superior National Forest endless?) P.O. Box 129, Lutzen, MN 55616.

Mother moose and twins

Larger of the two Grand Marais on Lake Superior (the other is in Michigan), this Grand Marais is one of the few harbors for boaters on this part of the coast and heavily into the hospitality and art business. The Harbor Inn Restaurant, Angry Trout Cafe, East Bay Hotel and Restaurant are all excellent; the Silverston Galleries, Great Northern Gallery, and Johnson Port Art Gallery show off local talents. History fans should pause at the Cook County Historical Society Museum. For events and maps: 800-622-4014.

Cree Indian designs in dazzling color mark the high-ceilinged dining room of the Naniboujou Lodge, on the shore fourteen miles beyond Grand Marais. A private club for well-heeled backers during Prohibition, it closed down during World War II. Go in for a meal (humongous sweet rolls), and you might check in. Or camp nearby. 218-387-2688.

French voyageurs and fur traders made Grand Portage a market place in the 1700s. Today's little community sits on the Ojibway Indian Reservation facing the awesome lake, hugged tightly by a ring of green hills. On a clear day, you can see Isle Royale, twenty-six miles away. Pull in to the Grand Portage National Monument. Reconstructing the first white settlement in the state, there is a stockade, kitchen, and Great Hall where a voyageur's life and the know-how of canoe-loading (a big one held tons of freight) are told in fascinating detail while you sit on simulated bales of fur. There are special events and demos amid a superb history lesson. 218-475-2202.

Grand Portage is departure point for two boats to Isle Royale, one serving a slightly longer season. Grand Portage Isle Royal Transportation Line, 715-392-2100. Advance reservations required.

The North West Company, a British firm with the fur trade in mind, established headquarters for a while in Grand Portage, then moved to Thunder Bay. There are two establishments to visit, to learn how those early traders lived and coped. Sit on bales of fur in the canoe shed and hear the story of the Portage stockade. 218-387-2788.

Another spectacular overlook of Lake Superior is at the Grand Portage Bay Travel Information Center. Information on Minnesota, local and statewide, on Canada and the road ahead, and on border-crossing particulars is always available.

For more information:
Minnesota Tourism, 800-657-3700.

23.

Isle Royale National Park

A loon sends its signal across a pond. A moose wades into the mists of a lake, and you hear it slurping (a moose slurps like a bathroom plunger) up succulent water weeds. Wind swishes in the manner of an attending nurse through the pine tops. "Why are we whispering?" Because the forest whispers. When you are in a place where there is much to learn—like a library—you whisper.

Isle Royale is such a place—a rocky outcropping forty-five miles long and from three to nine miles wide, with about two hundred satellite islets scattered along the edges. No cars, trail bikes, or outboard motors (except around the outside perimeter) are allowed. A bit of hilarity at Rock Harbor Lodge, the toot of the whistle when the *Ranger III* leaves for Houghton, or campfire talk accounts for what unnatural noise level there is.

It has been said that the U.S. can thank Ben Franklin, the shrewd ambassador at the Treaty of Paris, for maneuvering toward eventual ownership of Isle Royale. Just what Franklin thought the island was worth is not clear, but two hundred years later, it is a priceless pristine wilderness where nature is in balance because things have been left alone.

There are still dozens of pits left by Indian copper-mining operations hundreds of years ago. A small amount of commercial fishing was attempted, but nothing resembling a real town was ever settled.

A hundred and sixty miles of foot trails lace through the woods, including the forty-mile Greenstone trail along the island's central ridge. For able hikers, going the full length of this strenuous route takes about six days. One of the rewards at the top of Mount Ojibway (1,183 feet elevation) is a splendid view touching three states and Canada (fifteen miles away). Muskrat, weasel, beaver, and fox may be sighted darting across a trail, but there are no deer, skunks, or porcupine. An amazing variety of tiny woodland orchids grow among the hardwoods and conifers. They are only one species among hundreds of wildflowers. Botanists are surprised by the variety, including Devil's Club, ordinarily found only in the Pacific Northwest. Pike, brook trout, and walleye flourish in the under-fished lakes; just remember that all canoes and equipment must be portaged in.There are herring gulls, of course, but twenty-five kinds of warblers (!) have been spotted here as well.

Isle Royale's 539,280 acres of deep forest and rugged rocks hide thirty-six campgrounds, two hundred and fifty-three sites, with a few Adirondack-like shelters. Rules about fires and back-country permits are strict; this is no place for beginning or poorly equipped adventurers.

Rock Harbor Lodge at the north end of the island offers rooms with baths, dining-room facilities, a camp store, limited fishing accessories, gas, and boat and motor rentals (for going around the outside and to other islands only). For those who plan far ahead, there are a limited number of housekeeping cabins. Ranger programs and guided hikes are free.

One fun excursion is a ride to the Rock Harbor Lighthouse to hunt for greenstones, the Michigan state gem and found mostly on Isle Royale.

By late August, the often-maddening fly population has quit, a lot of visitors have gone home, and very early in September the fall color change is nibbling at the leaves. Bring insect repellent and plenty of film—and perhaps a seasickness aid if Lake Superior has been stormy.

Isle Royale National Park is open for visitors mid-April till October. Full services are available from

mid-June to Labor Day. Take a boat from Grand
Portage, Minnesota, or Copper Harbor or Houghton
in Michigan. The big trip is on the *Ranger 11* from
Houghton, the biggest boat and also the longest (six
hours) ride.

For more information:

**Isle Royale National Park, 87 North Ripley,
Houghton, MI 49931, 906-482-0984.**

**Reservations, Rock Harbor Lodge, off season,
502-773-2191; in season, 906-337-4993.**

24.

Thunder Bay/Fort William: Trade Secrets

Going from Minnesota into Ontario, the designated highway number remains 61, a symbol,
perhaps, of the no-stone-unturned efforts both countries have taken to make circling Lake Superior an
easy-going and hospitable sojourn.

Unless you're a grazing cow, that great view from
the east-bound lane as the highway curves toward the
city is a visual feast. Deep blue harbor with freighters
and sails, a ring of hills, and a broad spread of low-
rise urban landscape. You can see the grain elevators,
pulp and paper complexes, and shipping terminals on
a water-front shared with marinas and parks. A sleeping giant silhouette of hills on the Sibley Peninsula
rises in the mist beyond the bay. Over 120,000 hardy
folks who relish their snowy winters and green summers call Thunder Bay home and sometimes heaven.

Surprisingly, this EST-zone center is almost
equidistant from both the Pacific (approximately 2000
miles) and Atlantic (by water, 2,235 miles). Grain from
Canada's prairie provinces finds its way to world markets through Thunder Bay.

Thunder Bay was founded with markets in mind. In 1717, when the only roads were waterways, the North West Fur Company sent advance men from Montreal to build a trading post. Furs were for the markets of Europe—two hundred thousand pelts a season made up the biggest business on our continent. The first post was at Grand Portage, the next, in the early 1800s, was at the mouth of the Kaministikwia River. A detailed reconstruction sits upstream at Fort William, but more on that in a moment. Thunder Bay first.

There's a breathtaking lookout point on Mt. McKay, one thousand feet over the city on the west side and minutes from downtown. Thunder Bay's Community Auditorium, a building with drama of its own, will shout down any fears of a far-north cultural backwater. Home of the Thunder Bay Symphony Orchestra, the handsome building throbs with Broadway shows, ballet, and year-round entertainment. 807-343-2300. The Thunder Bay Art Gallery, a National Exhibition Centre and Centre for Indian Art, houses one of Canada's largest collections of two- and three-dimensional works by premier Native artists. It's a major gallery with a wide exchange-show schedule. 807-577-6427. In the open-to-all Canada Games Complex, the activity-conscious can swim, jog, ride bikes, and pump muscle all year. It's next to the Community Auditorium. 807-625-3311. The city also offers the Thunder Bay Historical Museum, Children's Museum, Railroad Heritage Building, Centennial Park (history on a hundred and forty-seven scenic acres), Northwestern Ontario Sports Hall of Fame & Museum, and Paipooge Museum (pioneer artifacts). A lot of choices.

No choice here: Visiting Fort William is a required course in the way they were. A ten-foot stockade wall encompasses forty-two buildings that filled various needs in the company's business, which was to secure beaver pelts for the hatters of the world. The popularity of the tall beaver hat (such as Lincoln wore) made fortunes for fur traders and (almost incidently) opened up the land for European settlers. Costumed guides re-enact the lives of original inhabitants, even mimicking the stiff class system of the fort: company VIPs at the top, voyageurs and Indians at the bottom. (Never mind that there would be no fur trade without them).

Fur rivalry with the Hudson's Bay Company reached pitched-battle proportions just before tall collapsible silk hats began to replace stiff beaver "stove pipes." Secrets of the fur trade are here, along with the makings and astonishing capacity of canoes, Ojibwa life in an encampment, and one thousand and one history lessons in one memorable ten-acre spot.

The big event of the year is the Great Rendezvous, which started at the Fort and is now a city-wide celebration. Historic games, arriving voyageur canoes, music, and spirited fun. Old Fort William: 807-577-8461.

Very close to the city's west side, Kakabeka Falls has been called the Niagara of the North, with a hundred-and-twenty-eight-foot high wall of water to gaze at from walkways and viewing pods on both sides of the river. It's even more awesome in spring and early summer.

Up and north from Thunder Bay, the trans-Canada Highway (17) will take you to the Pacific or eastward to Quebec. Go west on 11 to Quetico Provincial Park and the Boundary Waters Canoe Area. To the North, the official Ontario road map marks lakes with regular fly-ins. There's another world up there.

For more information:
Thunder Bay Tourism, 800-667-8386.
Ontario Tourism, 800-ONTARIO.

25.

Follow The Amethyst Road

A long the loosely winding road of the northshore of Lake Superior, the purples of lupines and wild asters are caught forever in rare caches of amethyst crystals. The treasured birthstones of May (amethyst dust was once thought to cure drunkenness) sit rough or polished in roadside shops or hide in hillside veins, waiting for land owners to let you find them.

In a region of uncommon beauty and activity, amethyst, however, is only a flashing corner of the picture. Twenty minutes east of Thunder Bay, Pass Lake (population two dozen, maybe) acts as gateway to the Sibley Peninsula where Sleeping Giant Provincial Park is wide awake, laced with hiking and biking trails, views from thousand-foot cliffs, camping, and cross-country skiing. 807-977-2526.

The highway is now 17, a continuation of the highway to Kenora and points west. Rock shops and mines aren't exactly elbow-to-elbow, but they are frequent, and every little cafe has its counter display of amethyst for sale. Look for Pearl Lake Mine or Diamond Willow Amethyst Mine (Road # 5) or the Ontario Gem Amethyst Mine, remembering that mine roads were not built for Corvettes. Or browse through places like Castagne's Rock Shop.

Geologically part of the pre-cambrian shield, rocks and cliffs of the region are among the oldest exposed surfaces on Earth. Shifting forces and eons of time have played with this surface, creating canyons, rifts, and waterfalls and enhancing the general grandeur. One such rift, the slate-gray rock walls of Ouimet Canyon (Provincial Park) that form a two-mile corridor, 550 feet wide and 350 feet high, is well worth the seven-mile detour.

Nipigon marks a take-off junction for those going east by heading north first to Lake Nipigon, Hearst, or Timmins on Route 11. Since 1915, when a fourteen-pound trout was caught in the Nipigon River, anglers have been casting for ways to get up here. Modest little Nipigon is home to several curling (the game, not the hair procedure) champions, it but received more notice as the place where cancer victim Terry Fox could not continue his fund-raising marathon cross-Canada run. A monument to brave Terry has been erected in Thunder Bay. Nipigon's waterfront provides the latest facilities for Lake Superior water sports, charters, and docking, all in close proximity to hotels, ball fields, swimming facilities, and tennis courts. A new regional Tourist Information Centre and Community Centre has information on the fall fishing fests, winter skiing, golf, and whatever else you may want. Pick up the brochures, go over to the Normandie Hotel, order a great homemade dinner, and decide your future. 807-887-3021.

The distilled essence of Lake Superior north-shore villages has to be Rossport, perched on a hillside along a picture-book bay, as if on a bleacher seat for the big game. Bay islands make this sheltered cove a favorite anchoring place; its total charm makes Rossport hard to set sail from. The Rossport Inn (once a railroad hotel) belies its simplicity with wonderful food and comfortable quarters. The Serendipity Gardens Cafe and Gallery offers international cuisine and a warm-weather Margaritaville Patio with its own menus. Recognized in Where to Eat in Canada, it's on Main Street overlooking the harbor. 807-824-2890. Art work, desserts, and gifts are at the Forget-Me-Not Gift Shop, half a block east.

Ontario's oldest fish derby and perhaps the biggest on Lake Superior takes place here in July. Meanwhile, several charter and tour boats are ready until ice closes the operations. Call the Rossport Tourism Association for more phone numbers and events, 807-824-3389.

Amiable Schreiber offers more hospitality, especially in a super eatery called Rosie and Josie (take-outs too) across from the provincial police station on Highway 11. There's picnicking, underwater diving, and a drift of winter sports. Experienced hikers might try the thirty-mile Casques Hiking Trail into some prime Canadian wilderness.

Terrace Bay, slightly larger, drew this comment from artist A. Y. Jackson, who worked here extensively, "I know of no more impressive scenery in Canada for the landscape painter.... There is a feeling of space, dramatic lighting, stark forms...and beyond, Lake Superior shining like burnished silver." Jackson was one of the famous "Group of Seven" Canadian painters. There's all that plus twenty-four-hour convenience stores, ice hockey, curling bonspiels, and a golf course overlooking the big lake. At the information center next to the library, ask directions to nearby Aguasabon Falls. A new boardwalk leads down to a spectacular gorge and hundred-foot spill. 807-825-3542.

Marathon, down to five thousand souls from a high of twelve thousand in the 1800s, is booming once more, partly thanks to that gleaming population enhancer, the discovery of gold. Mine tours are offered at the Hemlo Gold Mine. 807-238-1121. New businesses have sprung up, and the harbor front is due for a face lift with expanded marina. Travelers are invited to use Marathon's Olympic-sized pool, guaranteed warmer than the big lake. More hiking trails are along the coast, as well as winter skiing.

For more information:
Ontario Tourism, 800-ONTARIO, 800-668-2746.
Marathon Information Center, 807-229-0480.

26.

More Northern Lights
(Winnipeg The Pooh?)

The lands of northeastern Superior between Marathon and Sault Ste. Marie, inland up to Hearst, eastward to the border of Quebec, are studies in rugged boreal forests and upthrusting slate-colored rock. Everything looks as though it should be on a wildlife calendar. As Highway 17 dips and curves, arcing across hilltops to reveal more sweeping panoramas or misty gray segments of primeval hills, the "moose-crossing" signs tantalize. Don't bother to pull over to watch: They are deep-woods creatures who never cross roads when you want them to.

Highway 17 links north Superior's relatively narrow band of towns and resorts, commerce and amenities. It's a modern traveler's security belt. There's no running out of gas as in early motoring days and no need to take crisis amounts of food.

Use caution, however. Wide rugged vistas may inject a sense of excitement and personal discovery, but an inexperienced back-packer tramping off alone without a plan or guide could mean deep trouble.

Pukaskwa National Park, Ontario's largest national park, is the sub-Arctic home of bear, fox, moose, and a few caribou. Only one road penetrates its 1,878-square kilometers of rugged rock and forest, a dramatic untouched region where Lake Superior can go scenically rampant against the shore as canoeists maneuver inland on the White or Pukaskwa Rivers. There are forty miles (sixty kilometers) of coastal hiking trails, trails from campgrounds to inland lakes and scenic overlooks (Tip Top Mountain, highest point in Ontario, is two thousand feet). Primitive campsites (limited number) and sixty-seven improved campsites are available, some with electricity and even beaches; everything is first-come, first-served. The whole glorious spread is explained at the visitors center, fifteen miles east of Marathon, then seven and a half miles down Highway 627 to Hattie Cove. 807-229-0801.

What's that statue of Winnie the Pooh doing in a place like White River where the temperature once (and once only) reached 72 degrees below zero Fahrenheit? Ol' Win was born here, and the winter temperature averages merely sub-zero. Winnipeg was a stray cub adopted by Captain Harry Colbourn, who took the bear to England as a troop mascot and later gave it to the London Zoo. A. A. Milne and his son, the "Christopher Robin" of fame, saw Winnie, and Milne was inspired to write some bear tales. The results are literary history, known by millions of little kids to be absolutely true.

At the White River Visitors Center, they assure you it gets very warm in summer; they also tell you about the two nearby provincial parks, about their sawmill tour, Hemlo Gold Mine tour (no rock-hounding here), shops of teddy bears, the Historical Society's minimuseum on Elgin Street, and the Pooh Bear Festival which attracts an astonishingly far-flung crowd. 807-822-2794.

Wawa (Ojibway for "wild goose," a word simulating their call in flight) started as a small Hudson's Bay Company fur post, but it was the discovery of gold that brought in the population. The area also produces iron, which sustained the economy when the gold petered out. A solid little community, Wawa has an airport, hospital, good eating places, motels, and other reinforcements such as waterfalls and terrific hiking trails—that translates to snowmobile trails in winter. The upper falls of the Magpie River (seventy-three feet or twenty-two meters high), Silver Falls, and the Michipicoten River Falls are attractions.

On a high scenic bluff next to the new visitors center, a much-photographed steel Wawa goose looks toward Magpie Valley (with golf course) and the big lake beyond. If you are interested in a fly-in fishing experience, Wawa is famous for putting people into outpost camps, lodges, and remote lake sites. It will also lead them to a dozen provincial parks: Pancake Bay, Batchawana, Superior Park, Obatagana, and others.

Ask anybody where Young's General Store is. No sale on the stuffed moose on the porch, but Young's qualifies as a real ring-a-ding shopping experience.

For more information:
Wawa Information, 705-856-1080.
White River Visitors Centre, 807-822-2794.

27.
Taking The "A" Train

In smooth, refurbished coaches, passengers on the Agawa Canyon Train Tour settle in to the best of all worlds: seeing the pristine northern wilderness at ground level with no need to keep an eye on the road, no stop-action time lost for dining. And what a world! The train allows views of deep canyons and mixed forests of maple, birch, and pine; it goes over high trestles and edges deep blue lakes and waterfalls, passing through a land unchanged for eons.

Travel in summer when skies are bluest and Alpine meadows sing with color or in fall when glorious splashes of red-and-yellow hardwoods grab your attention away from deep green pines or in the depths of winter (January to March, weekends) when you move through a white fairyland with snow-bending trees and great masses of gleaming ice which seem determined to bring down the cliffs.

The train curves around one bend after another, finally stopping on the floor of Agawa Canyon for two hours of walk-around time. Climb to a lookout point, watch waterfalls, eat another sandwich. Park Rangers can answer all your questions.

If the call of the wild pulls you farther on, there is a special schedule for passengers to go as far as the French-Canadian town of Hearst, to stay overnight or longer. Don't come without your woollies, especially in fall or winter.

And listen to this, direct from the brochure: "a unique opportunity to experience the luxury of travelling aboard one of America's vintage private cars...from the days when only a few could enjoy such delights." The car you can hire for your own private party has dark mahogany woodwork, deep wing chairs, private kitchenette, and similar fine-tunings, with a rear standing platform (make a speech).

Home station for the Algoma Tour Train is in Sault Ste. Marie Ontario, very close to the bridge to the U.S. and only an hour north of the Mackinac Bridge. There are enough hotel rooms to go around, keeping you close for that 8:00 A.M. departure. Fares are $46.00 for adults, half or less for students, much less if you're under five. Babes in arms free. (Prices subject to change.) Advance reservations needed.

For more information:
Passenger Sales, Algoma Central Railway,
129 Bay Street, Sault Ste. Marie,
Ontario P6A 1W7, Canada, 705-946-7300.

28.

Sault Ste. Marie, Ontario

Although the nickname "twin cities" is quickly applied to towns sharing lot lines, the two "Soos" are more like true twins than most paired-off towns. The same Algonquin Indians fished from their shores, the same Jesuit missionaries, voyageurs, and traders built camps on their river. When an international boundary came between them, their roles as gateway to Lake Superior remained mutual.

The North West Fur Trading Company built a post here and installed the original Soo lock canal in 1799, replaced by a newer one in 1899. Today, there are five locks (and another in the talking stage), one Canadian, four American, lifting and lowering ships past the twenty-one-foot difference between Lake Superior and the St. Marys River. The rest of the river tumbles down a wide unnavigatable stretch of rapids ("sault" to the French).

From humble campsites to a city of eighty-two thousand, modern Sault Ste. Marie has rooms enough for eighteen hundred overnighters and places at the table for thousands more. There's a lot here to explore on foot, as locks, docks, art gallery, civic center and Algoma Railway Station are all on the waterfront.

The handsome Art Gallery of Algoma shows off a broad range of contemporary and historical Canadian art, while keeping a keen eye on local talent. 10 East Street. 705-949-9067. Canada's oldest surviving stone house west of Toronto, the Ermatinger House, built by a wealthy trader for his Ojibwa wife, stands open for tours at 831 Queen Street near Pim. See the "Mini Aquarium," sea-lamprey control center on Parks Canada Sault Canal property. See what the ugly little creature has done to fish and fishing commerce. The park provides a viewing stand, historic marine post office, and public facilities. Close by sits the *Norgoma*, last overnight cruise ship built on the Great Lakes, now a marine museum. There are guided tours in summer. It looks stubby by today's proportions, but must have been a fun ship. 705-253-9850.

Two boats leave Norgoma Dock (next to the Holiday Inn) several times a day for two-hour cruises, going through the American and Canadian locks, close to giant steel mills, close to freighters flying all flags. Lock Tours Canada, 705-253-9850.

The Great Lakes Forestry Centre, a large and advanced research facility, has an audio-visual program and tour to put visitors in better in touch with the trees. 1219 Queen Street East. 705-949-9461. Ask the desk clerk about steel-mill tours, too.

Then board a double-decker bus for a tour of anything you've missed or just for the fun of riding a bus upstairs. The same tour company offers a full day into the wilderness by minivan for a memorable time. Also next to the Holiday Inn. 705-759-6200.

Lest you get the wrong image, the Algoma Arts Festival Association, Community Concerts Association, and Sault Symphony know how to book big names, classic works, and top-rate performances. There are several theater groups, some winning high praise from critics as far away as Toronto. Art doesn't stop there: Weavers, potters, handspinners, painters, and sculptors all have their own guilds and bright shows. Dance theater, choirs, barber-shoppers, and Sweet Adelines also come under the wing of the Arts Council, a vitally active civic group. Check the paper for events at Algoma University, Sault College, or the library.

Last chance (or maybe first) to shop at Canadian prices, advantageous to U.S. dollars as of this writing. Hudson's Bay Company maintains a store in the station mall; the Totem Pole on Highway 17 North claims to have the largest souvenir shop in town. Keep all accommodation and sales receipts; you may be eligible for a tax refund. (See Canadian tax information in the back of the book.)

Winter hills come alive with the sound of snowmobiles and whizzing skis at Heyden and Searchmont. Let the visitors bureau tell you more.

For more information:
Algoma County Regional Information,
705-254-4293.

29.

Sault Ste. Marie, Michigan

Far into the continent, at the tip of the wide inland sea, Sault Ste. Marie put down roots as a mission in 1782, sixty-two years after the voyageur Etienne Brule portaged his canoe around the rapids. We are apt to think of settlements on the eastern seaboard as being "first in line" for Europeans, but the east was by-passed in this case. The Soo is Michigan's oldest city and third-oldest in the United States, home of the Sault tribe of Chippewa Indians.

In the first century of Sault Ste. Marie's existence, vessels trying to get in or out of Lake Superior had to be portaged or hauled on tracks overland. This certainly kept the size down. However, with the discovery of iron and copper in the ranges of the north, the need for navigational locks to compensate for the twenty-one-foot difference in lake and river levels was obvious (although funding was fought; Henry Clay declared in Congress that Lake Superior was beyond the farthest reaches of the moon). The first lock was built in time for the North (with a better iron supply) to win the Civil War.

Lock-watching can be intriguing. If Detroit's seventy-two-story Westin Hotel were turned on its side and floated into a chamber, it would be considerably shorter than most of the long freighters coming through the locks. You stand on observation platforms and watch as the ships, with only inches to spare on either side, come in, then slowly rise (like watching a warehouse rise out of a slot), or go down twenty-one feet and leave. The Sault locks or Welland Canal (by-passing Niagara Falls) put you as close to a freighter as you can get without climbing aboard. A scale model in the Corp of Engineers Information

Center shows how locks need no pumps—its all done with water seeking its own level.

The locks at Sault Sainte Marie bring shipping into Lake Superior.

Check in or have a meal at the waterside Ojibway Hotel and watch ships pass as you dine. 906-632-4100. Two blocks away, the Tower of History is a free-standing concrete eagle's perch for enclosed or open viewing of the area, plus history lessons about the founding of the city. The Soo Locks Tour Train guides retell the whole story as you go through the city and across the International Bridge. 906-635-5912. Go through on a Soo Locks tour boat, however, for a ship's-eye view you won't forget soon. The tour crosses to the Canadian side for a memorable close-up of the Algoma Steel operation. 500 and 1155 East

Portage. 906-632-6301 or 800-432-6301. Ask about dinner cruises.

Largest of the Great Lakes Museums is the SS *Valley Camp*, a retired five-hundred-and-fifty-foot lake-freighter-turned-showcase. Tour the galley, crew's quarters, bridge, the exhibits in the cargo hold. On deck is a lifeboat from the *Edmond Fitzgerald*, which sank in a Lake Superior storm with no warning, no lives saved. Remember the Gordon Lightfoot song? On Portage Avenue.

It's hard to capture the spirit of a city in a few short paragraphs, but the Antlers Bar (bring the kids) is an Irish eatery with no pretenses and an extremely eclectic décor. Stuffed critters, street signs, canoes, and whatsits festoon the walls; carefully orchestrated outbursts of whistles, bells, and the bartender thumping a gong mark birthdays or whatever. It gives full vent to the nonconformist Soo psyche. Great burgers, lake fish, and even Alaska crab. It's on Portage Avenue past the Valley Camp on the right.

Lake Superior University sits on the crest of a ridge with some excellent views of locks and city, plus it has a lively calendar of events. The River of History Museum is in the old post office (Federal Heritage Building), and the Sault Ste. Marie Foundation for Culture and History documents thousands of years of Indian life. Both the Alberta House Arts Center and Craig Gallery feature Michigan Upper Peninsula arts and crafts and help with the August Arts Festival celebrating international friendship through graphics and sculpture. There's camping, plus plenty of motels and an Indian casino out on Shunk Road.

For more information:
Sault Ste. Marie Chamber of Commerce,
800-MI-SAULT.

30.

Westward To Paradise

Here's a softer, gentler shore. The southeastern coast of Superior curls around Whitefish Bay with sand and pebbles and low dunes instead of rugged rocks. There are many places to walk shoeless through the refreshing grit, and more places to stare across this watery vestibule into Lake Superior and its parade of long ships entering and leaving the big lake. The Bay is also known for tragedy: Its glistening surface hides the remains of too many losses to the gales of November (namely the *Edmond Fitzgerald*), and there are the ships unable to avoid colliding in a stormy fog, as they try to make one last freight run before ice freezes commerce.

Yet on a clear summer day, the distant hills of Canada and the murmuring waves are only a balm. It would be hard to work up a real anger on such a coast.

About six miles south of Sault Ste. Marie on I-75, turn west toward Brimley on USFS 3150 (the Curley Lewis Memorial Highway), a quiet beauty of a road. Private homes, Brimley State Park (with a hundred and seventy campsites), and an Indian cemetery come first. The latter, a historic little burial plot surrounded by an aging picket fence, still has some small wooden shelters over graves, homes for the occupant's spirit. Do not enter, just look; these are sacred grounds. In this Bay Mills Indian Community, traffic laws are strictly kept. The Kings Club Casino, which you will pass, is their big local enterprise.

Lighthouse towers that you can climb up into are rare, so inspect the one at Point Iroquois. (Warning: watch your head near the top of the stairs!) The house has been turned into a small marine museum and shop, and a boardwalk protecting the low dunes gives access to the beach. Hard to leave, but the road ahead twists pleasantly, passing a couple of beach picnic areas. At M 123, turn north to Paradise.

Can a village that calls itself Paradise be described? Friendly, hospitable, homey. There are no visible angels, but groceries, gas, and places to eat. Check into Curley's Motel and stay awhile. Scuba divers use the area as a jump-in place for exploring shipwrecks in the Whitefish Point Underwater Preserve. Paradise is also a happy hunting ground for picking wild blueberries. Bring a pail and help yourself or attend their annual Blueberry Festival during the third week of August. About twelve miles north on Whitefish Road is Whitefish Point and an outstanding small museum highlighting shipwrecks. With excellent dioramas and videos, stories of doomed ships sink into your consciousness. The real belongings, of real men, salvaged from the bottom make a poignant display. Explore the gift shop and beach, where finding interesting stones may take over your attention.

West of Paradise on M 123, a Michigan state park treasure—Tahquamenon Falls roars through a beautiful mature forest. The largest waterfall between Niagara and the Rockies, it's nearly two hundred feet across and fifty feet high. Fifty thousand gallons of water per second pour over the edge, a rush best photographed when the morning sun lights the cascade head-on. (Hemlock and tamarack bogs upstream give the water that tea-like color.) Platforms and paths take you to the falls' brink and beside the meandering Tahquamenon River, which tumbles over a lower falls and eventually empties into Whitefish Bay. The enormously popular State Park site is a thirty-five-thousand-acre spread with naturalist-dream hiking trails, three hundred and twenty campsites, a new visitors center, gifts, and food.

Look up at the sun filtering through those tall stately pines, breathe deeply, and hear the birds. Maybe they had a point, calling it Paradise.

There are other approaches to the falls. Follow M 123 to Newberry and head east on M 28 to Hulbert. Ten miles north at Slater's Landing, the Tom Sawyer River Boats and Timber Train will take you there. So will the Toonerville Trolley, a narrow gauge rail ride through the woods and meadows to a boat on the Tahquamenon River. Accommodating Newberry makes a fine center for exploring some of Ernest Hemingway's favorite fishing streams or getting to Muskallonge (big inland lake) State Park.

For more information:
Newberry Area Tourism Association, 800-831-7292.
Michigan Tourism, 800-5432-YES.

31.
Michigan's Surprising Alger County

You don't expect dunes like that? You can't believe cliffs like that? Seventy-five miles of trout streams, two hundred and fifty inland lakes? Four waterfalls in Munising?

Michigan's angular Alger County shines like polished agate; not flashy yet full of kept promises. Even underwater there is much to explore.

Start at the east shore town of Grand Marais ("marais" meaning harbor), a petite hamlet ten blinks wide. The first Europeans in its placid little harbor (still uncluttered by condos or marinas) were French voyageurs who sought refuge from Superior's storms. "Voila! le Grand Marais," they must have cried. In 1890, at the peak of its population, tough, lumber-shipping Grand Marais had thirty saloons, two newspapers, and twelve boarding house/hotels. When the train stopped coming in and lumber stopped going out, commercial fishing took over, but that's gone, too. Today's four hundred and fifty residents live under a historic-preservation designation, and curious visitors can find a mother lode of early-day tales.

Gourmet-level smoked fish is at Lefebevre's Fish Market, the perfect ice cream for pig-outs at the Earl of Sandwich. There are enough rooms in town for two hundred and fifty vacationers, while Woodland Township Park on Lake Superior has a hundred campsites and all the facilities. Best of all, the Pictured Rocks National Lakeshore begins next door.

It's not rocks all the way. At the northeast end of the park are the grandest shore dunes on the continent (perched on glacial debris, but dunes nonetheless), rising majestically as high as two hundred and fifty feet above the lake. Walk at lake level west from Woodland park to view them from the base, then ask the way to Sable Falls. After climbing down a minicanyon to see the falls, follow the ridge path to the dune's topside and a wondrous, windy view of Lake Superior.

A visitor's center on Highway 58 has maps of the long, winding park road. At Log Slide, turn for the best dune overview of all. This is where the sand banks end. Westward is the lighthouse at Au Sable Point, and you can follow a hiking trail for a closer look. Beyond that is a twelve-mile beach (that water is fearsome cold) and the famous rock cliffs visible only from a boat. Another detour from H 58 at Miner's Castle Road (plus a sub-detour to Miner's Falls) leads to a famous rock formation and boardwalks. For National Lakeshore data, call: 906-387-3700.

In a place where Chippewas camped and the legendary Hiawatha took his first steps, Munising sits in a green amphitheater facing a blue bay and Grand Island, second largest island in the lake. Surrounding hills spill four waterfalls within the city limits and others are close by. One of them, Wagner Falls off Highway 94 on the south side, is the star of Michigan's smallest state park.

Munising serves as county seat, custodian of Alger County's lumbering and iron-foundry history, and shopping center of the territory. From the city pier, Pictured Rocks Boat Cruises go out daily, most frequently during July and August, edging close to the cliff's uncommon colors and the eerie formations carved by incessant waves. Late-day trips in midsummer get maximum sunlight for photographs. 906-587-2379.

Beneath the surface from Au Train to Au Sable Point, the Alger Underwater Preserve guards half a dozen Lake Superior shipwrecks, a sure lure for divers. Three diving charter businesses are nearby for qualified divers. 906-387-4477.

Undeveloped Grand Island, recently purchased by the National Forest Service, is being treated cautiously. Hiking and fishing are about all. Ask at the Pictured Rocks Cruise office.

Next, west from Munising, visit a Munising tourist campground (nice beach), a village called Christmas, and beautiful spots along the shore with a few picnic tables. At Au Train, a little delta of sand forms a shallow pool, the only place Superior waters get warm enough for tots. Go through Au Train's 1884 Paulson House, a surviving log cabin, and the Hiawatha Folk Craft and Art Center on Forest Service Road 2278. You'll see high-quality crafts and artisans at work. Continue to Road 94, then west to Sundell, and up to Laughing Whitefish Falls. After a half-mile walk through birch and hemlock, your reward is a lively, deep cascade of water, the favorite falls of many who have seen most of the hundred and fifty Upper Peninsula falls.

Snowshoes ordered from L.L.Bean might come from the Iverson Snowshoe Company in Singleton

where you can see how artfully they're made. Yuper
food ("Yuper" is what Upper Michigan residents like
to call themselves) has its own mystique. Try a pastie
(rhymes with nasty), which is a Cornish meat pie.
Details on restaurants, motels, cabins, lodges, antiques,
snowshoe races, fishing derbies, the Moose Flea
Market, and Winter Carnival are at the Munising-
Alger County Visitors Center, easily found off M 28
in Munising.

For more information:
Munising Visitor's Bureau, 906-387-4864.

32.

To Marquette, To Marquette... To L'anse

Men of iron—those were the seventeenth-century
French Jesuits who faced the hostile wilds of
northern Michigan to preach and comfort and take
nothing away. Pere Jacques Marquette and later Bishop
Baraga (the snowshoe priest) made maps, wrote letters,
and garnered the know-where that helped to open up
the lands of Superior. (Baraga was buried on the
north shore.) Decades later, men of a different iron
came and took their fortunes from mines and forests
or wrested a living from rocky farms.

Two counties named for Marquette and Baraga
are side by side on Superior's south shore.

Marquette, the city, is the largest in Michigan's
Upper Peninsula, with a university, malls, and discount stores. Restaurants, museums, parks, amenities, and good hotels are easily found, yet the feel of
pioneer country never quite lets go. Relocated moose
do well in the area's woods; loons call across lost
lakes; waves pound into untouched coves. Students
practice mountaineering survival skills minutes from
their classrooms.

Marquette first boomed as a lumber center, but the discovery of iron in 1844 forged its future. Hundreds of immigrants came to work in the mines, supplying iron for the North's cannons in the Civil War and feeding the needs of the industrial revolution. There once were forty-eight working mines in Marquette County, a story well told in the Michigan Iron Mining Museum just down the road from Negaunee.

The solid, substantial brownstone that was the former city hall and newly restored Marquette County Courthouse (where *The Anatomy of a Murder* was filmed) reflect the prosperity of Victorian decades. At Northern Michigan University, special facilities for Olympic trainees push skills for twenty-five out of thirty-seven competitive sports. NMU owns the largest wooden doomed stadium in the world, a wonder of modern design.

Drive along the waterfront to the Marquette Maritime Museum, housed in a former waterworks building. 906-226-2006. Beyond a Coast Guard station (a good stop for pictures of the red lighthouse) lie the mammoth ore-loading docks and Presque Isle Park. The Marquette Visitors Center can usually tell when a ship is coming in—always a special sight. The park (almost an island) has a marina, swimming pool, water slide, hiking and biking trails, and a great breakwater to walk out on in calm-only weather. Beautiful spot at Presque Isle's north end to watch sunsets.

Marquette High School's excellent Shiras Planetarium is open to the public. 906-225-4204. The Marquette County Historical Museum has its mirrors to the past in order, plus walking-tour maps of the town. 906-226-3571. At the waterfront park downtown, Marquette Harbor Cruises will feed you, entertain, or just let you look and listen, depending on the outing you select. 906-225-1777 or 800-544-4321.

Part of the Marquette scene is a drive up to Big Bay, also a locale in the *Anatomy* film. (Author Robert Travis lived up here.) It's a tiny lumbering town and past headquarters for Brunswick Bowling Pins. When Henry Ford invited guests to his Huron Mountain retreat, he'd put them up in the Thunder Bay Inn, which he owned at the time. 906-345-9376 or 800-732-0714. The Bay Point Lighthouse also takes in guests, a rare bed-and-breakfast experience. 906-345-9957.

West of Marquette, Negaunee and Ishpeming share the iron experience, the regional love of ski-jumping, ice sports, and Yooper (an Upper Peninsula native) humor. Listen to Da Yoopers singers belting out their "Da Second Week of Deer Camp" with a straight face. You can't. There's great antique shopping in Negaunee in a converted bank building.

The national Ski Hall of Fame catches the eye on US 41 with its ski-slide roof line. The handicapped skiers exhibit makes a strong statement for personal courage. A modern, classy Michigan Iron Industry Museum is just down a country road with miner insights to a rugged trade. Ishpeming gives complete information on both museums. 906-486-4841.

US 41 West and M 28 (combined for a while) pass Riker State Park and Lake Michigamme. It's moose country, but you'll be lucky to see one, even on a back road. Good for a pause or overnight is the Michigamme Lake Lodge, a cheery log hotel on the National Register. Crafts for sale. Breakfast for guests. 906-339-4400.

US 41 skims past beauty spots, none nicer than Canyon Falls, a short hike and rewarding detour. Eventually, you'll reach L'Anse (say Lahnze), seat of Baraga County and a good base for exploring the Huron Mountain area or as much of the north shore "hump" as roads will let you reach. Mount Curwood (on private land), at 1,996 feet, is said to be the highest point in Michigan, although nearby Mount Arvon is about the same height. Trees bar any view from the top. Take a good county map and compass in this part of the state to find treasures in tiny communities, agate shores, and great fishing.

The visitors center on East Broad Street in L'Anse is bedecked with motel and bed-and-breakfast information, fishing guides, and maps to twenty waterfalls and to the nearly hidden Sturgeon Gorge, Grand Canyon of the state. For eating time, indulge with a pie-sized sweet roll at the Hilltop Restaurant. Food is plain and plentiful, like going home to Auntie Em's.

A thirty-five-foot statue/shrine to Bishop Baraga stands on a high ridge overlooking Keweenaw Bay—quite an impressive sight. The good bishop, known as the Snowshoe Priest, faced starvation and freezing cold to care for his small, remote flock and left valuable notes, maps, and geographic information. Around the bay bend, Baraga State Park and new log Baraga County Museum are right on the lake. A new area addition to the town of Baraga is the Ojibway Casino Resort, contrasting comfortably with the Hanka Homestead, a genuine old Finnish farmstead and true picture of country life a century ago.

For more information:

Baraga County Tourist & Recreation Association, 906-524-7444.

Marquette County Tourism Council, 800-544-4321.

Michigan Tourism, 800-5432-YES.

33.

Vacation Gold In Copper Country

Six years before the '49ers made a dash for California gold and fifty years before silver fever hit Colorado, a stampede for copper was on in upper Michigan.

The prime target was that finger of land poking into western Lake Superior, the Keweenaw Peninsula.

Michigan's copper rush was the stuff of legend. Hardships of deep snow, ice, black flies, a babble of languages, and boom towns had to be endured. Include a lot of hell-raising and going broke—until wives arrived and things got civil. It was just like the Wild West, except that Michigan's tales didn't make it into the national folklore, even though these mines produced the purest copper in the world and, over many years, made more money than the silver or gold strikes. In haunted, beautiful Keweenaw, the history of copper mining is layered thickly between ghost towns, great fishing, coast-of-Maine scenery, ethnic potpourri, and laid-back fun. Few areas have so many reminders of the past so close at hand, such as the long strip of gray beach noticeable as US 41 curves along Portage Lake. That's stamp sand from old foundry dumpings. In Houghton, the road zips past Northern Michigan Technological University, founded as a college for mine trainees. An empty, rusted processing plant sits on the portage way, right across from downtown Houghton.

At NMTU, the Seaman Mineralogical Museum in the school's Electrical Resources Center is a gem for anyone and a must for rock hounds. Thirty thousand minerals and precious stones are displayed. 906-487-2572. Also home to the Keweenaw Symphony, the university puts on a major ice-sculpture contest and carnival in January, when downtown skywalks help dodge icy winds. On Houghton's waterfront, the *Ranger III* waits for summer trips to Isle Royale.

Copper history is there when you cross the big hydraulic lift bridge over the Portage Ship Canal (aka the Keweenaw Waterway), a way for earlier ore vessels to avoid lethal rocks and storms around the peninsula's tip. In Hancock, there are street signs in Finnish, one of the major ethnic groups lured by copper. Suomi College is the only U.S. school to offer Finnish as a major; its converted-church Cultural Center reflects Finnish gifts for design. US 41 winds steeply uphill to a great overlook of the scene and then passes the tall angular housing of Quincy Shaft No. 2. Under new sheathing, this historic hillcrest relic marks a mine shaft deeper than six stacked Sears Towers—one and a half miles down. A giant steam hoist built to haul men and ore such distances stands next door, open for inspection. (No, you don't go down). Anyone mechanically minded will love this stop.

Visit the restored opera house in Calumet, where Jenny Lind and Caruso sang, and Sarah Bernhardt emoted grandly. For news of current shows, call 906-337-2610. Calumet, now under one-thousand population, came within an ace of being named state capital in its forty-seven-thousand-citizen glory days. Along with Laurium and the Quincy Shaft, Calumet is part of a new National Historic Park. Stroll through town and through the Coppertown Museum. In Laurium, home of the "Gipper" of Notre Dame football fame, a grand old mine-owner's mansion, Laurium Manor, lives again as a fantastic bed and breakfast.

As US 41 curls to the top of the peninsula, it passes the Delaware Mine, an excellent chance to see how a real mine works. It's safe and educational for everyone. 906-337-3333. The end of US 41—it starts in Florida—comes just past Copper Harbor and Fort Wilkins State Park. The Fort was built to guard miners from Indians, who were no trouble at all, but miners often needed protection from each other. There are self-guided tours with costumed personnel, plus camping, a playground, and a beautiful setting. 906-289-4215.

In the village, there's a nice choice of motels, eateries, and shops, plus transport on the *Isle Royale*

Queen III to the National Park. (Reservations are essential. 906-289-4437.) Ask about trips to the harbor lighthouse, now a small museum. 906-289-4410. For a super-scenic panorama, drive to the top of Brockway Mountain (pause at the first turnout for a view of Calumet Harbor and region), six hundred feet above Lake Superior. The whole peninsular topography spreads before you—forests, lakes, the Eagle River harbor and, on a clear day, a shimmering hint of Isle Royale.

Keweenaw Mountain Lodge on US 41 was built by miners out of local logs and stone during the big Depression. It's operated by the county—wonderful, with a dining room and lounge, a nine-hole golf course, plus single and duplex cabins with fireplaces. 906-289-4403.

Explore the coastal villages of Eagle Harbor and Eagle River, as well as the singing sands and underwater preserve of Bete Grise, the ghost towns of Central or Mandan. Rustic outdoor furniture is available in Mohawk, thimbleberry jam at a bakery shop run by monks on M 26, and free blueberries in season atop Blueberry Hill near Eagle Harbor. Ask where the trail is. Old mine dumps sometimes yield pieces of copper (NEVER enter an old shaft.) In this surprising territory, the top producer of basketball and dance floors in the world operates in Dollar Bay, and the unofficial top ice-cream parlor is Lindell's Chocolate Shop in Lake Linden. The Houghton County Historical Museum on M 26 here has its own treasures for history buffs to mine.

Woods and waterfalls, a full airport, downhill skiing.

For more information:
Keweenaw Tourism Council, 906-482-2388 or
   800-338-7982.

34.

Falling Water, Flying Skis — the Porcupine Mountains

Split by Central/Eastern time-zone lines, the forested hilly world of western upper Michigan unites on ski slopes, wilderness areas, waterfalls, and the glory of having Michigan's largest state park, plus the deepest and most dependable snow for ski slopes, the world's tallest Indian, and the highest manmade ski jump in the Western Hemisphere.

The general feel of the region is remote even though things are cozy in such nooks as Gramma Grooter's Restaurant in Bruce Crossing and at resorts sequestered down county roads, and it's lively with winter sports and summer campers. South of Rockland on Victoria Road, the restored mining settlement of Victoria tells how it was in earlier times. This author had the pleasure of meeting a lady who lived in one of the log cabins as a child and was acting (in costume) as a guide. Weaving lessons and basket-making are part of the program.

Ontonagon, the county seat on Lake Superior, has a busy paper mill, open for tours if you call the public-relations office. There's a highly casual exhibit to mull through at the Ontonagon Historical Museum, and it's good coastal pickings for rocks and driftwood.

Porcupine Mountains Wilderness State Park entails some 58,335 acres of ancient rock, streams, forest, and the highest hills in these regions. One of the state's show-off lookout points is the view of Lake of the Clouds from the top of a craggy rise (a road takes you near the brink). High over the polished sapphire surface of a mountain lake, watch for changing light and cloud shadows, fragile mists, autumn red and gold—a vantage point to unboggle the mind. The park's hundred-and-eighty-three-mile trail system lets hikers into back country, where all camping requests need advance notice.

A handsome ski lodge (no overnights) with chairlift is a park special, plus fishing, a hundred and eighty-three regular campsites, and a long, long shore. More information is at the visitors center, including some on guided backpack tours. 906-885-5275.

Among the snowy hills of winter are three major Michigan ski resorts, Indianhead, Blackjack, and Big Powderhorn, with another nearby in Wisconsin, Whitecap Mountains. For lodges and motels, call the hotline for snow conditions. 800-BSC-7000. (BSC= Big Snow Country.) Ski lodges can be rented during the summer when golf and tennis are plentiful and the fishing fine to excellent.

Turn north at Bessemer onto CR 513, a road roughly paralleling Black River, the route to a concentration of waterfalls and an awesome twenty-story ski jump at Copper Peak. On a high shoulder of rock, the steel giant waits for the next world championship ski-flying meet. Via chair lift, elevator, and a small fee, you too can go up in midsummer to view the scenic panorama or imagine going down the slide into a hankie-sized landing zone. Let persons who think like eagles do the rest.

Conglomerate Falls, Potawatomi, Gorge, Sandstone, Rainbow Falls—before finally emptying into Lake Superior, the Black River drops nearly a thousand vertical feet from its source in Wisconsin in an unmatched series of scenic spills. Author's choice road.

Hiawatha stands tall and handsome, a fifty-two-foot tribute to the American Indian, in Ironwood. The visitors center on US 2 answers to motel and dining queries and has dates for area fishing derbies, ski meets, 4th of July parades, and maps to waterfalls (more than forty within close range). The Nurmi

Marathon in August (since '68) clearly wins as a favorite for runners and watchers. Community productions are seen all year in the Ironwood Theater; the Goegebic County Historical Museum uses the old depot to house its heritage collections. Ironwood's twin, Hurley, Wisconsin, had a hell-bent reputation in earlier years, times alluded to by the Red Light Snowmobile race in January. Both towns have hearty Italian cooks and fine restaurants. After lunch, go to court—the old courthouse full of looms, tools, a tower clock, and odds plus ends. For maps of marked snowmobile trails, bike and hike trails, see below.

For more information:

Wisconsin Department of Development, Division of Tourism, 800-432-TRIP.

Michigan Upper Peninsula Convention & Visitors Bureau, 800-272-7000.

Michigan Tourism, 800-5432-YES.

Lake Huron

35.

Port Huron/Sarnia: Internationsl Fun

On a Saturday morning late in July, crowds with binoculars and lawn chairs find places on the upper St. Clair River shore to watch a parade of sail boats heading out to a watery starting gate in Lake Huron. The boats are competitors in an annual Port Huron to Mackinac Island Race, sponsored by the Bayview Yacht Club of Port Huron.

Contestants are accompanied at a respectful distance by less elite craft, and the whole cluster is sometimes pushed aside by a long freighter, like a fortress easing through a field of pup tents.

It is an enormously popular spectacle, even among hard-core landlubbers.

Sarnia, Ontario, and Port Huron, Michigan, anchor the intersection where Lake Huron flows into the St. Clair River—a genuine crossroads. The high, handsome Blue Water Bridge carries east-west motorists (millions a year), while the north-south shipping lanes below only stop for winter ice. All the while, passenger and freight trains are going through under-river tunnels.

The family ties of these international civic siblings are strong. They share history, quite naturally, but also a surprising calendar of summer events. Except for some high-rise apartments on the Sarnia side, the cities have a similar ambience.

A fort was being built by the French in Port Huron at about the same time early settlers were arriving in Sarnia's vicinity. Port Huron's founding economy was lumber until disastrous fires in 1871 (when the whole Great Lakes area was affected). Today, it's best known for salt, brass, fishing rods, cheese, and marine products. Sarnia's bonanza came with the first oil gusher in nearby Petrolia. It was not the first oil well, but the first that spewed oil in fire-hose fashion, flooding fields and creeks, while drillers frantically fumbled for ways to control it. Sarnia became a refinery city, now dealing with petro-chemicals, shipping, shopping, and tourism.

An inventive young lad named Thomas Edison lived in Port Huron and was employed by the railroad...until one of his experiments set fire to a baggage car. His old station work-place sits close to the Blue Water Bridge, wears coats of bright red paint, and serves as travel information center. Next door, the Edison Inn's wide windows view the river and passing vessels. About four blocks away at Pine Grove Park, the Coast Guard's Huron Lightship opens its hatches for summer tours.

Port Huron wears its maturity well, from tree-filled old neighborhoods to the county courthouse. The Black River bisects downtown and has a nice walk beside the marinas. Just south of the river at the Museum of Arts and History on Sixth Street, relics from high and low times, old ship models, and new art vie for attention. In May, these imaginative folks sponsor a re-enactment of an annual fur-trading rendezvous with eighteenth-century feasts and dress. Splashiest wing-ding of all is the Blue Water Fest in July, with parades and fireworks, and including appearances by marchers from Sarnia.

Sarnia—beloved by boaters for spiffy docking facilities, by shoppers for malls, English china, and Canadian art prints, and by gardeners for the acres of blooms in Rosebush Gardens plus flower plots everywhere. A revamped downtown and fine hotels near the river have made Sarnia a meeting favorite.

Hundreds of kilted competitors toss cabers, play bagpipes, and do their fling every August in a gathering of clans for Highland Games. It's enough to make a Scotsman out of anyone. Canada Days (boat races and fireworks) and United Kingdom galas are as bright as Sarnia refinery lights after dark. (A Port Huron waterfront bonus is to see the lights of Sarnia reflected in the river.)

Persons crossing the border need to carry proof of citizenship; every car should have a copy of customs regulations. Shoppers may otherwise miss a tax refund.

Both cities make great anchors for exploring downriver, the lower coasts of Lake Huron, Michigan's Thumb, and Ontario's wonderful little towns.

For more information:
Port Huron Chamber of Commerce, 810-985-7101.
Sarnia Chamber of Commerce, 519-336-3232.

36.

Exploring Michigan's Thumb

Michigan's eastern geographic digit lies half-way upstate and all the way to a mind-set, as far from traffic and urban hoopla as country lanes are from race tracks. Unsophisticated (mostly), yet it's wise to what counts.

Like the rest of the state, the Thumb was covered with forests in early times; waterside towns were ports shipping out lumber. Horrendous forest fires in 1871 and '81 changed the economic base to farming, then (years later) a lethal Lake Huron storm destroyed everything in the ports but their names.

Sugar beets, white navy beans, fishing, and a shrugging acceptance of tourism dictate the fortunes of the Thumb today. State and county parks are dotted with inviting beaches, lighthouses, affordable cottages, and some choice eateries; the Saginaw Bay side has more motels. Drive around the edge first, reduce your pulse rate, then explore a few ruler-straight but delightful back roads.

The Thumb is easily reached via I 75 or M 53, but we'll take the shore route, pausing at Port Huron's Fort Gratiot Lighthouse, Michigan's oldest navigation light (1825). Feel the mood-change in Lexington, a pretty little walk-around town and harbor of refuge. "Harbor" refers to a Great Lakes sail-safe program providing shelter at least every thirty miles along the coast. The feat is usually accomplished with long breakwaters and marinas, making natural pier-fishing spots.

South of Port Sanilac, the Sanilac Historical Museum's lovely pale-yellow Victorian house was built by the area's first doctor. The office and living-room furnishings are still there, along with Great Lakes marine memorabilia and a dairy exhibit, plus a pioneer cabin and even a highly successful Barn Theater on the grounds. 810-622-9946.

Supreme Court Justice Frank Murphy was born in Harbor Beach, largest community on a coast of historic storms and shipwrecks. The Thumb Area Bottomland Preserve has plenty to offer scuba divers and the Point Aux Barques Lighthouse Museum displays photos of wrecks. Lighthouse Park, north of Port Hope, offers some trailer camping, but you can't climb the tower.

Pull over at Pioneer Huron City Museum's tidy collection of vintage buildings (store, Coast Guard station, church), a place Yale educator W. Lyons Phelps made famous with charismatic preaching during summer visits. 517-428-4123. Up the road, Grindstone City makes ingenious use of leftover grindstones, an early local product. However, there's no city. An 1884 Bank in Port Austin cashes in as a chic gourmet

restaurant getting rave reviews, 517-738-5353, and the
Garfield Inn would please a first lady. 517-738-5254.
Or you can catch your own supper from a long, long
pier next to a beachside park. Around on the Thumb's
west side, there are two state parks and a new excursion boat going out of Caseville, a ferry to Charity
Island out where Saginaw Bay meets the lake. Charity's gifts are an old lighthouse, stone quarry, rare
plants, and three miles of shoreline. 800-933-9442. Or
visit the spacious Huron County Wilderness Center,
nine miles east of town on Loosemore Road.

Summer fishing derbies, where the walleye catches
are legendary, and food galas (Sebewaing Sugar Festival and Bay Port Fish Sandwich Day) liven up the
social calendar, as do the duck hunters grouping for
fall shooting. Anybody remember Arthur Godfrey and
"I Found My Baby in Bad Axe"? The oddly-named
county seat has more Thumb information.

Into the bigger world, there's Bay City that
shipped out enough lumber by 1888 to circle the
globe four times. Today, it's chemicals, auto parts,
boats, river walks, antique shopping, and malls. In
riverside Winona Park, catch a whopping 4th of July
fire-works party and free summer events. Poke into
the old Romanesque City Hall—if the tower is open,
it's a super view.

Part of any Thumb excursion has to be a stop in
Frankenmuth (just close enough to Thumb territory
to qualify) and one of Michigan's biggest attractions.
Family-style chicken dinners are steamed up by Bavarian cooks, and there's a year-round Christmas store of
stadium proportions; then add clock shops, wood
carvers, dirndl skirts, and leiderhosen amid Alpine
architectural touches and overflowing flower beds. A
glockenspiel on the side of the Bavarian Inn Restaurant tells the time and the Pied Piper story three times
a day; a big Bavarian Festival in June oomp-pah-pahs

111

the whole Frankenmuth tune. A popular place in August, it's also wonderful in spring and fall. Visitors should call 517-652-6106. A huge discount mall is minutes away at Birch Run on I 75.

Resume speed.

For more information:

Bay City Area Tourism, 517-893-1222 or 800-424-5114.

Blue Water Area Tourism, 800-852-4242.

Frankenmuth Chamber of Commerce, 517-652-6106.

37.

The Morningside of Upper Huron

The morningside regions of Michigan's upper Lower Peninsula near the Huron shores have a folksy, lets-go-fishing hospitality. With pine-scented scenic appeal, it is also one of those areas that's "being discovered," which means that the rent is going up, although it's still a bargain. Travelers who like to play golf before breakfast or sip Mai Tais after canoeing are in safe territory.

Leave I 75 north at the Standish exit and lock into US 23. Up a few miles, Au Gres has a new offering, a ferry to Charity Island in mid-Saginaw Bay twice a day in summer (see chapter 36). Tawas and East Tawas (only a native can tell where the dividing line is) have good piers and cute play constructions for kids. There is a hiking/biking/horseback trail going from this point on Lake Huron across the state to Lake Michigan. (Happily, horses going through are rare, which makes for better hiking). Folks less inclined to such pursuits can dig into the Tawas Bay sand and watch racing sailors compete in the sheltered waters. A run-down on local events is available at the Tawas Visitors Center on the beach or try the Iosco County Historical Museum.

As the road turns north, Tawas Point State Park gleams in a special early-morning glory when a rising sun paints the lighthouse gold, and redwing black birds sing in full voice from the reeds. Bird watchers have identified at least two hundred species in this Cape Codish spit of land separating Tawas Bay from Lake Huron. There's a windy boardwalk over low dunes, places to sit and gaze, and camping facilities. It's popular in summer, a haven in spring or fall. 517-362-5041.

The long and winding Au Sable River, favorite with canoeists and trout fishermen, enters Huron between Oscoda and Au Sable. In summer and during fall color weekends, a popular paddlewheel river boat cruises upstream.

Harrisville State Park's ninety-four acres gives two hundred and twenty-four campers a chance to pull in near an offshore boulder where Indians once made sacrifices to insure safe lake travel. Another beautiful spot to watch the sun come up. 517-724-5126.

Around Sturgeon Point and an 1869 lighthouse, there are shipwrecks for divers to explore but not exploit—no helping yourself to artifacts. Dinosaur Gardens in tiny Ossineke were the life-time project of a devout gentleman long gone, and perhaps a few specimens need updating now. Even so, the beasts are artfully spread through a beautiful (and labeled) stand of trees, making a very good stop for everyone.

Alpena, an aging lumber town with great Victorian houses and young ideas, reigns as the largest city on the coast. Live theater, golf, good shopping, a generous supply of motels, and restaurants where helpings overflow are some of the offerings. The Jesse Besser Museum, a jewel for its size, showcases art, science, and history with genuine flair. You can also bet

113

on fishing derbies, boat races, and Fourth of July fireworks. Inland from Alpena, the stately elk ambles—ask how you might go to see them.

Fall colors, elk, tiny towns, hunting, fishing, this deep interior spread of eastern upper (lower peninsula) Michigan is low on high excitement. And that's the lure of it.

North of Alpena, the light at the Presque Isle Lighthouse Museum can be climbed. Exhibits in the former keeper's house showcase homeware and marine gear, and exasperated parents may want to walk off with the old-fashioned pilgrim stocks in the museum yard. Another, newer light a mile north is being renovated as of this writing.

Watch limestone dynamited out of its quarry, take part in a big nautical festival, munch on smoked fish or buy it freshly filleted at the third-generation fish market Gauthier & Spaulding. G & S is a Rogers City tradition in a town where working on freighters and having salmon derbies (or the fish of the hour) is what you do.

Ahead are roadside parks, Hoeft State Park (wide, uncrowded beaches), Cheboygan, and the Straits of Mackinac.

For more information:
Alpena Chamber of Commerce, 800-582-1906.
Rogers City Visitors Center, 517-734-2535.
Tawas Visitors Center, 517-362-2731.

38.
Straits Talk: Where the Waters Meet

Where Lakes Huron and Michigan curve toward each other at the Straits of Mackinac, tourism has replaced everything else for a hundred and forty years, including the fishing industry, lumbering, and the original commerce, fur trading. It is, however, tourism with a muted voice. It's not garishly banging for attention, but it provides plenty to do in an area of high historic interest, crystal clear air, and water in vast blue expanses.

Cheboygan, Mackinaw City, St. Ignace, and Mackinac Island (a chapter of its own) stand beside one of the first-discovered passages into an unknown continent, a strait that knew three flags and saw the change from canoes to sails, steamships, freighters, and family vans. Big industry never arrived to change their skylines; smog and major swells of population are unknown.

Cheboygan ("place of going through") facing Lake Huron on US 23 is well-named for a straits town with additional water connections to Mullet Lake, Burt Lake, and an inland waterway reaching for forty-five miles. At Huron and Court Streets, an old jail lives a reformed life as a historical museum, while Cheboygan's prize possession, a restored Opera House with flawless acoustics, has presented Roy Clark, the Detroit Symphony Orchestra, and even the Peking Acrobats. Visit the Coast Guard cutter *Mackinaw* or stroll the long boardwalk over a cattail marsh. There are ferries to a large off-shore isle, Bois Blanc (pronounced Bob-Lo), from both Cheboygan and Mackinaw City. Takers find a twenty-five-thousand-acre retreat with a few places to eat, stay, and buy basics. There are little lakes and rustic living, plus another old lighthouse. Call Plaunt Transport at 616-627-2354 or 616-627-9445 and plan ahead.

Between Cheboygan and Mackinaw City lies one of three showplaces under the auspices of the Mackinac Historic Parks Commission. Mill Creek State Park has no camping or usual park trappings, but it does have a sleek visitors center and a demonstration of practical ingenuity. In a camera-ready setting on a small creek, a minor waterfall turns a big wheel, the wheel activates gears, the gears move a sawblade (the only metal used), and voila!—heavy timbers become boards. The original mill was built in 1780. Costumed workmen put on various how-to demonstrations and answer questions. Nature trails and a video show are among the offerings. 616-436-5563.

(Note: All Mackinac names are pronounced Mackinaw, although Mackinaw City alone is spelled that way.) Mackinaw City's community roots go back to the building of Fort Michilimackinac (wade through one syllable at a time, and you'll come out all right) and a small settlement around the lighthouse. When big lumbering and commercial fishing days were over, Mackinaw City went into a retreat and was merely the place where you had to wait, sometimes for hours, to catch a ferry across to the Upper Peninsula. Now, with the bridge and several ferries to Mackinac Island, plus the reconstructed fort, the town at the Straits is a major home base for area travel.

Points of special interest include the Mackinac Bridge Museum located over a restaurant on Central Avenue, with pictures and movies on the construction of the bridge that "couldn't be built," and Teysen's Talking Bear Museum (a lot more than bears) on Huron Avenue. Three ferries connect with Mackinac Island: Arnold Line, 906-847-3351, Shepler's Ferry, 616-436-5023, and Star Line, 906-643-7635. The big annual event is the Mackinac Bridge Walk, which brings thousands of hikers (sixty-one thousand in 1995) every Labor Day.

Fort Michilimackinac is a 3-D wrap-around history lesson. In the early 1700s, the French built this stronghold to protect their fur trade. Later, the area was ceded to the British, who moved over to Mackinac Island after rebellious Indians massacred their troops. America's Revolution finally put the area in

U.S. hands. The whole story of the fort, village life within its walls, and even the massacre is told in sound/light shows, guides, demos, and special pageants. 906-847-3328.

St. Ignace is another departure point for Mackinac Island, another city of motels, souvenir shops, and good eating. Neat, historic St.Ignace, named by Pere Jacques Marquette when he founded a mission here in 1671, is thirty years older than Detroit, a hundred and twenty-eight years older than Cleveland. The Michilimackinac Historical Society Museum on Spring Street, the Fort De Baude Museum, and the Museum of Ojibwa Culture contain treasures of area history from bone needles, beadwork, and muskets to a three-hundred-year-old canoe and a longhouse.

Curved along the shoreline, the town center sees a lively list of imaginative events. For Memorial Day weekend, there's a history pageant and an annual pasty bake (the favorite Upper Peninsula meat pie); mid-June has its annual MESSABOUT, a hand-made boat-builders gathering; the Straits Area Antique Auto Show is in late June; and the Straits Underwater Preserve Treasure Hunt is in late August; the Annual Mackinac Bridge Walk is held on Labor Day; then comes the Dockside Arts and Crafts show. The Father Marquette National Memorial, Wilderness State Park, and nearness of Sault Ste. Marie and the locks, with Mackinac Island right at hand, gives a Straits destination special value. See the chapter "Top of the Lake" for more.

For more information:

St. Ignace Chamber of Commerce, 906-643-7635 or 800-638-9892.

Mackinaw City Information Center, 616-436-5574.

Cheboygan Information Center, 616-627-7183.

39.

Camelot North: Mackinac Island

As the ferry approaches from St. Ignace or Mackinaw City, you get a good look at graciously sized Victorian "cottages" and the hundred-and-ten-year-old Grand Hotel with the world's longest porch (six hundred and sixty feet), unrivaled queen of seasonal inns. The boat pulls in next to a nineteenth-century town, with shops and vintage hotels, rental bike racks, and waiting carriages. The gleaming white stone ramparts of Fort Mackinac crown a bluff; sailboats fill the marina. There's not a car in sight.

You may wonder if its real. It is.

Not a theme park, Mackinac's carefully tended buildings reflect more than two hundred years of true history. Indians powwowed, fur traders gathered, and Americans fought the British here. St. Anne's Church grew from a 1670 mission, the fort was built in 1780, and the Island House Hotel went up in 1848. The picket fences and gingerbread trim aren't make-believe.

Mackinac Island was the nation's second national park (after Yellowstone), but reverted to Michigan in 1895. Today, eighty-one percent of its five square miles is State Park. The only paved road in the state with no auto traffic runs for eight miles on the island's rim.

Walk slowly up to the gates of Fort Mackinac on the south-side ramp, plainly visible from Mission Street, or take a carriage tour and enter on the north side through an avenue of flags. There are fourteen white and bright original buildings to go through at your own pace, with interpreters everywhere, plus firearm and marching demos and rustic musicians. Every so often, folks stand by while they fire off a cannon.

In the hospital ward at reconstructed Fort Mackinac.

One of the fort's delights is the tea room and out-door porch with a perfectly grand view of the town and straits. Food service is by the Grand Hotel.

Dr. W. Beaumont, an army surgeon, treated a voyageur who was shot in the stomach, causing a wound that wouldn't heal. With a window into a live human stomach, the curious medic ran experiments on food digestion, and contributed greatly to our knowledge of such things. The patient outlived the doctor. The doctor's house on Market Street explains more.

A French-Canadian log cabin near the Beaumont house is believed to be the oldest on the island, dating to about 1775. On down the block, the charming Biddle House was owned by an independent fur trader. The blacksmith shop is still at work, and the Indian Dormitory exhibits native artifacts. John Jacob Astor (of the Waldorf-Astoria), who owned the American Fur Company and employed up to five hundred clerks just to keep track of incoming hides, had three floors of warehouse space, and the furnishings can still be seen. Up the road, just beyond the Grand Hotel, a museum of antique carriages is operated by the people who drive you around today. New and wondrous is the Butterfly House where hundreds of specimens flutter around a tropical greenhouse. It's up Mission Street.

There are unique rock formations of interest, namely the seventy-five-foot towering Sugar Loaf or Arch Rock, pointed out on tours and maps. History fans who love old headstones can find them in three cemeteries, or they can find a battle to research at British Landing.

Shopping, dining, lodging, and the high consumption of fudge fill the gaps of island conversation, in between golf (three courses), sailing, and flowers. For the T-shirt that says YOU or for an original painting, island shops are really special. The Mustang Lounge has its own set of local legends; hotel dining rooms are never bad choices.

The Grand Hotel positively must be seen close up, although they've been forced to charge $5.00 apiece for nonguests to stroll the porch or sit in a rocking chair (dinner or lunch guests excepted). Built in 1887 by a consortium of railroad companies, the four-storied Greek Revival structure with bright yellow awnings, boxes bursting with geraniums, green porch carpeting, and the dazzling blue waters of the straits just beyond is a visual trip of its own. Add the liveried footmen and the classic carriages of the Grand's

On the porch at the Grand Hotel, Mackinac Island

own taxi system to the list of attractions. Cornelius Vanderbilt, President Theodore Roosevelt, movie stars, royalty, and dozens of dignitaries are in the guest registry. High tea is served in the afternoon; no shorts may be worn at dinner. Elegance lives on. 800-33-GRAND.

On the other side of the village, the Mission Point Inn makes some rather grand statements of its

121

own. Go into the tall tepee lobby and stare upward at the huge beam "tent" poles. 800-833-7711. Bed and breakfasts, condos, suites, and more than one thousand rooms are available in wonderful places with long traditions of coziness and charm.

Near the docks, things get pretty busy (well, hectic) in midsummer with bikes and carriages everywhere, but most of the island remains serene, almost secluded and a refreshing change. Two major sailing races fill the island on two weekends in July: the Chicago-to-Mackinac and the Port Huron-to-Mackinac races. The June Lilac Festival is a winner, as is the fall color season. In August, there are bicycle races and a horse show. There are fewer boats and places to stay as winter comes and islanders rev up their snowmobiles. When the ferries stop, you can fly over for sleigh rides. Camelot never really shuts down.

For more information:

Mackinac Island Chamber of Commerce, 906-847-3783.

Mackinac Island State Park/Fort Mackinac, 906-847-3328.

40.

Les Cheneaux and Drummond Isle

A brief glance at a map and one thing is clear: In the squiggly, odd-shaped section of Michigan east of I 75 and on the north Lake Huron shore, community names are spelled out in very small print. This means a low density of humans and a high density of trees, a destination with great appeal to those who can live without traffic and neon lights.

Leave I 75 for M 134, skim the north shore of St. Martin Bay, pass a few houses at the mouth of the

Pine River, and go on to Hessel, an anchoring place and village.

There are at least two restaurants and a general store in Hessel, maybe a little more. Lumber yards and limestone shipping are the main occupations of Hessel and Cederville (a tad larger, just up the road), besides going fishing, ferrying people over to an island, and gearing them up to hunt or catch their own. These folks know where all the resorts and rental cabins can be found and are happy to tell.

Once a year, the little gazebo in Hessel's Marina Park holds a band to play for the big August Antique Boat Show and Art Fair, an event that should charm the world back into straw hats and middy blouses. Launches, cruisers, and classic sails swish or putt-putt into port in the largest gathering of its kind in the country. It's sponsored by both communities and the Historical Museum in Cedarville, (a neat place for browsing). Remember, to old boat aficionados fiber glass is an ugly term.

A Victorian sells-all, the Woodshed Gift Shop has hand-crafted baskets, rugs, and more. Half a block south of the M 134 and M 129 intersection. Another art-full shop is Northwind Pottery, east of Hessel and worth turning back to. 906-647-3416.

Les Cheneaux, (pronounced Le Snows) refers to tricky channels between thirty-six off-shore islands. Best seen on a county map, these diversely shaped land pieces seem to be leaning in the same direction, northwest to southeast, and are hauntingly scenic hideaways. Boaters, however, need to know what they're doing.

Appealing turn-outs along the Huron coast can delay your arrival in tiny DeTour village, last coffee stop before Drummond Island. The name means "the turn," and freighters headed for or coming out of Lake Superior must turn here at DeTour Passage. It's a prime spot to watch the stately long ships pass close at hand.

Drummond Island was named for a British general who kept on building his fort here, even after the bad news arrived that the American Revolution had turned the island into his enemy's territory. Apparently, he was finally convinced and left without much of a trace. This is the largest U.S. Great Lake island, with Michigan's Upper Peninsula stretching over three hundred and sixty miles to the west.

Eighty miles of paved roads and three times that in rutted trails curl into every Drummond cove and cranny. Botanists and bird watchers warble happily over the island's variety of species. For example, twenty-four kinds of orchids (bring your magnifying glass) can be found, and raptors, finches, cranes, and owls are here en masse. In a little cluster hamlet called Four Corners, you can restock the picnic hamper or arrange a golf game or just talk if you've been alone in the woods too long. For housing and cottage rentals, call: Drummond Island, 906-493-5245.

The water route between DeTour and Drummond is not just a straight river path to the Soo; shipping must pass Lime Island, Munuscong Lake, Neebish Island, Lake Nicolet, and Sugar Island before reaching the turbulent St. Mary's River where locks were required to deal with rapids. Lime Island is very small, but Neebish and Sugar have a quiet life of their own, seldom mentioned in guidebooks. There are roads and farms, with little tourism, but the fishing, hunting, and biking are excellent.

For more information:
St. Ignace Area Tourist Information, 906-643-8717.
Sault Ste. Marie Tourism, 800-MISAULT.

41.

A Glorious Strand of Sand

A long golden boulevard of sand, part of the incredible border of a province that still reaches a thousand miles farther west and fifteen hundred miles farther north, is Ontario's coast of Lake Huron, marked on early maps as the "sweet water sea." Over three hundred and forty kilometers of mostly beach, over two hundred miles of lakeshore living, of watching sunsets and launching sailboats, fishing from piers or seeing long ships pass are here.

For those coming from the south, a stop at either Ipperwash or the Pinery Provincial Parks will introduce a feast of a five-mile (eight-kilometer) beach in well-equipped style. Between them, there are more than a thousand campsites, so count on room except on big holiday weekends. 519-243-2220.

Just before Grand Bend, enjoy the outstanding Lambton Heritage Museum. Exhibits in several buildings feature a large collection of pressed glass, artifacts of Native American and pioneer life, a slaughterhouse (rare in reconstructed villages), and a blacksmith's. Annual galas include an Antique Engine Fest. 519-243-2600.

Grand Bend gets a little dizzy with its own popularity. No wonder. It's a place where you can play golf or tennis, bowl, roller skate, ride horseback, shop, slither down long slides, or eat from dawn till sunset... watched across more beach. In the Huron Country Playhouse (not your regular barn), an energetic summer-stock company concentrates on comedies and musicals. Lots of motels nearby. 519-238-2201.

How do you judge a sunset? A leading American magazine once named Bayfield as second-best sunset place (first was Hawaii); sit atop Bayfield's bluff and decide for yourself. A chic community, it's bedecked

125

gently with craft shops and old buildings. Have a bite to eat in the Little Inn before you leave. Excellent marina.

North off Highway 21, the full-size functioning Goderich Township windmill was privately built with the aid of eighteenth-century plans. A summertime Dutch treat.

Years ago, Queen Elizabeth II dubbed Goderich (GOD- rich) the prettiest town in Canada, and she's still being quoted. She had an eye for charm. The largest Canadian community on Lake Huron, on a high bluff overlooking the lake and the Maitland River, Goderich flourished as a salt-shipping port. Begin exploring in the octagonal courthouse square, the hub of eight streets like spokes on a wheel with judicial functions in the center. The nifty old Hotel Bedford is one of the buildings on the Square, along with shops and services.

The Huron County Gaol (jail) also has an unusual hexagon shape and was a step forward (in its day) toward prison reform. You won't think so after the thought-provoking tour. Huron County's Pioneer Museum and Marine Museum (in a ship's forestructure) tell more tales. Add the Carnegie Library, Benmiller's Inn, St. Christopher's Beach and Cove, and nearly two thousand nearby campsites, as well as the farmer's market and concerts in the park—fun town. A full-blown Celtic Festival, with medieval knights and jig lessons, is high on the list of events. 519-524-6600.

Travel northward to Kincardine, a tidy urban center where the lighthouse once held a distillery, and the Scottish heritage is celebrated with a Pipe Band parade and concert every Saturday night. More good beaches, of course.

Inland from Goderich down Highway 8, through Clinton, Seaforth, and Mitchell, Stratford continues to win fame for superb Shakespearean productions in a setting that deliberately imitates England, with a river Avon, swans, lawns, and gardens. There are thousands of blooms in the Brickman's Botanical Gardens and the bird sanctuary, with still another park-like setting around the Gallery Stratford, showplace for traditional and modern art. The main event, of course, is the Stratford Festival, now involving three theaters and a season from May till mid-November.

For more information:
Huron-area Tourism, 519-649-7075.

42.
Adventures On the Bruce Peninsula

The tapering finger of land trying to separate Lake Huron from Georgian Bay is certainly part of chapters 41 and 44, yet it has a personality of its own. To many people, "going up to the Bruce" is a complete goal that shouldn't be sidetracked. Even campers come away with a sense of part ownership. It will get to you.

For such a narrow peninsula, the Bruce is an interesting bit of geology, with high rugged cliffs on the east side, beach and wetlands on the west. Highway 6 runs up the middle so that exploring the edges means a lot of detours, all part of the fun, which really begins back down the road between Inverhuron and Macgregor Point Provincial Parks. There, the large Bruce Nuclear Power Plant has a visitors program, a futuristic introduction to a region that looks ahead.

Port Elgin is southern anchor for the Bruce. Literally. It has an excellent marina for sailors, charters for deep-lake fishing, plus wind surfing and beaches. Take a ride on the miniature steam train, hear a band concert in the park, or plan to attend the rousing Scottish

Festival in June with all things dear to a Scot's heart. Spreading maple trees put on a spectacular fall color show. Port Elgin Information Bureau, 519-832-2332.

Not far from Southhampton, the Chantry lighthouse beacon marks the halfway point for vessels traveling between Sarnia and Sault Ste. Marie. At the mouth of the Saugren River, the town has achieved fair fame for being a fine canoe area and for the big annual Chantry Chinook Classic Salmon Derby where the prizes are pro-golf size and the fish try to match up. There's lots of tennis, some lawn bowling, and enough motel and cottage rooms to let you be picky. Take time for the Southhampton market bazaar or check out the summer workshops in the Southhampton Art School. 519-821-9792.

The Bruce County Museum, in an old schoolhouse with a modern wing, does a professional job in twenty-one thousand square feet of floor space, with ten galleries, a new marine showspace, and a catalog-size list of collections from art works to zithers. Victoria Street North in Southhampton. For museum and town events, call 800-268-3838.

Past the Chippewa Indian Reserve and Sauble Beach, a wide pleasure zone of beach and surfers, the coves of Olipant and Howdenvale are filled with resort lodges and private property. Visit sparkling Sauble Falls (a long flight of watery steps) before heading over to Highway 6 and up to Tobermory.

The village named for Tobermory, Scotland, and called "Tub-er-murry" by the locals has two bays. Business action surrounds Little Tub, a small inlet of large charm, while Big Tub (in comparison) is lined with homes and cottages. Beneath the surface of the latter are several old shipwrecks—in fact, they are strewn all around the peninsula. At the tip of the Bruce, maneuvering space between Georgian Bay and Lake Huron narrows down; before radar and sonar, a storm could make a ship as helpless as a sock in the rinse cycle. At least two dozen wrecks lie in the deep clear waters of Fathom Five Provincial Park, an underwater world of its own plus a few islands. From one of them, Flower Pot Island, an unusual pot-shaped rock formation is probably the most-photographed object in the Bay.

Nondivers can see wrecks in movies at the Crowsnet Theater (and print shop) on Little Tub or peek through a glass-bottom boat with a schedule to fit the comings and goings of the Manitoulin ferry, *Chi Cheemaun* ("big canoe"). Trivia note: Nearby, Wireless Point was one of the first radio stations on the Great Lakes and, sadly, one of the rare ones to hear distress signals from the Titanic. Tobermory Information Bureau, 519-596-2452.

The two sides of the Bruce Peninsula have little in common. The west is sand or marsh, the east dramatic and rocky, a part of the same escarpment that shapes Niagara Falls. Here in Ontario's newest national park is superb scenery and an exciting and a challenging hiking trail. Park visitors center and maps in Tobermory.

A bit of England can be found in the shape of St. Margaret's, a meticulous replica of a British stone country church, East Road north of Lion's Head in Lindsay Township. Lucky little Lion's Head enjoys the most scenic position on a lovely coast, big enough for playgrounds and motels, small enough for a feeling of intimacy.

Once, seven sawmills and three furniture factories stood in Wiarton, and Colpoys Bay turned brown with floating logs. Those days long gone, the new Wiarton is where "Brucers" shop with close-by golf and a full-service airport (Canadian customs). In waterside Bluewater Park, leave the picnic long enough to inspect the 1904 Wiarton Railway Station's elaborately mitered ceilings and other craftsman's touches. A Heritage Walking tour shows you around a town that's proud of its architecture. On County Road 26 east of town, the inquiring mind will want to see Bruce's Caves, pillars of stone, and gaze at overhanging cliffs. Frog-jumping contests, Sunday park concerts, downtown sidewalk sales, and half a dozen boat races mark the calendar. Wiarton is alive and well and fun. Call Wiarton Tourist Bureau, 519-534-1400, for more of the scoop.

For more information:
Ontario Tourism, 800-ONTARIO.

43.

Manitoulin Island: What Is a Crowd?

Stretched across the northern waters of Lake Huron is a large land mass with no definite shape and irregular height bearing the name Manitoulin (of the Great Spirit). Here lives a breed of uncommonly friendly, hearty folks including five Indian tribes who love cold winters, scenic fishing holes, and cooking meals for strangers.

Because of Manitoulin Island, Lake Huron is blessed with two north shores. The inner one follows the north side of the famed North Channel; the surf-side coast is the south side of Manitoulin. It was the Channel's inner shoreline that the first European canoes cautiously followed westward.

If today's voyageur paddles his van from the north, he/she crosses the Channel by bridge. From the south, there is an auto ferry, the *Chi Cheemaun*, the largest built for service on the Great Lakes. Running exclusively between Tobermory and South Baymouth, a port on Manitoulin, the vessel opens its jaw and swallows up to a hundred and fifteen cars. For about two hours, the *Chi-Chee's* six hundred passengers can enjoy a cafeteria meal, browse the gift shop, and relax while kids are in their own special playroom. Clearly, getting there is a good chunk of the fun.

The ferry terminal in South Baymouth has the answer to everything you wanted to know about Manitoulin but forgot to ask before you left home. The town is complete enough with restaurants and motels to stay in while you explore from here.

The island's general shape defies description, but all the tiny peninsulas and inland sections add up to the largest freshwater isle in the world with nearly a thousand miles, or sixteen hundred kilometers, of coastline, half a dozen hamlets (Little Current is the metro area with a population of 1,511), and five First Nation reservations.

At the extreme western tip, citizens of Meldrum Bay (population thirty-six at last count) maintain the Mississagi Lighthouse Museum. LaSalle's ship *Griffon* (first recorded loss on the Lakes) is said to have been damaged here in 1670. Marine treasures and lighthouse-keeping aids are on display. The setting of Gore Bay (the second largest town with nine hundred and sixteen souls) is picture-book lovely; it's a supply depot for boaters. Not far to the east in a wooded setting, a lacy cascade called Bridal Veil Falls is worth the detour. The Gore Bay Museum was once a jail, with cells now guarding historic bric-a-brac.

Once a Hudson's Bay Company trading post, then a port for coal shipments, Little Current is a boaters haven today. The Little Current-Howland Museum is set in a wooded park off Highway 6 at the village of Sheguiandah. In its various buildings are ethnic, pioneer, and native crafts, plus tools and other clues as to how our forebears managed. There's great hiking on the Cup and Saucer Trail, leading to the highest point on the island. (The cliff is also a part of the Niagara Escarpment that runs along the Bruce Peninsula.) Another super view is from McLean's Mountain Lookout, two miles west of Little Current on Highway 540.

Manitowaning, bright button of a town with an old church, lighthouse, and museums also has tennis and even a racetrack. You seldom find a town this small that's this diversified. The Assignack Museum complex started in a jail on Main Street; it now includes a house, log cabin, and transportation shed. In Heritage Park, the Great Lakes ship SS *Norisle*, gives tours; it's next to the old Burns Wharf, Rolling Mill, and other exhibits.

If it's a beach you need, the one at Providence Bay on the south shore is the longest and best. For a calendar of events, including powwows, call Chamber of Commerce, 519-859-3161.

For more information:
Ontario Tourism, 800-ONTARIO.
Manitoulin Information Centre at Little Current, 705-368-3021.
Ferry Service, 800-265-3163.

44.

Georgian Bay South: Ontario Favorite

S ome think that Georgian Bay qualifies as a sixth Great Lake. If the Bruce Peninsula reached to within wading distance of Manitoulin, that would have been the case. It was once named Lake Manitoulin by Captain William Owen of the Royal Navy, the Britisher who made the first charts of its waters with his name on one of the bays.

Renamed after George IV, the big Huron annex (a hundred and twenty miles or a hundred and ninety kilometers long; fifty miles or eighty kilometers wide) has remarkable variety along its shores, and the south coast is as different from the north as a rock is from a soft place.

Cautionary note: Anyone who thinks that because it is a bay the storms are less severe is taking a large chance. Georgian Bay is strewn with wrecks and too many of them are twentieth-century pleasure boats.

Curving away from the Bruce Peninsula lies Owen Sound, marked by a grain elevator, three miles of docks, plus a long freighter or two. Owen Sound's role as a shipping port thus defined, museums and events are ready to tell more. Two rivers wind their way through town to the bay, a mecca for scuba divers, summer sailors, photographers, and those with an urge to set up an easel and paint.

Tom Thomson grew up painting his way around Owen Sound and helped to steer Canadian art to a new vibrant realism. Although associated with the Toronto Group of Seven, he worked alone, a life story told in the Tom Thomson Memorial Gallery and Museum, at 840 First Avenue West. The Grey-Owen Sound Counties' Museum brings together a first-class exhibit of arts and crafts—wampum belts, farm tools, bowls, and beads—and demonstrates the arts our predecessors did for survival and we do for fun. 965 Sixth Street East. A Marine-Rail Museum fills the old Canadian National Railway station on the west harborfront. It's run by the Historical Society, the folks who also conduct complimentary walking tours. There's a farmer's market behind city hall on Saturdays. Dog shows, music fests, and other lively doings provide more entertainment. Owen Sound Information Bureau, 519-371-9833.

If all the Great Lakes towns that began with a lumber mill were to vanish, the map would go quite blank and Meaford would be listed among the missing. Emphasis today is on apples instead of pines;

there are thousands of acres of orchards (glorious in springtime!) and even an apple-shaped travel information booth. It's a winsome town with the blue bay in front and green hills behind it. What looks like city hall also encloses the restored seven-hundred-seat opera house, an item of much town pride. Professional dramas and musicals are part of Meaford life. Call ahead. Meaford Tourist Bureau, 519-538-1640.

Another big apple town, Thornbury, is home of the Northern Spy variety. In a scenic setting where every road south takes you up to wide, panoramic views, some of them are from the edge of another segment of the Niagara Escarpment. Heady stuff in apple-blossom time or during the fall color show.

In winter, these hills (the Blue Mountains) shine as a popular ski resort area with alpine and cross-country opportunities. Ask for the bed-and-breakfast list and ask about the annual chili cook-off, boat regattas, and roads to look-out points. 519-599-2795.

Past Craigleith Provincial Park is Collingwood, a village where cityhood bloomed when a builder of boats called skiffs moved into town. Collingwood grew as a ship-building center, eventually producing lake freighters, tankers, patrol boats, and even the *Chi Cheemaun*. There are no tours of shipyards, but you can stand in a parking lot and see freighters in drydock, sometimes with their hulls peeled back for repairs.

Behind the city, the highest hill (Blue Mountain) rises 541 meters or 1,775 feet, and the slopes are alive with the sound of schussing from first snowfall till last. Summer visitors follow the signs uphill to the Scenic Caves and a wonderful hiking workout.

The Collingwood Museum won an Ontario Award of Excellence and can be found in an old train station (they are such useful structures!), where the area story is told with artifacts and artful skill. They sponsor a Power of the Past Steam Show and Classic

Car Rally (all that and more) in June. There's wind-surfing, lawn bowling, golf, horseshoe pitching, and shopping for Blue Mountain pottery (local clay), along with plenty of restaurants and accommodations all year. 705-445-0221.

Wausaga Beach Provincial Park has a long beach, with no camping, but no worry as motels are a big local business. Everybody comes to Wausaga Beach, sometimes on the same weekend, and tourist attractions are there (water slides, minigolf, et al) in full or jammed array. One of the things you don't want to miss is the Museum of the Upper Lakes, on a little island of its own. Cannons go off periodically, and an unusual theater gives vivid history lessons. Wander among the anchors and buoys; inspect the model lighthouse. The Museum is part of the Huronia Historic Parks. As you follow the coast eastward, you'll find the others.

For more information:
Parks' Information Bureau, 705-726-9300 ext. 220.

45.
Penetang, Midland, and an Outpost of Saints

Around the eastern bends of Georgian Bay or up on Highway 400 from Toronto are two civic chapters of the same historic tale. The first is a bit hard to spell or pronounce at first: Penetanguishene (pen-et-ang-wish-een), which means "place of rolling white sands." "Penetang" will do. The other town is Midland.

Pretty, tree-shaded Penetang was blessed with a bicultural heritage, French and British. The mix made for lively clashes in the long-gone past, but now Penetang shares mutual pride in area history. The naval and military establishments at Discovery Harbour (end of Church Street) were built by the British after the War of 1812. It seemed ideal at the time—it's an almost hidden harbor big enough to moor the inland fleet, serve as a supply base, and be a repair dock. Life for men stationed here (unless you were an officer), however, could get bitter and boring in winter, fly-plagued and harsh in summer. There are reconstructed buildings and re-enactments and guides to explain as you wander. 705-549-8064.

The army joined the navy for a while, so today, "soldiers" in full red-coat regalia fire muskets for you. Part of the strategy was to look so splendid in uniform and bearing that the enemy would be overcome by the sheer brilliance of the opposition. Next door, King's Wharf Theatre puts on professional summer plays from June to September.

Midland, Ontario's oldest gathering place for Europeans, started as home base for Jesuit missionaries. It's a tiny morsel of the Old World in a vast devouring wilderness. Sainte Marie Among the Hurons was intended to be a retreat where priests and lay workers could find a few creature comforts plus companions who spoke French. It was a site that influenced the exploration and development of the whole continent, while bringing cruel martyrdom to its founders.

Visitors to the site can see a film on the ten-year life of the enclave showing the French setting their buildings afire before fleeing to evade ferocious Iroquois. As the film ends, the screen and wall move away and audiences walk into a painstakingly authentic scene with robed priests, traders, and livestock. This was never meant to be a fort, only a peace mission with the first hospital ever to care for Indian patients.

At Little Lake Park, the Huron Indian Village is a full-scale replica of a sixteenth-century compound with explanatory film and gift shop. A wigwam, longhouse, and carefully checked artifacts make the story vividly real. 705-526-7838. Martyrs Shrine, a tall two-

136

spired Catholic church rises in homage to North America's first canonized saints.

Midland's downtown area centers around an inlet of Severn Sound, a pleasant place of shops and marinas, restaurants and services. From here and from Penetang, you can take cruises through the Islands National Park, largest concentration of islands (thirty thousand, really!) on earth or take a sightseeing flight for spectacular views of mountains and the big bay. 705-526-0161.

Natural adventures nearby involve an outing at Awenda Provincial Park and the grand Nipissing Bluffs—deep woods and glorious views of Georgian Bay. Or an easier trek can be made through the Wye Marsh Wildlife Centre where boardwalks lift you over wetlands. There's an observation tower plus underwater window, guides, and films. Next to Sainte Marie.

In the area, Barrie and Orilla, both on Lake Simcoe, bounce with sophisticated city bonuses. Barrie has additional history in its Base Borden Military Museum and the large in-depth displays of the Simcoe County Museum. Performing arts are at the Gryphon Theater and visual adventures at the MacLaren Art Center.

Orilla, at the top of Lake Simcoe, fills a place in the Trent-Severn waterway system and boasts a heritage opera house (1895) where live performances go on all year. On West and Mississaga Streets, Canada's famous humorist, Stephen Leacock, built a nineteen-room lakeshore mansion which is now a museum. There are boat cruises on the lake, farmer's markets, summer festivals, and winter ice fishing. Ask in town for a calendar of events.

For more information:
Parks' Information Bureau, 705-726-9300 ext. 220.
Ontario Tourism, 800-ONTARIO.

46.

Holiday On the Trent-Severn Water Route

I t zigs, it zags, it goes north, it goes south, east, and west. After three hundred and eighty-six kilometers (two hundred and fifteen miles) and forty-four locks, the waterway connects Lake Ontario with Georgian Bay, a gleaming path doing no business except serving the getaway trade.

Planners of the Trent-Severn Waterway (sometimes called the Rideau-Trent-Severn) thought they were proposing a speedy way to get the burgeoning commerce of the nineteenth century into the upper Great Lakes and back, but it took so long to build (eighty-seven years) that railroads took over much of the job, and then freighter sizes far outgrew the lock system. So much for thinking ahead. Today, the waterway is the exclusive domain of houseboats, canoes, sails, and dinghies, with family on-board gatherings waving and passing the time of day with friendly folk along the banks. It passes marsh-land birdlife, the green fields of Ontario farm country, ancient rocky ledges of the Canadian shield (the oldest visible rock on earth), quiet towns, and wide open lake vistas—a wonderfully varied landscape for those who go the whole route. It's possible to do in a week, but two weeks are better. Three are best.

A seventy-five-foot difference in water levels between Georgian Bay and Lake Ontario is taken care of by forty-four stair-step locks (one named for bandsman Glenn Miller). Near the Bay at Severn Falls, the Big Chute Marine Railway picks up boats with a sling, puts them on railcars, and hauls them up to the high water level—the only such arrangement in North America. Two other locks (Kirkfield) use massive hydraulic devices to lift a section of the lock. Take a scenic cruise to Big Chute from Port Severn. Big

Chute Marine Railway, 705-538-2378.

Fishing bulletin: Rice Lake, one of those on the route, produces about eleven thousand kilograms (twenty-two thousand pounds) of walleye, northern pike, and muskie a year. Aside from prime fishing, everything you could ask for is available along the route. Bed and breakfasts, hotels, restaurants, tackle shops, marinas, and even such tantalizing extras as cheese factories and candy stores can be found. Or take a break at the movies or stop for an art fair.

Orilla, population twenty-five thousand, is a popular place to start or stop for those who don't want to go the whole route. Houseboat-rental information is at the visitors center, and any marina can tell you more.

In 1615, the explorer Samuel de Champlain, who came through a great many of these streams and probably walked while tougher voyageurs carried the canoe between waterways, wrote that the trip was "very fine and of pleasing character." Still is.

For more information:
Orilla Tourism, 613-384-3682.

47.

Muskoka Lakes, Parry Sound, and Thirty Thousand Islands

Pine-filled islands, glistening blue lakes, towns you'd like to say you were born in, plus a dash of snob appeal, and the reasons for the Muskoka area's popularity are clearer than the crystal air. The district reaches from Algonquin Park to Georgian Bay and from Gravenhurst to a bit north of Huntsville. Before World War I, wealthy vacationers built palatial cottages on Muskoka, Joseph, or Rosseau Lakes or checked into luxury resorts. It was the ultimate.

There is still a lot of class around. The area has a zillion moderate resorts, campgrounds, and boats for rent. By the very nature of the land-water ratio, almost everything seems more secluded (and exclusive) than it really is—one of the Muskoka's charms.

In Gravenhurst, an elegant old opera house on Muskoka Road offers summer theater, calling the season the Muskoka Festival. The restored birthplace of Dr. Norman Bethune, famed medical missionary to China, remains open on weekdays nearly all year. 235 John Street North. At the visitors center, there's an exhibit of Chinese gifts to the honored doctor. Gravenhurst's summer Sunday evening moods are tuned to a band concert from a stage on an off-shore barge in Gull Lake.

The RMS *Segwun,* a nattily restored historic steamship promenades through the lakes, offering a variety of cruise choices. Town Wharf, Muskoka Bay.

In Bracebridge, there's a highway sign that says "halfway to the North Pole." The moppets in your car will love Santa's Village and kiddie park. Mister Rudolph's Funland, next door, has go-carts and minigolf. More Lake Muskoka cruise opportunities go from the dock at the Muskoka Riverside Inn. Every lake town, in fact, has a cruise launch, or charter to take you around.

Home-improvement fans ought to see Woodchester Villa, an 1882 octagonal house ahead of its time with indoor lavs, poured concrete, and a water-pressure system. It stands beside Bracebridge's first Presbyterian Church, now a museum. The western entrance to Algonquin Park (huge wilderness preserve) lies near the pretty town of Huntsville, center of the Lake of Bays Resort Region. There are two special treats for the camera: the Dyer Memorial Botanical Gardens, northeast via Muskoka Road 3 to Williamsport Road, and Lion's Lookout, a fine vista of Huntsville, Fairy Lake, and the Muskoka River. It's in town on Brunel Road.

A rare square-timbered log church, the Madill Church, is in perfect condition and still in partial use. South, off Highway 11. The Muskoka Pioneer Village Museum will tell you more about local history with pioneer homes, store, and sawmill in a lovely woodsy setting. Open all year, on Brunel Road.

Muskoka brightens into stunning color every fall, especially grand when reflected on the surface of a glassy lake. A lot of cruises make special trips for autumn.

Parry Sound's history is partly the story of William Beatty, a staunch young Methodist who came with his father and brothers to the area on an 1863 timber search and never really left. When he became manager of the mill town laid out by the family, Beatty tried hard to be the very model of a patron/manager, banning liquor and demanding church attendance. For those who lived up to Beatty's rules, it was a good place to live. It still is.

The popular Georgian Bay summer resort has excellent waterfront facilities. Sunken vessels are visible in the clear cold water, and fishing is what you do, period. Unless you are on an Island Queen Cruise through the thirty thousand (a world record) islands. An international-class music festival attracts top popular and classical talent every summer from mid-July to early August and is well worth a long detour. Summer drama can be seen in the Rainbow Theater, St. Peter's Hall, 52 Church Street, during July and August.

In a parklike setting overlooking Georgian Bay, the West Parry Sound District Museum goes from aboriginal art to shipping and homesteading. On Tower Hill, a lookout platform puts viewers at bird level.

Oastler Lake, 705-378-2401, Killbear, 707-342-5492, and Sturgeon Bay, 705-366-2521, are part of

141

Provincial Parks, not far away for hiking, canoeing, and camping. Facilities vary, so call ahead, but each is a scenic wonderland.

For more information:
Parry Sound Tourism, 705-522-0104.
Muskoka Lakes Tourism, 705-726-9300, ext. 220.
Ontario Tourism, 800-ONTARIO.

48.

Sudbury Regions: From Stark to Stunning

Sudbury, the surprise city. Theater, parks, a terrific science museum, university, horse racing, and huge boulders in back yards—all this way up here?

Because of some far-past trauma (volcano, meteor...), the Sudbury basin has rare mineral treasures close to the surface, producing gold, silver, platinum, tin, iron, and a major share of the world's nickel. Finding this bonanza was almost an accident.

In the 1870s, when lumbermen were chopping through Ontario forests like locusts at a picnic, British Columbia was saying "Yes, we'll join the Dominion IF you bring us a transcontinental railroad." In the push to build rail connections, an error was made in surveying the right-of-way around Lake Nipissing, and a metal-wise blacksmith on the construction crew drove his pick into nickel-copper ore. The first mining rush was a fade-out, however, because of the expense of extracting mixed ores. New technologies and the discovery that nickel added to iron made better steel turned "poor-quality" ore into a seventy-five-billion-dollar deposit.

Nothing is more looked-at in Sudbury than the impressive nine meter (thirty foot) 1951 Canadian nickel balanced upright atop the only authentic hard-rock mine shaft open to visitors. The famous landmark is not far from a second Sudbury special, the world's tallest smokestack. At one time, the area's stacks spewed out enough acid to discourage plant growth; Sudbury's rock-pile landscape looked dismal and bleak to the point where the first astronauts trained here for moon landings.

Not so today. With more emission control and major citizen efforts, Sudbury has blossomed, literally, into a beauty queen. A crown of sorts is its stunning Science North Museum on Ramsey Lake. Two snowflake-shaped buildings enclose the story of the two-and-a-half-billion-year-old Canadian shield, the rock on which the region stands. Built directly around a geologic fault line which is part of the show, visitors can also pet tarantulas (well, no thanks) or watch 3-D nature movies in a dark cave. These extraordinary films put you, for example, right next to the leader in a flight of geese to see the muscles in his neck and the efforts of his wings or shifting eyes. Or you can follow a bee in a meadow... (where IS that cameraman?). One hour cruises of the lake depart from Science North's dock.

Sharing Ramsey Lake is the bilingual campus of Laurentian University, where the Museum and Art Center, housed in a grand old mansion, shows changing exhibits. The Doran Planetarium and an arboretum are also campus attractions.

The Sudbury Civic Center and Sudbury Centre Mall reflect the new era; tours are offered to those who ask. A Copper Cliff Museum, Flour Mill Heritage Museum, and Galerie du Nouvel Ontario run the field from pioneer beginnings to avant-garde art.

Shaughnessy Street on weekends rings with the bright sounds and colors of a farmer's market and the Sudbury Theatre Centre holds a session of live performances from September to June. The Sudbury Fringe Nord Festival (in early August) packs in visitors with continuous theater performances on ten different stages, with an eclectic mix of improvisational, childrens' shows, mysteries, musicals—the whole spectrum.

There are ninety lakes in the Sudbury District, a lot of parks, and miles of trails for hiking in summer or snowmobiling in winter. Ice hockey, anyone? Just stand on the edge of a frozen pond and shout, and a team will gradually appear.

Killarney Provincial Park requires a rather long detour, but the splendor of the area stifles complaints. The Group of Seven Canadian artists were inspired in Killarney, where quartzite mountains, turquoise lakes, and hidden waterfalls come together in landscapes unspoiled by manmade structures. The hundred and twenty-two interior campsites are certainly primitive, and the tiny village at the end of the road is your nearest source of supplies. No motors, just superb canoeing. 705-287-2900. The Killarney Mountain Lodge in the village is the biggest surprise of all—an elegant oasis of creature comforts and great dining. 705-287-2242 or 800-461-1117.

For more information:
**Sudbury Information Bureau, 705-523-5587 or
800-465-6655.**

49.
Savoring the North Channel

Paddling out of the French River (south of Killarney Park) into Georgian Bay, the first Europeans saw what they reasoned to be an ocean and prudently stayed close to shore. Edging along through the North Channel and portaging past the Soo rapids, they entered Lake Superior before venturing into Lake Huron or Lake Michigan. Missionaries and fur traders made much use of this broad passage on the north side of Manitoulin; it was the first Great Lake area mapped with any accuracy.

The channel is a study in rock and pine, high bluffs, and deep bays. Elevations are dramatic, and the forest cover is as thick as rug pile. Sailors love its relative protection. Travelers on Highway 17 find unrehearsed friendliness in towns without pretense.

Espanola, where you turn toward Manitoulin Island, a name definitely out of the French-English-Indian title norm, is believed to date from the time a Spanish-speaking woman was brought to the area by Ojibwa traders. Later, French traders met the Spanish-speaking descendants of this woman and called the village Espagnole; finally it became the Spanish word. There's an indoor mall in Espanola, where a lumber company employs most of the citizens. On Anderson Lake Road off Highway 6, the Anishnawbek Spiritual Centre trains Native Americans in the ways of their ancestors. Feel free to visit and see the fine works of these artists. The town also boasts a rare (for this stretch) nine-hole golf course.

In Massey, talk fishing, or you'll meet a lot of polite silence. It's a good spot for area directions, boat or cottage rentals. Explore Chutes Provincial Park, hike through it to the seven sisters (waterfalls), or swim at the park beach. In late summer, Massey puts on one of the oldest agricultural fairs in the north, big and joyfully behind the times.

Walford, Spanish, Cutler, Serpent River—you pass through them as soon as you approach. West of Cutler, Highway 108 streaks up to Elliot Lake, a modern city of thirteen thousand. A corporation town in 1954 when rich uranium deposits were found nearby, Elliot Lake nearly disappeared when the demand dropped. However, there were too many assets to abandon this gateway to the untamed north.

Elliot Lake celebrates its short colorful history with a week-long summer Uranium Festival (dare I say it's a blast?). Over at the Elliot Lake Mining and Nuclear Museum they explain what the city is all about, show the process that takes uranium ore to nuclear power, as well as have wildlife studies and an exhibit of logging history. For motels, resorts, shopping, and fly-in charters, call 705-848-3974. Ask about the Deer Trail scenic route, the Fire Tower Lookout, snowshoeing, and a hundred and thirteen miles of groomed snowmobile trails with warm-up stations and food in just the right places.

Blind River, lumbering and mining center, is now a resort favorite. Why not, with sure-catch fishing, hunting, and rock-hounding on agate beaches. The Timber Village Museum is a full-scale replica of a logging camp, with river boats, real steam engines, and other parts of great-great-grandpa's life. East of town. A snow-melting winter carnival in February, and the Mississauga First Nation Traditional Gathering (powwow) beats its drums in July.

Iron Bridge or Thessalon are where waterfall addicts turn off to take pictures of Aubrey Falls and Red Rock Dams. Intrepid searchers for wisdom, truth, and maybe moose can leave the Channel at Thessalon and head for Timmins or Wawa. Highway 129 arcs through wilderness as alluring as a calendar painting, but where the generous supply of lodging, housekeeping cabins, and motels are not too visible.

Back on the Channel, Thessalon's marina can hold and repair yachts; a twenty-three-acre lakeside park offers a beach for tot craft. Area snowmobiling trails win top ratings.

Can you connect a doll house with the man who wrote the rules for boxing? The gap closes in the Bruce Mines Museum, housed in an old church in the town of Bruce Mines (population 684). The museum dotes on the history of the area and happens to own the Marquess of Queensberry's doll house. His son ran the mines in their declining years.

Into the sunset of this segmented destination, St. Joseph Island lies in the channel between Lake Huron and Lake Superior. A country place where visitors can swim and, with any luck at all, catch a fish dinner. Turn south at the bridge from 17; a short ride farther, the St. Joseph Island Museum Village is history to poke through. Church, log cabin, store, and tools—all proof that life here was never luxurious. The ruins of a fort (1796-1812) have their own reception center and display of Indian and settler wares. A bird sanctuary and wilderness area share the location on the southwest corner of the isle.

For more information:

North Channel Area Tourism Information, 705-254-4293 or 800-623-ALGOMA or 800-465-6655.

50.

North of North: Timmins

Timmins seems a little far inland to qualify as a Great Lakes destination, but without the big-lake connections, it wouldn't have survived. In a region where cities don't come easily, places like Kirkland Lake, Iroquois Falls, Cochrane, and Kapuskasing seem just up the road apiece.

Close to the Trans-Canada Highway, the wide city limits of Timmins make it the biggest spread of a town in Canada. Although today Timmins glistens through record books as having the richest silver-zinc mine in the world, it was once the largest producer of gold in the Western Hemisphere. Timber is also a major area biz.

The citizens have used their prosperity well. A nice surprise is the Timmins Museum and National Exhibition Centre, with art from local and major national sources, traveling exhibits, and art lectures, as well as local history and a gallery of minerals from around the world. It's on Legion Drive, South Porcupine.

On the Timmins Underground Mine Tour, excursionists are taken to the quartz veins that stir a miner's pulse. They even have a mock explosion to demonstrate drilling procedures on the Giant Yellowknife Mines Hollinger site. For those with underground qualms, the Porcupine Outdoor Mining Museum displays a collection of mining paraphernalia outside the Timmins Museum.

No motor boats are allowed in Kettle Lakes Provincial Park, a relief for the silence-deprived. There are little round lakes to fish and swim in (cold, cold, cold) and great blueberry picking in season.

With forty-seven thousand people to feed, Timmins is not short on restaurants, food outlets, motels, and places to replace the parka you forgot. Although summers get hot, winter is slow to let go and in a hurry to return. It's a great place for ice hockey, curling, and cross-country skiing.

Remember Sir Harry Oakes whose unsolved murder in the Bahamas years ago remains an intriguing unsolved mystery? Well now, Harry's mansion in Kirkland Lake (he owned a local gold mine) has been converted to a museum with more mining history than most mortals can absorb, along with aboriginal tools and clothing. At 2 Chateau Drive, Kirkland Lake.

Since Kirkland Lake is literally built on gold-bearing rock, you might wonder how many sub-sub-sub basements have been dug in this town.

Iroquois Falls and Kapuskasing both have museums in railroad settings. Garden-conscious Iroquois Falls has converted an old Ontario Northland Station into housing for pioneer-life artifacts. A restored Shay steam engine sits just outside. In Kapuskasing, the pioneer goodies are passengers in two coaches and a caboose, on rails, attached to a Canadian National Railway steam locomotive. The train, however, never chugs away from CNR Station Park. In between these communities, Cochcrane's Polar Bear Express leaves town, and clicks its way through tall forests, across semitundra, around lakes and twisting rivers up to the tidewater area of James Bay, part of Hudson Bay. Go to Moosonee and by freighter canoe to Moose Factory, Canada's oldest English settlement, founded by the Hudson's Bay Company (business where employees were often wilder than the local animal life). You go and come back in a day, but the traveler with soul will stay overnight to ride with a colorful crowd of trappers, Indians, geologists, adventurers, and like-minded tourists.

There are five provincial parks and three airports in the Timmins regions, plus summer wildflowers and festivals and winter sports. From Kapuskasing, take a Heritage River Boat Tour to Beaver Falls and back. You could start here in September and follow the fall colors south. Ask about festivals and winter doings, from dog-sled racing to snowshoe contests. Church bazaars in November may not be on the chamber-of-commerce calendar, but here they are great fun and a source for the best mittens ever produced by grandma's bunch.

For more information:
Timmins Information Bureau, 705-360-1989.

Connecting Waters

51.

Flow Gently, Sweet River: the St. Clair

Like silent phantoms, the long ships come nearer, pass, and soundlessly glide away. Now and then there is a deep-throated signal to another freighter coming from the other direction, but mostly they are eerily noiseless in their journey. They carry the flags of the world: Greece, Japan, Liberia, U.S., and Canada.

To the inland lubber, the slow low-wake passage of the big freighters is a tableau of another life. Watching, even on a light-traffic day, becomes addictive, and ship-gazing is nowhere better than along the shores of the St. Clair River. Both sides of this modest international destination have warmly pleasant (even romantic) places to eat sandwiches on park benches facing the water.

The thirty-mile (fifty-kilometer) channel between Lake Huron and Lake St. Clair flows between banks with small and smaller towns. Port Huron and Sarnia aside, it is a low-keyed stream. At the Canadian south end, the Walpole Island Indian Reservation leads a quiet life, as does the town of Algonac on the American side. A small auto ferry goes between the two.

A circle drive around the river can be easily made in one day, but taking a whole weekend is ideal.

Start in Algonac, a town that likes being called Pickerel Capital of the World. To make the title perfectly clear, it puts on a pickerel summerfest. Algonac sits where the river divides around Harsen's Island, an enclave of fourth-generation family cottages with few facilities for visitors, then pours into Lake St Clair. Henry's Restaurant on the bend is a comfortable place to dine and stare at boats. Just north on M 29,

Algonac State Park has three hundred campsites about as close to the river as you'd want to be and wonderful wide stretches of lawn. 313-765-5605.

The road takes a couple of minor turns through Marine City, a neat community of lovely old houses, a Victorian town hall, and lots of tall trees. Across from downtown shops, the park is the place for the watchers. Visit the Marine City Museum, a building that served as school, village hall, jail, and firehouse and is now displaying everything from antique dinnerware to quaint signs. ("Do not cross this bridge at any speed faster than a walk!") Marine City's lighthouse does not function; it was brought here from another site. Another ferry to Canada leaves from here.

More streets of another-century vintage, another park facing the water, and chic shops are found in St. Clair. Here, the man who decided that the U.S. flag should wave over every schoolhouse left his desk to the Historical Museum, housed in a former Baptist Church on Fourth Street. True fame belongs to the beloved Tudor-style St. Clair Inn (hotel and restaurant) on the river's edge. Romantic dining rooms overlook the river in this Michigan landmark. Sturdy American menu. 800-482-8327.

On up through Marysville (M 29 ends, M 25 takes over) and more viewing spots are found. If you're here after dark, find a place to see the lights of the Agro-Chem plant of south Sarnia sparkling with a galaxy of lights on the river.

Port Huron and Sarnia have been described (incompletely) in an earlier chapter. Explore further by yourself with help from the racks at the info centers.

On the Canadian shore, the St. Clair Parkway ambles close to the river leaving room for frequent parks and picnic places. In spring, add blooming crab apple trees, and there are flower beds all summer. Some of the best fairways in Ontario are at the championship Parkway Golf Course in Mooretown (complete with full dining service). 517-867-2160.

English-themed Sombra will charm the wits out of tea-room devotees, antique searchers, and lovers of quaintness. The Bluewater Ferry Service connects Sombra to Marine City, but stay on this side a little longer, taking a detour to Dresden and the Uncle Tom Cabin historic site. The early slave life of the Reverend Josiah Henson inspired Harriet Beecher Stowe's famous abolitionist story. The escaped Henson established a school here for runaway slaves. 519-683-2978. At Oil Springs (once the oil capital of the world) and Petrolia (site of the first real gusher), museums tell the sludgy and curiously fascinating history of a local bonanza, explaining the giant complex in Sarnia. Bonus: You are almost sure to run into a yard sale on these country roads.

Back along the river, Walpole Island holds an all-Indian community plus parks, beaches, and duck-hunting heavens. The craft shop is open all year, and there's a big powwow in July. Another ferry across the river leaves from here.

For more information:
South Ontario Travel Association, 519-649-7075.
Blue Water Area Tourist Bureau, 810-987-8687.

52.
Lake St. Clair: Little Sister

Twenty-one miles wide, twenty-four miles long, and averaging ten feet deep—not quite big enough, not quite deep enough to qualify as a great lake, yet Lake St. Clair gets more use per square mile than any other lake in the fabulous group. With two hundred and sixty miles of shore, kid sister St. Clair can take on thousands of boaters in the same afternoon, giving them all a sense of wide-open space. Sailboats in summer, fishing shanties in winter. Popularity plus.

At the north end, the St. Clair River filters through a delta-like area called the flats, where conditions are ideal for spawning walleyes and muskies and for acting as a natural freshwater purifying system. M 29 curls between Anchor Bay and the famed St. John's Marsh, a critical life-force in the St.Clair ecosystem. Bird-watchers dote on the marsh, and fisher-folks hang around for bass and pickerel.

No single road tightly belts its shores. You pick out the places you want to see, and often it's an in-and-out process of getting there.

Going around from Windsor, the first suburb is Tecumseh, named for an Indian chief who was dubbed a brigadier general by the British to thank him for his help in battle. A town of high apartments and quiet streets, it has its sights on the lake. Just beyond are a marina and lighthouse and a pleasant little park at Belle River; and then there's another lighthouse (built in 1818), marina, and park where the Thames enters the lake. Beyond this point, the road leaves St. Clair, and it's time for a detour to Chatham, another name in abolitionist history.

Chatham began life as a naval dockyard in 1793. Sixty years later, it was a goal for fugitive slaves on the Underground Railroad; John Brown plotted his raid on Harper's Ferry here, helping to fire off the American Civil War. This garden-loving city, big enough to have adornments such as malls and fast-food chains, boasts a quartet of extra-specials in the Chatham Cultural Centre: a theater, workshops, art gallery, and the Chatham-Kent Museum. The latter has a dozen ways to look at Chatham's past with changing exhibits in five galleries. William Street North. The Raleigh Township Centennial Museum in Buxton, one of the rare existing Black Canadian settlements that dates to pre-

Civil War days. Tecumseh Park's band concerts, lawn bowling, art shows, and all the fun that a lively population can conjure up keep this a steady showplace.

Back to the lakeside, there are country roads to the Canadian shore, and the St. Clair Parkway picks up again (see the St. Clair River chapter) at Mitchell Bay, near Wallaceburg. A glass factory outlet and great duck-hunting, plus some neat little eateries, mark the community, where the marina holds about two hundred boats. If that's your transport from the States, be sure to have identification ready and obey all customs rules.

Going northeast from downtown Detroit on the U.S. side, the lake opens up gloriously as you drive out Jefferson to the posh residential area of Grosse Pointe. You pass the elegant estate of the late auto baron Edsel Ford (tours available) and go through St. Clair Shores, where there are enough boats and marinas to restock the fleets of the world. Almost any lakeside restaurant is the place to lunch.

Spacious Metropolitan Beach Park tries to fill every bill, from hiking trails to tot lots and big bands, food, and acres of soft sand. Naturally, this largesse is popular on summer weekends, so if you hate crowds, think it over. Delightful in fall color.

Mount Clemens (no mountain; who is Clemens?) was in the spa business for a great many years, as a place to go for the cure in mineral baths. Today, you go to hear the symphony orchestra, wander through the art center, and attend an ethnic festival or a play at the college. At 15 Union Street, the Macomb County Historical Society has a suitable Victorian house to reside in. Very close by, terrifically exciting air shows are put on by the Selfridge Air National Guard base (dates vary), and their Military Air Museum has oldies for ex-fliers to examine. The eighty-five-year-old base has seen Coast Guard, Marine, and Naval units, so the displays have wide appeal.

155

The village of New Baltimore on M 29 at the top of the lake has beachy reasons to stop, especially if traveling with the kids, plus small shops and ice-cream fixings. Rent a boat or fish off the pier.

Places to rent boats, launch your own, or dock them around Lake St. Clair, high and steady quantities of fish, and the closeness to the backyards of a million-plus humans keeps Lake St. Clair's popularity high, but proceed with a note of caution—the shallow waters are easily ruffled by the winds, and it is essential to keep tract of weather reports, not gamble with storm warnings, and keep your radio handy.

For more information:

Central Macomb County Chamber of Commerce, 810-463-1528.

South Ontario Travel Association, 519-649-7075.

53.

Detroit: River City Revs Up for Company

In May, flower growers flood Detroit's huge downtown Eastern Market with tides of color at the world's largest sale of bedding plants. Bedding plants? To those who thought Motown life began and ended with front ends and rear suspensions, news of Detroit's other leading activities has been slow to get around.

Summertime sees dozens of ethnic dance groups whirling at free events, while formula-one auto racers steer toward Detroit's Grand Prix. Attendance records are made by the country's original State Fair and the big Ford Montreux Jazz Festival. Winter warms to ice shows, art openings, concerts by the Detroit Symphony Orchestra, opera by the Michigan Opera Company, and a whole district of renovated theaters.

This is the city that pioneered the suburban mall (Hudson's Northland), municipal aquarium, national-ity festivals, and ice-cream sodas. More hot dogs and potato chips are produced here than anywhere else.

On the Detroit River ("Detroit" means "straits"), Sieur Antoine de la Mothe Cadillac established a tiny French fort and trading post in 1701. Where Cadillac planted his staff, now stands the Renaissance Center, a seven-tower cluster of glass offices, shops and restaurants around a seventy-story hotel. Cadillac's little fort would fit on one floor.

Next door, also on the waterfront, chess games are being played and brown bag lunches opened in Hart Plaza, a wide paved space with an amphitheater and dramatic fountain, benches, and a walkway along the river for watching freighters glide past. Trivia note: This is the only spot in the U.S. where you gaze south into Canada.

Cobo Convention Center and Arena and beyond that the Joe Louis Arena mark the west end of the Plaza. Overhead, the monorail People Mover circles downtown neighborhoods in a 2.9-mile loop, stopping at the Joe Louis Arena, the convention center, financial district, and Greektown, where lovers of flaming cheese and baklava gather in old family establishments or new chic bistros.

From this hub, Detroit's main lines stretch out like the spokes on a half-wheel. Along Jefferson to the east is the bridge to Belle Isle, America's largest island park designed by Frederick Law Olmstead, the genius of New York City's Central Park and other national landmarks. The nation's first municipal aquarium, back-to-back with a nonstop flower show in the conservatory, makes a year-round double-header outing. The overhead-walk zoo keeps summer hours, but the marine gear and long ship models of the Dossin Great Lakes Museum can be seen all year. Steer a ship in the duplicated wheelhouse realistically placed with a watery view. North from Hart Plaza, Woodward

Avenue, which divides the city's east and west sides, goes through a steadily brightening theater district. The Fox Theater is a 1927 movie castle extravaganza of oh-my-gosh opulence. Attend an event there if at all possible—the structure is its own show. Look at the calendars of the Gem Theater or Second City Comedy, Music Hall, Wayne University's Hillberry Theater, Masonic Auditorium, and Fisher Theater— something you've always wanted to see may be on now. The Detroit Symphony's Orchestra Hall, an acoustical treasure that ducked the wrecking ball, also faces Woodward. For dinner, the super-posh Whitney housed in a mansion, up a few streets, was built before income taxes. Cuisine, American; mood, Edwardian. 313-832-5700.

The Detroit Institute of Arts and Public Library, both prestigious establishments, face each other across Woodward and are a pair of Italianate palaces to get lost in. The DIA has an old-world courtyard for lunch hours. There are plenty of old masters and new pacesetters, but the most stared-at works are the murals of assembly lines by Diego Rivera. 313-833-7900.

In adjoining blocks are the Detroit Historical Museum, 313-833-1805, Children's Museum, Museum of African-American History, 313-833-9800, and the Detroit Science Center and Omnimax Space Theater, 313-577-8400. Michigan's largest artwork, the golden-towered Fisher Building, stands off by itself on Grand Boulevard, a block west of Woodward. Its soaring lobby, the size of two cathedrals, gleams with rare marble, art-deco brass, and Detroit-made Pewabic tile.

The modest house on the Boulevard about six blocks west labeled "Hitsville, U.S.A." is a Motown Music Museum in the home where Berry Gordy launched the Supremes and others into fabulous stardom. 313-875-2264.

A good zoo being a civic gotta-have, Detroit is steadily adding to its, with three hundred species, twelve hundred animals. Chimps cavort in a state-of-the-art romper room, and penguins play in an icy rookery. It's a large and pleasant spread, with a mini-train ride to add to the fun (Ten Mile and Woodward). 810 -398-0903.

Nestled in the comfortable environs of the northern suburb of Bloomfield Hills, the Cranbrook Institutions of Art and Science have become two of the U.S.'s top cultural influences. Eliel and Eero Saarinen (he designed the St. Louis Arch), Carl Milles, Charles Eames, and others worked and taught here. At the science institute, 3-D hands-on presentations, mineral displays, and a planetarium stand out. 810-645-3312.

Antique cars join the huge collection of Americana at Greenfield Village outside Detroit.

Take Michigan Avenue from downtown to reach Dearborn, home of the largest indoor/outdoor collection of Americana anywhere. Greenfield Village and the Henry Ford Museum trace our progress from a rural to an industrial society, from hand looms to design by computer. Here, you'll find the Wright Brothers bike shop, Thomas Edison's lab, an historic carousel, airplanes, firearms, old trains, and ...Golden Arches? Burma Shave signs?

Watch marchers with muskets or the firing up of old steam cars during special events. Admission is pricey and separate for museum and village, but worth it. History is seldom such fun. 313-271-1620.

Lifestyles of the rich and famous, Detroit version, means a tour of the auto baron's homes—Edsel Ford's, the Fisher mansion, Matilda Dodge Wilson's Meadow Brooks Hall (with a hundred and ten rooms and twenty-four hand-carved fireplaces), or Henry Ford's place with its own powerhouse. You may want to redecorate your apartment.

Easy excursions can be made from Detroit to Ann Arbor (University of Michigan) or to a nearby circle of great metroparks (such as Kensington or Huron Metropark) for golf, skiing, canoeing, or whatever.

Also found here are the Tigers baseball, Red Wings hockey, Pistons basketball, Lions football, and the Goldcup Races (speedboats). On Jefferson at Hart Plaza, the visitors center has fistfuls of ideas, lists of restaurants, motels, and hotels, as well as maps and calendars.

Detroit has a good time.

For more information:
Metro Detroit Convention and Visitors Bureau, 313-259-4333.

54.

Windsor, Ontario: Gand and Getaway

When Detroiters want to smell the roses, have a bargain dinner in great French or Italian

restaurants, or do a little gambling and still be home
by midnight, they scoot over to Windsor. From
Windsor, you look north into the U.S., browse
through shops with a difference, or sit on a riverside
bench to watch the setting sun turn orange and light
up glassy towers of Detroit's downtown. Around
dusk, the lights outlining the Ambassador Bridge add
their own touch. Crossing the border via bridge is the
best way to get a quick wide view.

The two cities put their acts together for a gigantic International Freedom Festival in July, both celebrating their independence days with parades and
all-out fireworks, boat races, and band concerts.

Like Detroit, Windsor is known for cars—in fact,
is called the automotive capital of Canada—with General Motors, Ford, and Chrysler all having large plants
in the city.

The main downtown thoroughfare is Ouellette
Avenue, where many visitors first head to find the
china and woolen import bargains that can't be found
elsewhere. Hang on to all receipts as you may be able
to get a tax refund and remember, that after forty-
eight hours, you can buy up to $400 worth duty-free.

Then go for your area of interest. In the Art
Gallery of Windsor, three floors of art treasures
include a fine permanent collection and exhibits from
top-rated museums on tour. Children's gallery, gallery
cafe, spiffy museum shop. 445 Riverside Drive West.
519-258-7111. The Francois Baby House, a charming
neoclassical house downtown on Pitt Street West, was
used by U.S. forces in 1812 and now is a museum of
local history.

For green-thumbers, Jackson Park rates more than
a sniff through. Bright floral mob scenes, special lighting after dark, bowling greens, a ball park, and a
World War II Lancaster bomber in a flying stance are
here. The Memorial Rose Garden shows off five hun-

dred varieties from around the world. There are more flowers on Riverside Drive where Coventry Gardens and Reaume Park skirt the river. In a shallow inlet, North America's largest floating jet of water, the Peace Fountain, goes through endless spray ballets daily (with floodlights after dark), and you get to watch the boats at the same time.

Willistead Manor, a Tudor house of grand proportions, designed by famed Detroit architect Albert Kahn, stands amid lawns and trees—a perfect setting for Art-in-the-Park shows in June. Lovers-of-things Gothic will dote on the house's Great Hall, the dramatic staircase, and hand-carved details. Take the tour. Walker and Niagara Street. 519-255-6545.

A Detroit River landmark and oldest industry in town, Walker's Canadian Club Distillery has limited tours, but no free samples. You must call ahead. 510-254-5171.

On Wednesdays and Saturday mornings especially, downtown between Chatham and Pitt, the Windsor public market fills with fresh produce, flowers, poultry, pastry, and people. A place for rare cheese and unusual pasta.

Ask about events at the Cleary Auditorium (Windsor Light Opera, the Windsor Symphony, and Essex Hall Theater) or at the University of Windsor. The newest act in town is the Windsor Casino, on Riverside West, a twenty-four-hour enterprise magnet for the whole international territory. Or you can bet on the harness ponies at the long-established Windsor Raceway, straight east from the bridge on Huron Road.

Information and money-exchange (same building) centers are well-marked and close to bridge and tunnel entrances. In this over-or-under border-crossing choice, the Ambassador Bridge offers a wonderful view for persons who don't have to keep their eyes on the road. It's at the foot of the Jeffries Freeway (I 96) in Detroit or the edge of the University of Windsor campus, University Avenue West. The Detroit-Windsor Tunnel (the first underwater international vehicular tunnel in the world) connects downtown Windsor (plenty of signs) to a spot wedged between Hart Plaza and the Renaissance Center in Detroit. You can take a bus through the tunnel, but if you drive, fare for both bridge and tunnel are the same, with a discount on the Canadian dollar as of this writing. Get your copy of the customs rules.

Windsor provides an excellent home base for exploring the near coasts and fishing possibilities of Lake Erie or Lake St. Clair or for hopping the train for some special time in Toronto.

For more information:
Windsor Travel Information Office, 519-255-6530.

Lake Erie

55.

The Western Corner: Redcoats, Soup, and 100,000 Birds

Amherstburg may face the Detroit River, but the town acts as maitre d' to a banquet of delights along Lake Erie's northeastern coast. Only thirty minutes from Windsor and forty from metropolitan Detroit, pleasant Amherstburg is sweet light years from either one. It's a good place for a minicircle tour to begin.

The town itself began as part of a colonial arms race when the English were unhappily removed from Detroit after the American Revolution. They built a fort and naval yard here, certain that Americans had invasion plans. (The British returned to Detroit for a year during the War of 1812, after which boundaries settled down.)

In the years since, the fort, called Fort Malden, burned down, was rebuilt, served as a mental asylum, and is now a historic site with summer soldiers firing muskets, restored barracks for visitors to inspect, and special events. 519-736-5416.

It wasn't just the troops who left Detroit in 1796; one Loyalist merchant put his house on a raft and floated it down to the Amherstburg site. The Park House Museum is that transported dwelling, full of the fixings of early-1800s life. 214 Dalhousie Street.

At 277 King Street are buildings of the North American Black Historical Museum, Inc., including an 1848 church built by former slaves who found refuge in Amherstburg via the Underground Railroad; also a cultural-center building is on these grounds of the first black settlement here. 519-736-5433.

The wine business of Essex County is growing like a hothouse grape. Here, in the region known as Ontario's Sun Parlor, De'Angelo Estate Winery near Amherstburg, Colio Wines and LeBlanc Estate Winery near Harrow, and the Pelee Island Winery and the London Winery in Middlesex County all add up to a delightful taste tour for aficionados. More details are available at the visitors centers or call 519-6656-3456.

Heading east on Highway 18, you'll pass an excellent restaurant called Ducks on the Roof. Note roof. Note ducks. Make a note to stop for a farm-gourmet dinner.

In this area where tomatoes grow to the size of a teenager's foot, and roadside stands fill every cook's dream, farm museums are special. At Iler Road and Road 50 south of Harrow, the John Park Homestead has its front porch almost in the lake. There are farm buildings, steam engines, a sawmill, and old-time summer socials. 519-738-2029. The Southwest Ontario Heritage Village, sponsored by the Historic Vehicle Society, dotes on old modes of transport—if you arrive dead, there's a hearse in the collection—but their fifty-three-acre layout includes a complete antique settlement. 519-776-6909.

Fishing tugs and the Pelee Island Ferry front Canada's most southerly town, two-restaurant-one-winery Kingsville, where the population quadruples in summer. Old mansions such as the Town and Country bed and breakfast on Mill Street tempt visitors to stay awhile. For ferry information, call 519-724-2115. Nearby, Jack Miner established the earliest bird sanctuary in Canada in 1904. Come all year, but in late March and October the sight of ten thousand or more migrating geese is a big-nature show-biz extravaganza. Ask the way to Colasanti's Tropical Gardens. Acres of plants, parrots, and pets in the petting zoo are available and pre-cleared for export to the U.S. Snacks are for sale, too.

In Leamington, the tourist-info booth is tomato-shaped, and the biggest industry makes soup for Heinz. A ma-pa kind of homey town with a rising business in motels, it's close to Point Pelee National Park. Two-thirds marsh and vegetation like the Carolinas, some of the plants and animals here are not found any farther north. There's superb bird-watching, but migrating monarch butterflies turning tree trunks to gold get the most attention. A long boardwalk, lookout tower, and transit system help folks get around. Bikes and canoes can be rented; no camping, however. Point Pelee National Park Information, 519-322-2365.

Try a detour to Pelee Island or go all the way across to Sandusky (i.e. make this an east-Erie circle tour). Largest isle in the lake, Pelee offers good bass and walleye fishing and, in late fall, draws hundreds to an annual pheasant hunt. (For a goodly fee.) With four small-craft docks, one tiny airfield, and one winery, Pelee is not for the jet set.

Highway 3 runs quietly between cottages, farms, and the long blue horizon of the lake. You'll reach tiny Port Alma and Dealtown, then Rondeau Provincial Park, a stretch of trees and beach on a peninsula that forms a grandly protected harbor for small boats. Camping, biking, programs, plus lodging and cafes are just outside the gates. 519-674-5405.

Go up to QEW 401 where there are buffalo, deer, elk, and maybe a llama or two at the Buffalo Head Ranch near Ridgetown, then back to Windsor, hardly an hour away.

For more information:
Ontario Tourism, 800-ONTARIO.

56.

The Central Shore: Ties To London and Stratford

With unabated sweetness, Highway 3 cuts its swath through farm and vineyard country. The lake looms large in this destination, but not more than the nearby towns, as seductive a selection of communities as you'll ever find.

One of the first whites to arrive was a wily developer named Thomas Talbot who managed to lure settlers, lay a plank road, and name several communities after himself. Talbotville, Port Talbot, and, it's suspected, St.Thomas. Today, we have the cheerful heritage of the Talbot Trail (follow the double-headed ax signs). St. Thomas, a real Victorian card of a town, has two major parks, a beautiful old city hall, and houses built for staring at. Stare also at the full-size statue of Jumbo, the famous circus elephant, on a hillside pedestal. Jumbo was killed in a local train accident, and school children raised money for the memorial.

Exhibits change monthly at the Art Gallery St.Thomas-Elgin, with a bright showing of historic and contemporary work. 301 Talbot Street. The Elgin County Museum shows off a large collection of Canadiana in a pioneer doctor's home at 32 Talbot; the Elgin Military Museum keeps tabs on past conflicts, at 30 Talbot.

North of St. Thomas, it's a quick run to London, big hotels, night life, and all the big-time shopping you could want. A partial list of reasons for a London break would include the London Regional Art and History Museums and the Regional Children's Museum, with dinosaurs, caves, and the street where you live. Then there's the Royal Canadian Regiment Museum for military-history buffs and the Komoka

Railway Museum where a model railroad room supplements the bigger stock. Native Guy Lombardo (remember his Royal Canadians? If not, you're very young!) has a music center named in his honor, and it's still performing "the sweetest music this side of heaven." London's beautifully refurbished Grand Theatre puts on the big shows, and the Fanshawe Pioneer Village has twenty-two restored buildings and interpreters. The Ska-Nah-Doht Indian Village is a re-creation of a prehistoric Iroquoian village with sixteen structures and special audio-visual presentations, events, and powwows. It's west on Highway 2 past Delaware.

London Princess Cruises on the Thames River does a scenic float to Storybook Landing for the kids and to Springbank Park. London is a favorite city—big, but not out of hand. The big event the first weekend in June is a giant International Air Show.

North on Highway 19, but still not too far from the coast, Stratford, Shakespeare, the Avon, and those serene swans are doing beautifully. Stratford's festival for the bard, of course, has a well-deserved world reputation. Even though W.S. is the main attraction, operas, ballets, and even bluegrass folkfests have been added to the schedule. June to October.

South of St. Thomas, Port Stanley is another charming spot. Ride the *Kettle Creek Queen* for an hour of a paddle-wheel tour or try taking the scenic train of the Port Stanley Railway to Union or St. Thomas. The station is easy to spot.

Tillsonburg sits amid tobacco fields (a surprise to many who did not know about Ontario's tobacco industry), boasting of having the widest Main Street in Ontario. Cooks will smack their lips over Coyle's Factory baking supplies, confections, nuts, and cake decorations. Three kilometers (two miles) north on Highway 19.

169

Three Provincial Parks are between Port Stanley and Port Rowan, and don't forget charter boating, excellent fishing, and taking pictures. If you can't unwind along here, consult a guru—but you might find them running the bed and breakfasts, bait shops, and rental boats, and wondering what's your problem.

For more information:

Southwestern Ontario Travel Association, 519-649-7075.

57.

The East Erie Coast: Peach Near the Action

It can raise a silence at parties if you announce your next vacation goal as Lake Erie's northeastern coast—not a big-name draw. However, most of the east shore is within two hours of Toronto, one hour or less from Niagara Falls and Buffalo, and in a region of festivals, lucrative fishing, and uncommon peace. Very good.

At the west end of this segment, Port Burwell, for example, snuggles quietly against the lake astride Big Otter Creek, another port that once saw lumber exports and commercial fishing and now caters to pleasure craft. It's on the map but not in most guide books, and Burwellians probably like it that way. Their mind-set on the matter of progress is probably typified by the antique fire truck still on call as a back-up vehicle. Look for it in the fire house.

South a mite off the Talbot Trail on Highway 53, a long finger of land pokes deeply into the lake like a natural breakwater. Long Point Provincial Park has a small town of campsites, showers, laundromat, and an interpretive building. There are glorious sunrises if you don't stay in your sleeping bag too long.

There is another path, the Heritage Highway as Route 3 is called, running north of the Talbot Trail, although they were often following the same pavement in the western sector. The Heritage route runs through Simcoe, named for the first governor of Upper Canada (Ontario). The leisurely River Lynss flows through town, lapping against some lovely parks. You can't stand next to a Simcoe fruit stall and not make a purchase; it's unlikely that you'd fish in the nearby streams without catching a black bass or trout. As warm as a tea cozy, Victorian Simcoe has a reputation as a model city. It's hard to argue with that, especially over a bed-and-breakfast morning coffee.

At 109 Norfolk Street South, a restored mansion houses the Donly Museum of Art and Antiques. The oldest part of the house was built in 1843, and a wing was added in 1967, making the building itself an item.

One of the town's big moments comes at Christmas when sixty lighted displays make up a community-wide panorama. Anyone planning to travel to Niagara Falls for the Christmas show there should make a note of Simcoe.

Winsome Port Dover is supposed to be the largest freshwater fishing port in the world. One wonders. For sure, the town is not large, but there are plenty of bright fishing boats bringing in the smelt, pickerel, bass, and whitefish. This means, of course, that fish dinners lead the restaurant entree list, and fishing derbies and fish fries are what you look for in summer. The Harbour Museum puts together a wheelhouse and net-making shed and tells more about Erie fishing, happily back after a near-death pollution era. It's on Black Creek near the lift bridge.

Summer fun is always at the Lighthouse Festival (professional) Theater.

Two more Provincial Parks on this part of the lake are at Selkirk, 905-776-2600, and Rock Point, 905-774-6642. In Dunnvile, up the Grand River from Port Maitland, there's a two-hour river cruise available aboard the *Willy Anne*. In Port Colborne, the Heritage and Talbot Trails converge at the southern gateway to the Welland Canal, site of a super-size navigation lock. Hike up a manmade observation hill in a lockside park and watch ships coming and going from Lake Erie, remembering that they are being lifted or lowered the full height of Niagara Falls (fifty-four meters or a hundred and seventy-six feet) and then some to make up for the hundred-and-fourteen-meter (three-hundred-and-thirty-two-foot) level difference in Erie and Ontario lake levels. Fascinating, educational, and fun.

The Welland Canal at Port Colborne, Ontario

The Historical and Marine Museum's tearoom serves homemade biscuits before and after walks around its collection of buildings, glass, and marine bric-a-brac. Professional theater is at the Showboat Festival, June through August. 96 Janet Street.

Where Lake Erie meets the Niagara River, across from Buffalo and linked to the States by the Peace

Bridge, Fort Erie is the name of the sizeable city and the military establishment that first gave it importance. French fur traders built a trading post, then when the land was ceded to the British, the English built the fort—actually, three forts. The first and second were both destroyed by masses of lake ice driven ashore in a storm. The third, on higher ground, has a history of hardship, bloody skirmishes, and swamplike conditions in a war that should have been fought at a conference table.

Visitors enter the fort via a drawbridge, watch the changing of the guards, and stand on the ramparts. For hours and a list of special events, call 416-356-2241.

The city is an important entry to Canada, and its history includes the entry of runaway slaves. Also, a fellow named Kraft who sold homemade cheeses from the back of his buggy did well, they say. One of North America's oldest and prettiest race tracks is here; and check out the Fort Erie Railroad Museum, the Mahoney Doll House Gallery, the Firefighting Museum, and Battlefield Museum. Crystal Beach used to be a separate site, but is now a Fort Erie destination, and an extremely popular one.

For more information:
City of Port Colborne Tourism, 905-835-2900.
Ontario Tourism, 800-ONTARIO.
**Mid-Western Ontario Travel Association,
    519-756-3230.**

58.
The Welland Canal

With a magnificent obstacle called Niagara Falls blocking the Niagara River, shipping between Lake Ontario and Lake Erie clearly must have help. There's a hundred-and-fourteen-meter difference (three hundred and thirty-two feet, more than a thirty-story building) in lake levels, partly caused by the same cliffs that the falls plunge over. The Welland Canal enables ocean ships and lake freighters to go from the Atlantic to the heart of the continent.

A lock is basically a simple device whereby water from the high side fills a compartment, then is drained (thus lowering the boat) till the water is level with the low side, and the compartment doors open for the ship to move out. Going uphill reverses the procedure. It's simple on paper, yet the Welland Canal is a world-class engineering achievement, operated with computer technology.

The first canal, opened in 1829, carried vessels to a point on the Niagara River above the Falls. However, the frightening current of the river was too much to reckon with, so that part of the canal was abandoned and the water rerouted to Gravelly Bay (now Port Colborne) on Lake Erie. The present canal you see is the fourth one.

At one time, it took forty locks to do the job; the present system uses eight giants, seven of them in the northern third of the canal and one (the largest) at the Erie port. The canal depth has increased from three meters (nine feet) to more than ten meters (thirty feet), a bottomside reflection on the whopping growth of modern ships.

Although towns along this commercial conduit are steeped in canal history and lore, they do have a life of their own. This is wine country where you can count on vineyard festivals, art in parks, bagpipes in parades, picnic tables, and kiddie lots.

Port Colborne and its canal viewing have been described, but pick up a canal-tour guide at the visitors center and plan to follow Canal Drive road signs, heading first on Highway 58 to Welland, the town. The canal goes through the center of the community, so that's an excellent place to hike around. Also, walking is the best way to see Welland's huge murals painted on various city buildings by Canadian artists. Themes are Welland's history and the canal.

The Niagara Regional Exhibition is held in this little heart of industry, featuring agricultural and live-stock shows, grandstand performances, and a midway. Niagara Street North, mid-September. The Welland Rose Festival blooms in early June, with a queen (of course) and high jinks to get you to stop and smell the flowers.

Thorold marks the center of the Niagara Penin-sula and is home to sets of twin locks where you watch ships coming and going at once. A nine-acre town park occupies the site of earlier canals and also an 1812 war spot, the Battle of Beaverdams. Sixteen Americans as well as Canadians are buried here, near blocks of heritage homes.

At the base of a long high cliff, St. Catharine was originally a Loyalist settlement, later a station on the Underground Railroad. The first electric streetcar sys-tem in North America clanged its way through St.Catharine's streets, and the big Royal Canadian Henley Regatta is only a length behind the English regatta in popularity.

Welland Canal Lock Number One welcomes and waves goodbye to ships on Canal Road north of Lakeshore Road. Lock Two is farther south, near Carlton Street. At Lock Three, you'll find a slick visi-tors center (where ship arrivals are up on a board), snack bar, raised viewing platform, and a close look at the hows and whys of the whole works. Lock fans will want to see the St. Catharine's Museum, also at Lock Three, QEW, Glendale Avenue exit north. Then pause at the Old Welland Canal Area at Port Dal-housie. Look at the locks, lighthouses, and nine-teenth-century gate-tenders houses, early area industry. Mountain and Bradley Streets.

St. Catharine's beaches and parks, motels and entertainments (such as Purdhomme's Landing-Wet & Wild slides, plus the whole bit from minigolf to go-carts) keep it a popular summer place, and it's wonderful in fall when the crowd lightens up. In mid-September, the Niagara Grape and Wine Festival means ten days of tasting, toasting, and touring, with ethnic music, dancing, and general frolic. 905-684-8070.

Watching the long freighters rise and drop and come and go at what amounts to arm's length, puts visitors at a closeness that imprints the brain forever. It probably has sent quite a few young men to their hometown navy recruiting offices or down to the docks on a job hunt.

For more information:
St. Catharine's Chamber of Commerce,
905-688-6462.
Welland Canal Vessel Information, 905-688-6462.
City of Port Colborne Tourism, 905-835-2900.

59.
Southeast Michigan Meets Lake Erie

About twenty-five miles long, Michigan's part of Lake Erie is a mere toe hold compared to its other Great Lakes coasts. However, short can be sweet, especially when added to a region of small-city, back-country pleasures.

I 75 and US 23 are the arteries in charge of getting you to southeast Michigan in a hurry—without glimpsing the lake, however. For that, you exit eastward from I 75 and work your way to the shore, not always easy. Although a map will show the coast as a fairly straight line, it is deeply indented with roads that dead-end at little docks, and it includes a lot of marshland. That's part of the good part, for the marshes of Erie are havens of bird life and spawning fish. Leave I 75 at Rockwood, the town base of the Lake Erie Metropark, a sixteen-hundred-acre spread with three miles of beach and a wide-angled Erie view. Bird-watchers have spotted dozens of bald eagles, peregrine falcons, and turkey vultures. The brand new Marshland Museum and Nature Center's aquarium highlights local birds and fish. There's golf at the park, with eighteen holes.

Without returning to I 75 (even though streets that keep dead-ending at canals make it tempting), turn south on Dixie Highway for a tour past farms and country homes, with the giant spool-shaped cooling towers of the Detroit Edison Fermi Energy Plant looming as silent observers in the background.

Farther south, Sterling State Park also stretches along the Erie shore and around the life-breeding marshes. There are two hundred and eighty-eight modern camp sites, with excellent fishing and hiking. The same bird species that touch down in Lake Erie Metropark show up here (redtails, raptors, geese, ducks). Other flight-bent types that come frequently are model-airplane fans with their remote flying gear. It's a splendid place for kites.

From the beach at Luna Pier, a concrete breakwater bends its protective arm against the storms of a temperamental lake. There are benches to sit on while watching the kids play in the park. It's a little village, but big enough for places to eat or buy groceries.

Between Otter Creek Road and La Plaisance on northbound I 75, a Michigan Travel Information Center bulges with brochures, bed-and-breakfast lists, and directions to anywhere.

Monroe, so-called capital of the area, had its beginnings in the mid-1600s when French missionaries and traders built a cluster of crude cabins next to the Raisin River. (The Riviere aux Raisins was named for the wild grapes once covering trees and bushes along its banks.) This rough little hamlet, just a few canoe-lengths from Erie's shore was tagged French-town. After the American Revolution, big disputes smoldered between British and Americans over who owned what. Before it was settled by the War of 1812, a bloody battle and massacre reddened the river, a grim story retold by history displays in Monroe's River Raisin Battlefield Visitors Center, at 1403 East Elm Avenue.

It took years for the area to recover from the slay-ings and cabin-burnings, but eventually Frenchtown became Monroe, and the city took shape. More history is at the Monroe County Historical Museum (a former post office): Victoriana, Indian lore and crafts (superb beadwork!), and items regarding Monroe's controversial adopted son, General George A. Custer. Examine the large Custer mural, then walk around Loranger Square, one of the prettiest little town centers anywhere.

Next to a modern city hall, you'll find the classic old county courthouse and a genteel house-turned-library; in the Edison Company's lovely Georgian structure, the chamber of commerce provides local travel information by the front door. A noble-appear-ing Custer sits astride his horse next to the bridge on the road north, while a Huey Cobra helicopter mounted in action position on a tall black post (used in Vietnam to rescue soldiers under fire) has a clothed figure behind the controls— in Captain Heck Jr. Park.

Save the last weekend in August for Old French Town Days when everybody dresses and talks as though it were before 1812. Music, games, crafts, and even the way soldiers behaved on parade grounds are all re-enacted with authenticity. Merry notes come from Irish, French, and Scotch tunesmiths playing dulcimers, penny whistles, or maybe bagpipes. Add tomahawk-throws, merchants and traders, and Ottawa longrifles to the festivities. And watch the ladies at looms or quilting frames, making dolls, and tanning hides.

In the next county west, happily named Blissfield has treasures in boutiques and a superb restaurant in a stately Greek Revival mansion, Hathaway House. Table settings are elegant; the cuisine is American. 517-486-2141.

Still in Lenawee County, near Tipton, are the Hidden Lake Gardens, a Michigan State University arboretum with green houses, ideas, and how-to. 517-431-2060. Just beyond are the Irish Hills, wearing thirty shades of green, with parks, lakes, towers, and amusements that include a museum/stagecoach stop on US 12 across from the Golden Nugget Saloon. 517-467-2190. Bauer Manor is a genuine stagecoach inn, and now there's another restaurant of top repute (regis-tered with the state Historical Society) on US 12, near roads that go back to the southeast corner of Michi-gan. For dinner at Bauer Manor, call 517-431-2506.

For more information:

Monroe County Convention and Tourism Bureau, 800-472-3011 or 313-457-1030.

Lenawee County Visitors Bureau, 800-682-6580.

60.
Whole-ly Toledo

E ver think of autographing a hot dog? When Toledo's native son Jamie Farr mentioned Packo's cafe on *M.A.S.H.*, the popular eatery hit big times. Its home-made adult Hungarian hot dogs (flavor that hits later, like a stiff drink), drew in celebrities. Burt Reynolds was the first big name to sign a bun; now, dozens of mummified specimens are framed and on walls. Established in a old Hungarian neighborhood, amid unstuffy camaraderie and great food, it's no wonder Farr couldn't forget Packo's... or Toledo.

Toledo, fourth in size of Ohio's cities, bridges the Maumee River, largest to flow into the Great Lakes. Hardly any town is easier to get to. I 75 zips past on its way from Florida to Michigan, the Ohio Turnpike, US 20, and Ohio 2 all come through here on their east-west passage. Boaters can sail in from Lake Erie under industrial silhouettes and high-rise offices, close to a freighter or two, and dock right downtown if they call ahead. 419-244-3625, for the dock.

The Toledo Office of Tourism hunkers down in SeaGate Center, a big convention hall on Jefferson, one block north of the riverside marina. Drop by for lists of motels, maps, restaurant guides, and tips. 419-255-3300.

Even if you don't know anything about art, the Toledo Museum of Art, a grand Greek temple on Monroe Avenue at Scottwood, is the place not to miss. Only a handful of galleries in the country match Toledo's jewel, where high-impact gatherings of great masters (including El Greco and Rubens) make headlines, and the house collection ranges from a medieval cloister to works by Picasso, Monet, and Hopper. The collection of glass (a main Toledo industry) is stunning. 419-255-8000.

Try lunch in a lion cage at the Toledo Zoo; the children will roar. All lions have been moved elsewhere, of course, and a former carnivore building now features a deli where you can eat in painted-up cages. In Toledo's innovative animal kingdom, lumbering hippos don't simply slosh into their ponds to disappear or look like gray islands with eyes. They can be seen from the bottom up through a glass panel in an underground viewing room. (P.S.: The water is filtered of mud and debris.)

Apes and gorillas have their own meadow; there's an African savanna, an award-winning Diversity of Life exhibit, koalas, naked mole-rats, and monkeys, plus a merry-go-round, a train, and an outdoor amphitheater, where the Toledo Symphony Orchestra plays from July through August on Saturday evenings. In December, five hundred thousand little bulbs are strung around for the annual "Lights Before Christmas" show. Great for specimens called people. 419-385-5721.

Gather with the downtown crowd in Promenade Park on Friday evenings in summer for one of Toledo's "Rally By the River" events with finger-lickin' food stands and live-wire music. A major rock, rhythm n' blues blowout takes place here in late May. Follow Huron Street south from the docks to the farmer's market for fresh-picked Ohio produce and homemade bread.

Across the river, anchored alongside International Park as if waiting for a new set of orders, the Great Lakes freighter SS *Willis Boyer* carries only cargoes of summer visitors into times past. 419-698-8252.

The Toledo Mud Hens baseball, a farm club of the Detroit Tigers, plays in Ned Skeldon Stadium at the Lucas County Recreation Center. Next door, the Ohio Baseball Hall of Fame has Cy Young items, plus the "Babe's" 1930 paycheck (haven't you wondered what happened to that?). 419-893-9483.

History of another ilk is at Fort Meigs, one of several area military forts and the site of battles before and during the War of 1812. Uniformed soldiers and log barricades make the past present, especially when cannons go off. At Perrysburg off I 475 on the south side of the city. 419-874-4121.

Still another backward look that might save your life some day—at the Toledo firefighter's museum, you'd expect old water pumpers and vintage uniforms, but not the complete safety and learning center where children actually play role situations and learn instructions should they encounter a fire at home. They're taught how to roll out of bed, keep low in case of smoke, and feel the floor for heat with the back of their hand. A must for families, it's at 918 Sylvania Avenue. 419-478-FIRE.

Milwaukee makes the beer; Toledo molds the glass to pour it into. Three major glass companies operate here, so checking a factory store is on most tours. The U.S. Glass Outlet (watch it blown) is on Miami Street, a half mile off I 75; mark-downs are at Libby's Factory Outlet on Buckeye near I 75 and I 280.

The Toledo Botanical Gardens (lilac time, rose time, mum time, anytime) or one the area's metroparks should be on the list, the latter especially in spring or when fall colors are at peak glory. The gardens are at 5403 Elmer Drive. 419-536-8365.

Or head for a state park. Ohio's chain of state park resorts includes the big Maumee Bay Resort and Conference Center just east of town. The allures of a public park, with a wildlife refuge, boardwalks over the wetlands, and hiking and jogging trails combine with an eighteen-hole golf course and with slick full-service dining rooms, bedrooms, suites, cottages, and meeting rooms. All of this is with the long blue edge of Lake Erie out the front windows. Close to the city, a world away. 800-At-A-PARK.

A total view of Toledo would have to list repertory theater, ballet, the University of Toledo, hockey, ethnic fests, golf, Victorian heritage houses, river cruises, charter fishing, mega-mall shopping centers (such as the Franklin Park Mall on 5001 Monroe Street), the performing arts, horse racing, and dining places (Fifi's, elegant continental; Chicago's, chic excellence; Mancy's Steak, hearty; Ricardos, downtown best). That will come in a thicker book.

For more information:
Toledo Convention and Visitors Bureau,
  419-321-6404 or 800-243-4667.
Ohio Tourism, 800-BUCKEYE.

61.
Put-in-Bay: Sweetly Monumental

This is about the Ohio Erie coast's only bay, the only splash of islands, unique geology, and a giddy population of fish.

Since 1812, when Americans and Brits finally settled their differences, these delightful assets have had a loyal fan club. Quiet and easy to reach, it's midway between Toledo and Cleveland, and some of the earliest vacationers never went home. Their grandchildren's grandchildren still live in Port Clinton or on Put-in-Bay Island, determined to keep fast lanes elsewhere.

Odd-shaped South Bass Island, alias Put-in-Bay, is largest of three (logically named North Bass, Middle Bass, and South Bass), and it's big enough to have a naturally protected harbor where vessels put in to escape storms (or British guns in the War of 1812). The preferred name of the bay and village has been applied to the whole isle; nobody says Bass Island anymore.

Many Victorian summertime-only comers were socialites staying in fancy hotels. (The sprawling Victory Hotel's ruins are part of a state park on the island's west end.) Wealthy financier Jay Cooke owned Gibraltar Island with his own harbor. However, Cooke and his wanna-be followers, left for more sedate pastures when day-trip excursion boats from

Detroit and Cleveland started bringing in riffraff who were boisterous even on Sundays.

There's one hotel today, four motels, and an assortment of cabins; a good number of visitors sleep on boats or camp in South Bass Island State Park. Everyone's sightseeing agenda, however, starts at the Perry Victory Monument and International Peace Memorial (one and the same). Commodore Oliver Hazard Perry was the U.S. officer who fought the British fleet in the Battle of Lake Erie. In a beautiful example of peace becoming more important than who-won-what, the monument was given dual dedication. Finished in 1915, the three-hundred-and-fifty-two-foot Doric column takes visitors up to a panorama of Lake Erie, the coast, and harbor.

Put-in-Bay's year-round population is around five hundred, subject to a ten-fold summer increase. There are all the services you need, plus good food, fun taverns, and souvenir T-shirts perhaps you don't need. The Round House Bar, for example, is terrific. One yacht club, the Crew's Nest, sells one-day memberships to those who want to enjoy the lounge or sit on the club's front porch. A bright park gazebo acts as centerpiece for summer events.

To visit a winery (a long-time Island specialty) or just to explore, rent a bike, golf cart, or antique car and travel the seventeen miles of flat, paved roads through the trees and beside the vineyards. You can also get around on a tour train. (It is not recommend that you bring your own car, but it's possible.) The hundred-year-old Heineman Winery (newly expanded), off Catawba Avenue near the island center, qualifies as a must. Of the nearby caves, two are not big enough for spelunkers. However, Crystal Cave, purported to be the world's largest geode, can be seen by hunching down on entering the room-size area; it's totally encrusted with large glassy formations. Perry's Cave held ammunition and British prisoners. May 30 to Labor Day for both.

Another tasting room for the devout to pursue is complete with a Spanish flair and National Register of Historic Places listing; it can be visited on Middle Bass Island from Put-in-Bay. The Lonz Winery, 419-285- 5411.

An airport opens for private planes from April to December; the Miller Boat Line runs frequent ferries from Catawba, 419-285-2421, the Parker Boat Line from Port Clinton, 419-732-2800. A jet-express catamaran also leaves from Port Clinton, 800-245-1 JET. Or fly over, midseason, on Island Airlines (also to Kelley's Island, Middle and North Bass) from Port Clinton, 419-734-3149.

For more information:
Put-in-Bay Information, 419-285-2832.
Port Clinton Information, 419-734-5503.

62.
Port Clinton, Marblehead, and Kelley's Isle

Ohio Highway 2 rather waves at Port Clinton as it goes by; you find your easy own way into the heart of town. A friendly little burg, only twenty minutes from Cedar Point Amusement Park, Port Clinton acts as main office for a pair of Siamese peninsulas called Catawba and Marblehead, sends boats off to Put-in-Bay and other Erie Islands, equips meandering fisherpeople, and doesn't change much over the years.

The town spreads with vintage shops and shady streets behind the Erie lakefront, a waterworks park, and the city beach. The Ottawa county courthouse's clock tower peers over the scene, a Romanesque sentinel on duty for around a hundred years. Of the peninsulas served in this low-keyed jurisdiction, they are juicy with orchards (peaches, apples) and seem to know how to put a good ma-pa cafe just where its needed. There are new condos on the shores—signs that times are catching up, perhaps, but the ambience of yesterday prevails.

The peninsula sticks out into an area called the Lake Erie Basin, where reefs, shoals, and isles make it the most productive fish-spawning nursery in the Great Lakes. In the spring, walleyes, yellow perch, and white bass move into shallow areas that warm up faster than the open lake. In the spring, accordingly, the pole, net, and bucket brigade heads out to greet them. Old-timers know just where the largemouths and bluegills feed, where the gravel banks are, and where to pull up a channel catfish.

Marblehead fishing is both legend and art, providing a mass of jobs to those who rent charters, sell tackle, or provide docking.

At the tip end of Marblehead is a lighthouse now appearing on a U.S. postage stamp in a series featuring four Great Lakes lights. Oldest continuously operating light on Lake Erie, it has paid its dues, warning against the gales of November and winds with an uninterrupted sweep of two hundred miles. Visitors may climb to the top (eighty-seven steps) four Saturdays during the summer. Call Port Clinton (below) for the schedule.

From the nearby shore, you can see Kelley's Island, largest of the Erie group. The Kelleys were Cleveland brothers who bought their emerald isle in 1830 for $1.50 an acre, then established a winery, limestone quarry, and the nation's first fish hatchery. Today's enterprise centers on wine and hospitality. Motel, cottages, and tourist rooms are available for those who plan ahead. There is an Ohio state park with camping. The Island is also known for the distinct scratching of glaciers, giant grooves in bedrock gouged out as the ice moved over them. For lovers of gothic settings, another sight is the old Kelley Mansion with its circular staircase and maybe a friendly ghost or two.

The whole of Kelley's Island is on the National Registry. Several boat services can take you over, or maybe you can get a lucky ride in a Ford tri-motor Tin Goose on Island Airlines from Port Clinton or Put-in-Bay. 419-734-3149. ("The World's Shortest Airline.")

Back on Marblehead, the village of Lakeside was a religious camp meeting ground and still is as wholesome as fresh apples. The Hotel Lakeside, circa 1875, uses plenty of antiques and wicker and is another name on the National Registry. A new Victorian pavilion sits dockside, and the Lakeside Symphony is a summer treat, along with Chatauqua-type programs.

Keeping the National Registry busy, we must mention the Old Stone House On the Lake (full name), a bed and breakfast with a gift shop and bike rental. Open year round, too. 419 -798-5922. For the whole motel list (you'll be surprised at the length of it!), call the Port Clinton Chamber of Commerce.

For a definite change of pace, an African Safari Wildlife Park can be found at 267 Lightner Road. 419-732-3606. Or wander through the largest array of crystal in Ohio at the Catawba Glass Works Outlet, 3865 Winecellar Road. 416-797-2425.

For more information:
Port Clinton Chamber of Commerce,
  419-734-5503.

63.

Sandusky and Cedar Point: Home of a Friendly Mean Streak

Notice to persons who love being slam-dunked through walls of negative gravity: More than ten stomach-defying roller coasters are waiting to rearrange your brain cells at Cedar Point Amusement Park, on the eastern edge of Sandusky. One of them, the largest set of wooden roller hills in the world, goes by the appropriately evil name of Mean Streak.

Tucked into the best natural harbor on the Great Lakes, sweet, soft-spoken Sandusky has catered to the summer trade's desire for safe excitement ever since its founding days. No place along the coast has such a concentration of (often hokey) things to do. Today, the Sandusky area ranks in the top ten most popular vacation areas in the nation. (Curiously, Sandusky is not in Sandusky County, but in Erie County right next to it.)

Now a playground, but once a battlefield, Sandusky's locale was the eye of storms between the French and the British, the British and the Indians, the Americans and everybody else. When things were settled after 1812, a destroyed fort became the site of the present town. It was part of the tract of land that citizens of Connecticut purchased after the Revolutionary War for future use, with the far section delegated to residents burned out by the battles. These Easterners called this chunk of Ohio their Western Reserve and the Sandusky shores the Firelands, a name occasionally seen on signs.

Downtown, the vaguely Italianate store buildings are mostly free of modern overlay. In the shady Erie County Courthouse square, a cobblestone fountain bubbles near a memorial floral clock. A local jewel much doted upon is the restored State Theater on Columbus Avenue where Ray Charles and Roy Clark have appeared. Ballet, musicals, movies, and programs for children. 419-626-3945.

At 404 Wayne Street, the Follett House displays a collection of Civil War mementos and items from great-grandma's attic. Not to miss: The Merry-Go-Round Museum on the corner of Jackson and Washington Streets has a wood carver on the premises and a round-up of joyous horses and other treasures. There are narrated tours as well as rides. At the waterfront, the Surf's Up Aquatic Center, a wave-action pool, provides twelve minutes of surf between periods of calm, plus picnic space. Or try jet skis, rent a paddleboat, or charter a fishing trip.

Marinas bob with boats and, across the inlet, on the Cedar Point peninsula, four carousels (and more on their history), a jungle safari, live stage shows, IMAX cinema, Canadian Pacific and Lake Erie Railroad, water park, Red Garter Saloon (what do they miss?), and coasters, coasters, coasters (the Manum XL-200, Corkscrew, Disaster Transport, and Wildcat) will draw thousands of visitors on any summer's day.

There's even a genuine National Register of Historic Places landmark (on the premises, of course) to help you sleep it all off. The Hotel Breakers dates from 1905, a real beach-side charmer where the Tiffany glass chandeliers and French chateau architecture set the sedate, relaxing tone. There are four hundred rooms, but call very early in the season. 419-627-2106. More accommodations, from suites to chalets and condos or RV sites are available.

For a total shift in gears, drive down to Milan's Historical Museum to browse through a country store, the Newton Arts Building gallery, restored homes, and a blacksmith shop. 419-499-2968. Quaint town, Milan, but you'll like going there anyway.

189

In winter, the inlets turn into tip-up towns where die-hard fisherpeople hunker down, waiting for bites. They come. Meanwhile, shows at the State Theatre go on.

For more information:
Erie County Convention and Visitors Bureau,
    419-625-2984 or 800-255-ERIE.
Cedar Point Amusement Park, 419-626-0830.

64.

Vermilion — Color the Skies Blue

Edging toward Cleveland, Vermilion makes an excellent base. It's part of a greater metro-system, yet an easy hop to Sandusky, Toledo, and points west. However, beware—it is hard to keep traveling on.

As lake traffic expanded and the industrial revolution forged ahead, Vermilion's ample harbor was sure to attract investment. Shipbuilders established themselves on the red clay banks, hoping to leave the rival commerce of Cleveland in their wake, but that didn't happen. So when the biggest builder finally gave up and moved his boatworks to Cleveland, Vermilion went into moth balls. For years, it was a place to retire, not a launching pad. The town withdrew into itself. Former lake captains and a few industrialists built their final homes in Vermilion, keeping the atmosphere sedate, unlike the rowdier environs of Sandusky. One of the families donated their mansion to the Great Lakes Historical Society, insuring that the past would forever be in Vermilion's future.

The Historical Society prospered, added a new wing to its house, and encouraged historic preservation throughout town. People began to drop by and walk around enjoying the shady streets and well-kept houses, with styles ranging from New England salt box to Queen Anne Victorian. The venerable Steamboat Hotel on Huron and Main Streets has sections dating from 1840, but is now a private housing structure. Nearby on Huron sits the first home of Ava Bradley, a leader of Vermilion's boom times. Today, the home is the Gilcrest Bed & Breakfast. 216-967-1237. The tender preservation of shops on Liberty Avenue, plus restaurants, brought in the admirers.

Everybody starts exploring at the Inland Seas Maritime Museum at the lake end of Main Street. Stand on a reconstructed ship's bridge, let your eyes walk the decks of scale models, and learn about funnel insignias, the meanings of whistles, the anatomy of a lighthouse lens. In June, it sponsors a model ship-building contest, with winning entries on display for the next two days. There are paintings, books, area history, a gift shop, and the Great Lake itself right there to stare at. 419-967-3467.

There are a lot of canals and inlets with houses backing up to their piece of the water and a definite New England-coast-town look to Vermilion. On the square sits a town hall and an opera house. A railroad track keeps it from being a real square but that's a minor matter. Shops and bookstores on Liberty Avenue keep their Victorian facades painted and polished. Pure nostalgia is in the Musik Box Haus, full of dolls and music boxes mostly disguised as something else. 5551 Liberty Street. Those who wax nostalgic over hardware choose the Vermilion Hardware at 678 Grand Street, an emporium of the old school.

Vermilion's Woolly Bear Festival in late September or October centers on a big parade and has become the largest single-day event in Ohio. Three to four hours of marching bands and parade-minded groups come in from everywhere, while the children of Vermilion dress up like those fuzzy caterpillars said to forecast warm or severe winters. Info is at the chamber of commerce, on Liberty east of Main Street.

Ask about the big annual fish festival in June.

A hint of Vermilion's ethnic mix or worldly sophistication may be in an ad for Papa Joe's Pizza & Pies that offers strudel as well. Chez Francois, Main near Huron Street, 216-967-0630, and the Old Prague, Liberty near Main, 216-967-7182, are gourmet and classic. Ohio-ethnic McGarvey's broils popular seafood specials at dockside and also has boat rides available. 216-967-8000.

There's no rush to build motels in Vermilion, and a casual poll of citizens seems to want to keep it that way. Try the Motel Plaza or the Village Square Annex Bed and Breakfast. After all, Sandusky and Cleveland, with rooms aplenty, are close at hand.

For more information:
Vermilion Chamber of Commerce, 216-967-4477.

65.
Let's Hear It for Cleveland

In downtown Cleveland's Public Square, an athletic bronze Adonis stretches upward from a flame-encircled globe. Officially, the centerpiece for the Press War Memorial Fountain symbolizes man's reach for peace. Unofficially, he could be Mr. Cleveland, stretching upward to new success.

Few turn-around cities have done it as dramatically as Cleveland. Once dubbed "the mistake on the lake" by cynical wags, the Cuyahoga River running through it was dirty enough to catch fire, and civic pride was in tatters.

No more. There are handsome new additions to the skyline, new restorations of old theaters, expanded museums, and a cleaned-up river. Old-timers who return see a new, more open downtown, with views of Lake Erie that were once blocked off.

Touring is easy because Cleveland has managed to keep special-interest features fairly close to each other. An outstanding example is University Circle, five miles east of downtown, where no less than seventy cultural institutions are within a one-mile radius. Close to the city's heart, the lavishly rejuvenated theater district puts half a dozen show palaces in easy reach. The "new" downtown lakefront is home to Cleveland's Municipal Stadium, a retired ore carrier serves as a marine museum, and the stunning new Rock 'n' Roll Hall of Fame was designed by I. M. Pei.

Why Cleveland for this type of museum? The term "rock n' roll" was coined in Cleveland on Moondog Freed's radio broadcasts in 1951. Here's where David Bowie met American audiences and Bruce Springsteen became mainstream. The new museum manages to spotlight its honorees (Elvis Presley, the Supremes, and others) without total worship in a building that again shows Pei's inventiveness—a seven-story glass tent anchored by a hundred-and-sixty-five-foot tower. Class Act. 216-781-7625 or 800-349-ROCK.

After meeting the new kid in town, walk over to the Terminal Tower, a building that says Cleveland the way Eiffel says Paris. Converting this icon of the big-time passenger-rail days into an elegant super mall was a major goal in the city's face lift. From the lower concourse, you can catch a train to the airport or to the far east side of town. (Amtrak leaves from a station only a few blocks away.) Upstairs, the wide span of an enormous roof looks down on a hundred-and-twenty-store shopping complex. There's a eleven-screen cinema center, as well as direct passageways to the Ritz Carlton Hotel and the sumptuous, palatial

Stouffer Tower Plaza Hotel on the same tight block. You could spend a week and not cross the street.

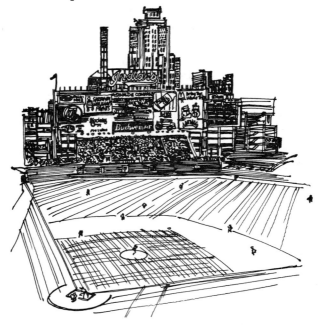

Cheer for the Indians at Jacobs Field in Cleveland

East on Euclid (Cleveland's Main Street), the Arcade, circa 1890, is a classy grand-aunt of enclosed malls. Sunlight streams down over three levels of cast-iron balconies and beautifully spotlights open space on the lower level. There are all manner of shops and services, once you stop staring at the building. Other nearby arcades, Dillard's Department Store, the Erieview Galleria on East 9th, and those Tower shops—the world's merchants are here.

Still on Euclid near 14th, the Palace, State, and Ohio Theaters are tributes to restorative skills on Playhouse Square, but better yet are the presentations: *Cats*, Bob Dylan, the Cleveland Opera, and Ohio Ballet and more. A newspaper will tell what's on.

Euclid Avenue gained fame in the late 1800s as Millionaire's Row when more than two hundred and fifty Victorian mansions housed the likes of John Hay, John D. Rockefeller, and Samuel Mather. One of the great residential streets of the world, it has disappeared except for the pavement, which leads to the Cleveland Playhouse at East 85th and then to University Circle. No other city in the world has a cultural gathering place like this.

In no particular order: The Cleveland Museum of Art, one of the very best, holds over forty-eight thousand works of art from every period and culture. 216-421-7340. The Cleveland Museum of Natural History, Ohio's oldest and largest of its kind, with dinosaurs, geodes, human ecology, and backyard botany—our world as we seldom see it. 216-231-4600. The Cleveland Health Museum where a transparent talking woman and an eighteen-foot tooth are among two hundred life exhibits. 216-231-5010. Severance Hall is home of the Cleveland Symphony Orchestra. Even in Cleveland's bleakest times, the Symphony was renowned as a superb assembly, consistently lauded by critics and musicians. If you're just passing through, its sheer luck to get tickets. In summer, look for the Symphony at Blossom Center, located in Cuyahoga Falls. 800-686-1141.

Still to go in the University Circle area: the Cleveland Center For Contemporary Art, 216-421-8671; Cleveland Opera, 216-241-6000; Cleveland Children's Museum (borrow a child, if you must), 216-791-KIDS; the Western Reserve Historical Society's mansions, classic autos, rare aircraft, extensive furnishings, and costumes, 216-721-5722; Cleveland Ballet; Karamu House; Garden Center of Greater Cleveland; and many others. Get the whole list and complete directions from the Cleveland Visitors Center or at any hotel desk.

The most-transformed area in town has to be the lower banks of the Cuyahoga River, the twenty-six-acre Flats. The city began here in 1796 when General Moses Cleaveland plotted a site for a New-England-type town. Harsh conditions (insects and disease) drove Cleaveland back east, but his project was not abandoned. (The name changed when a newspaper dropped the "a" to fit a masthead.) Conveniently set between routes to iron mines and the coal fields needed to make steel, Cleveland grew into a manufacturing giant. However, the world situation turned, there was a drop in auto production, and Cleveland was left holding the financial bag.

It took nerve and a lot of civic determination, but some hard-core believers started changing old factory sites into condos and restaurants, shops, and a couple of comedy clubs. The pollution problem received intensive care. You can now wine, dine, and watch lake freighters go by, almost within reach. The winding river, with its canopies of bridges, has become one of the biggest attractions in town.

The Cleveland Zoo, five miles south of downtown, has a new rain forest, complete with Malaysian ruins, waterfalls, thunderstorms, dwarf crocodiles, macaws, and everything but prowling tigers.

Turning back toward the city center, Gateway sports and entertainment facility at Ontario and Huron Streets, is home to the Cleveland Indians and the Cavaliers.

Tasty browsing is at the West Side Market, an old-world-style grocery outlet. The massive yellow brick building with the Italianate clock tower shelters more than a hundred and eighty vegetable, fruit, honey, and egg stands. This, perhaps, is the real heart of Cleveland. Old ethnic or social neighborhoods are alive and well and taking in visitors—Tremont, Little Italy, Coventry Village.

Then there's that long, long stretch of park on the lakefront, a green system that seems to braid itself into a wreath around the whole city, with boat excursions on the Cuyahoga and out into Lake Erie, plus a list of restaurants too long to handle. (Author's favorite: That Place on Bellflower–real name.)

As former Clevelander Dizzy Dean was reported to have said about his city, "It's not bragging if its true."

For more information:
Cleveland Visitor Information Hotline,
800-321-1004.

66.
Within Cleveland's Easy Reach

There was a song in a Broadway musical that lamented, "Why Oh Why Oh Why Oh, Did I Ever Leave Ohio?"–especially true when it's the Cuyahoga Valley in the full burst of spring. Or along the shore of Lake Erie when the fish are biting. Or when an Amish buggy goes lightly down a country road, and you remember Ohio's infinite diversity.

Going east from Cleveland (the suburbs seem endless), Headlands Beach State Park and a marine museum at Fairport Harbor are good stops. Geneva State Park, Geneva-on-the-Lake, Ashtabula, and on up the Pennsylvania line are for people who need to wind down. Going south, just north of Aurora, Sea World of Ohio is easy to take. It's gardenlike in most areas, and aquatic creatures are no longer put through ersatz-human paces, but cavort naturally (which can be funny), with trainers explaining why whales and dolphins leap and what they need to survive. You learn a thing or two. There are killer whales, several varieties of penguins, comical sea lions, walruses, and otters, as well as water skiers, fireworks, show biz, and lunch. 800-63-SHAMU. Next door—almost—Geaugo Lake Amusement Park has a hundred ways to ride, wet or dry, and four roller coasters. A two-million-gallon wave pool and nine super slides are here, plus Turtle Beach for kids and Palace and Western Theaters.

Both parks are located thirty miles southeast of Cleveland on Route 43 or nine miles north of the Ohio Turnpike at exit 13. There's a discount with an Ohio Pass Card. Ohio Tourism, 800-BUCKEYE.

Sleep in a silo in Akron's Quaker Square. A fellow named Schmacher had a granary, started packaging a compressed oat cereal, later put a smiling Quaker on the box, and Quaker Oats was on its way. Now the remodeled silos are Hilton Hotel rooms—and it's interesting to see how they fit these basically square pegs into their round holes. 216-253-5970.

A steam train, the Cuyahoga Valley Railroad, leaves from Independence, chugs through the Cuyahoga Recreation Area, between steep forested hills that are golden visions in midautumn, and finally puffs to a stop in the Quaker Square Shopping Center. Those who wish to can take a shorter trip to Hale Farm Village, a living-history museum depicting life in the first part of the 1800s. Glass is blown, horses get new shoes, and other nineteenth-century-life tasks are performed by costumed guides in buildings straight out of a New England primer.

Near Akron, Blossom Center, the Cleveland Symphony Orchestra's summer home, sends the classics skyward with concerts under the stars. Bring a blanket to sit on, a hamper to raid, and someone to put your arm around. Akron's sixty-five-room Hywet Tudor mansion, anchored in a sea of gardens, would make Henry VIII feel at home. You're invited to visit. 216-836-5533. Then have dinner at the Tangier, a restaurant/cabaret and Ohio legend.

Kick-off time is when you enter the door of Canton's National Football Hall of Fame, a round structure with a dome inspired by a football. Here you'll see one hundred years of the professional game, Jim Thorpe to Paul Brown, with replays of the action in a four-building complex. For avid sports fans, this is a call on the relatives. 216-456-8207.

The focus changes radically in Holmes, the next county south and west, where the world's largest settlement of Amish puts new charms into country driving. Those sprightly horses have often been purchased at auctions of retired harness racers, which the practical Amish see as just right for their uses. Call the Mennonite Information Center, 216-893-3192, for information on Amish restaurants, craft stores, quilt barns, and antiques. Be considerate with your camera—it's an offensive intrusion on their beliefs.

Circling back up and over to Youngstown, the Butler Institute of American Art, in a handsome Italianate building, was the first structure built in the U.S. specifically to house a collection of American Art. 216-743-1711. This former big steel town has tempered its pace to new-tech ways, hospitality, and history—as in a restored grist mill in Mill Creek Metro Park or the Mahoning Valley Historical Society's display case, The Arms Museum (local history). In a mansion, splendid for period furniture and costumes, the museum also managed to fit in transportation and the Civil War. 216-473-2589.

There's the tip of the list. Those who leave too soon sing "Why Oh..."

For more information:
Youngstown Tourism, 216-747-8200.
Canton Tourism, 800-533-4302.
Lake County Tourism, 216-357-2582.
Ohio Tourism, 800 BUCKEYE.

67.

Pennsylvania On the Lake— Short Coast, Long Fun

T here's barely fifty miles of Pennsylvania coast along the Lake Erie shore, but it gives a taste of wide blue horizon to a state known for its enclosing green hills and intimate valleys, for mists curling through the woodlands, and trim farms. Without half trying, most of northwest Pennsylvania evokes a rural life. The winding Allegheny River and coiled feeder streams twist across its meadows.

Erie has a population of 280,000—nothing approaches that number in the neighboring counties. Named for the Eriez Indians, it has been dubbed the "Flagship City" or the "Gem City" because of its sparkling sapphire-blue bay and a moment in history during the War of 1812 when Commodore O. H. Perry, commanding the flagship *Niagara*, forced the British squadron to give up. Perry's famous words "We have met the enemy and they are ours" made history of its own. (It was parodied in recent years by cartoonist Walt Kelly whose wise little swamp possum, Pogo, observes, "We have met the enemy and they is us.")

By the 1850s, Erie was sprouting rapidly with manufacturing and tourism, thanks to a protected shipping harbor and appealing beaches nearby.

The long, thin peninsula that juts out from the mainland, arcing like a spray of water or maybe a quill pen, is Presque Isle State Park, 3,202 acres of sand and woodsy locations. Ranked among the top one hundred American swimming places by Conde Nast magazine *Traveler*, there's everything here but camping—food, biking, a lighthouse, a marina for four hundred and seventy-three boats, programs, winter sports, and birding (a top national site), with more info at the visitors center. 814-838-8776.

At the foot of Holland Street in Erie, the hundred-and-ninety-eight-foot brig *Niagara*, used by Perry, is docked. A double-masted beauty with at least ten sails (the difference between a brig and a brigantine is largely the way the sails are rigged), it was part of Perry's fleet in 1812. It was scuttled, but one hundred years later, the hull plus the lead used to hold it together were recovered, and the ship was reconstructed to sail in another era. Under a cloudless blue sky, its main mast rising a hundred and eighteen feet above the water line and all sails set, the *Niagara* is a vision of art and function, although it seems smallish and vulnerable. Visit when the brig is in port or call to watch the next sailing (but not to board), with your camera ready. 814-454-3099.

The Old Custom House on State Street, a Greek Revival prize listed on the Registry of Historic Buildings, lives life today as the Erie Art Museum. Gannon University (Sixth, Eighth, and Peach Streets) has more about Erie's maritime background in the University's Historical Museum, housed in a Victorian mansion. Inspect the Land Lighthouse off East Sixth Street, first light on the Great Lakes, built in 1813 and then rebuilt in 1867. Gannon University also has a planetarium. Space travelers, call 814-871-5794.

Lemurs, llamas, and lowland gorillas, plus polar bears, pumas, and a panther, the Erie zoo is complete right down to a train and carousel. 814-864-4091.

Out in Erie County, there are four covered bridges and towns with little gem museums (Fort LeBoeuf in Waterford, the Sturgeon House in Fairview, Rural Life Museum and Kibler History Museum in Girard). Also, look for the wineries and vineyards and a place to buy chrysanthemums— Paschke's, near a town called North East (exit 12 off Route 20), has thousands of them in wide rows of brilliant color. 814-725-9860. Blooming bed-and-breakfast businesses, too.

A hundred and twenty-eight miles south as the van flies, I 79 will land you in Pittsburgh, a city with much soot in its past and a bright gleam in its present. Gone are the belching steel mills of yesterday that forced housewives to wash curtains twice a week. The new Pittsburgh is on the cutting edge of chic—clean and reasonably priced, with great restaurants, thriving midtown department stores, a good subway system, and enviable scenic advantages. Visitors can go to the top of Mt. Washington (a cliff along the river and close enough to hike to) and view the Golden Triangle of downtown Pittsburgh, see the Ohio, Allegheny, and Monongahela Rivers meet, look at a dozen bridges and the clustered sampling of gothic, art-deco, and far-out architecture that make up the present-day city. Don't miss Station Square's remodeled depot (a Victorian stunner) or the Allegheny County Courthouse. There was a big rivalry between tycoons in Pittsburgh, so that anything Frick (steel), Mellon (banking), or Carnegie (steel) could build, the other one would try to out-do, and the resulting opulence has left a rare legacy of art museums, science centers, public gardens, and wondrous houses. Three miles from downtown in Oakland, there's the University of Pittsburgh campus, plus the Tiffany Church and towering Cathedral of Learning that would make anyone want to go back to school.

River tours, theater, and dining in sky-high splendor prevail; the downside of the old town is out of sight. The Greater Pittsburgh Convention and Visitors Bureau will help with details. 412-281-7711 or 800-366-0093.

Meanwhile, back at the lake, the east edge of Erie's coast is seductively scenic. Dwindling ridges of the Alleghenies rise in the background, towns have a neat Connecticut look. For a wine festival, water parks, horse racing, and other data, contact the Erie Area Convention and Visitors Bureau for information. 814-454-7191.

68.

Chautauqua and Allegany: Talk and Walk

The westernmost county of the Empire State has a name you wouldn't think of as a household word. However, in the days before night classes and television with educational programming, Chautauqua was famous as a way to improve your mind without going back to school.

The Chautauqua Institution, a lakeside center for the arts, education, religion, and topics of lasting interest, started off as a Sunday-school-teachers' conference and training camp on the edge of Chautauqua Lake. It grew into a nationwide tent meeting, featuring presidential candidates, literary lights (such as Samuel Clemens), inspiring personalities (Helen Keller appeared on Chautauqua programs), great singers and musicians, actors, and college professors. The goal was to teach and learn, to improve one's mind. It was enormously successful, then faded away for a time, but now is enjoying a resurgence. As an example, look back at chapter twenty to see that Chautauqua is a big summer event in places like Washburn, Wisconsin.

Things have expanded at home base until today there is a sixty-five-hundred-seat Chautauqua Amphitheater, home of the Chautauqua Symphony Orchestra; Norton Hall, where operas are presented; a Palestine Park walk-through model of the Holy Land; and a bell tower on the shore. Over two hundred summer courses are offered. Call 800-836-ARTS.

203

At the other end of the lake in Jamestown is another stage, one that launched a funny redhead into show business and is now called the Lucille Ball Little Theater. For a schedule of plays, call 716-483-1095. More of the performing arts can be found at the Reg Lenna Civic Center. On Washington Street, the Fenton Historical Society functions in a Civil War-period mansion listed on the National Register of Historic Places. It has Swedish and Italian heritage rooms and a genealogy archives. 716-483-7521.

Pick up a brochure in Jamestown for information on walking tours through this town of houses, from Gothic Revival to art deco, survivors of the changing times.

Keep driving east on Route 17 to Salamanca and Allegany State Park, a jewel of the New York park system. Sixty-five thousand acres, two lakes, and eighty-five miles of hiking trails are here, along with a lot of mileage in scenic back roads. There are two stores and a pair of restaurants, plus everybody's outlet, be it for cross-country skiing, tobogganing, stream fishing, or tennis. For boat rentals, nature center, and tent or trailer camping, call 716-354-9101.

Salamanca, the only city on a Native American reservation, has a fine collection of western New York's railroad artifacts in the Salamanca Rail Museum at 170 Main Street. Scenic rail excursions in summer and fall are offered. 719-945-3133. Seneca beadwork and Iroquois arts are demonstrated and sold at the American Indian Crafts Center, 719 Broad Street. 716-945-1225. Or visit the Seneca-Iroquois National Museum, off exit 20 on Route 17. 716-945-17738.

A short spin east near Orlean, Rock City Park sits atop the Allegany Mountains, yet it was the floor of a prehistoric ocean which left some interesting traces, including the world's largest deposit of quartz conglomerate—and there are downright beautiful walking trails.

Wine buffs will enjoy stops like the tasting rooms of Roberian Vineyards Ltd., near Sheridan and Vetter Vineyards Winery, Westfield. The Chautauqua Wine Trail includes six farm wineries along Lake Erie, from Ripley to Silver Creek. Lighthouse fans must pause to visit the Dunkirk Historical Light and the Veterans Park Museum, buoy tender, and Coast Guard boats. And don't forget the Adams Art Gallery and Dunkirk Historical Museum, then on to Silver Creek and Buffalo.

For more information:
Chautauqua City Tourist Bureau, 800-331-0543.
Jamestown Area Chamber of Commerce, 716-484-1101.
New York State Tourism, 800-CALL-NYS.

69.
Wing It In Buffalo

Grandparents sang about shuffling off to Buffalo. Sport pages follow the exploits of football's Buffalo Bills and baseball's Bisons. A local cook first dreamed them up, and now there are stampedes across restaurant buffets for Buffalo wings.

Named for a creature reportedly never seen in these parts, Buffalo, New York, unwittingly shares a few characteristics with the beast—it stands its ground, can move and turn with surprising speed, and looks with a stoic eye upon detractors.

Biggest bad rap that Buffalo gets is that the weather is awful. Yet it rarely hits the ninety-degree mark and never goes to one hundred. The margin is narrow, but Buffalo gets more sunny days in summer than Washington, Baltimore, or Albany. And, contrary to popular belief, Buffalo does not make the top ten cities in terms of snowfall.

Directly across from Canada and facing both
Lake Erie and the mouth of the Niagara River (the
Peace Bridge spans the border), the second largest city
in New York State has a wide, inviting front entrance
where a long splinter of land throws a protective
shield around busy marinas and carpets of lawn. Exit
the N.Y. Thruway (I 90) onto Highway 5, coming
from east or west, to reach this area easily.

Buffalo is an important Great Lakes port,
although it is not freighters but a Navy destroyer that
grabs the waterfront visitor's attention. A guided mis-
sile cruiser, submarine, fighter plane, and museum are
part of the Erie County Naval and Servicemen's Park,
a generous assortment of battle hardware from all
branches of the armed forces. No other inland city
has a display of this size.

It is a short saunter from military memories to
Buffalo Place, a pedestrian mall surrounding the
above-ground metro rail transit system. Rides are
available every five to twenty minutes, depending on
the time of day, and the ride on Main Street is free
until it goes underground. Get a view of downtown
from the 28th-floor observation deck on the tallest
city hall in the country. Not quite like looking at a
map, but seeing things from the top will help get you
oriented. From here, architectural mavens may spot
the Guaranty Building on Church Street, designed by
Louis Sullivan, a mentor of Frank Lloyd Wright. City
Hall is Niagara Square. 716-851-4200. Buffalo right-
fully boasts about its buildings and styles, from mod-
ernists Saarinen and Yamasaki to the Italian
Renaissance basilica out on Ridge Road, Lackawanna.
There are five houses in town by Frank Lloyd Wright.

On Elmwood Avenue near Expressway 198, the
Albright-Knox Gallery, a classic Greek vision in marble, is one of great city art museums mentioned in
this book. (Toronto, Buffalo, Cleveland, Toledo,

Detroit, Milwaukee, and Chicago make a powerful cultural claim for Great Lakes residents.) The six thousand works in the collection include paintings by Picasso, van Gogh, Matisse, and Monet. Although the main body of work is contemporary, items go as far back as 3,000 B.C. 716-882-8700.

Buffalo's theater district (Shea's Theater, 646 Main Street, 716-847-0850; Studio Arena Theater, 710 Main, 716-867-5650; the Pfeifer and others nearby) is alive and well with several stages in active production. Your chances of being able to see good Broadway theater, ballet, or any of the performing arts are excellent, whatever time of year. The Buffalo Philharmonic Orchestra plays at Kleinhans Music Hall on Pennsylvania Avenue, 716-885-5000; and the Buffalo Inner City Ballet at 25 High Street promotes African American classics, 716-881-5131.

A survivor of Buffalo's 1901 Pan-American Exposition is the home of the Buffalo and Erie County Historical Society Museum. The collection dotes on such practical arts and crafts (and often a sense of fun) as were needed to pioneer or expand on life in America, including kazoos and Cheerios—all originating in western New York. 716-873-9644.

Wander around in Allentown, Buffalo's little enclave of nineteenth-century shops and houses, cozy eateries, and tiny gardens behind iron fences. About the second weekend in June, Allentown holds an extremely popular art festival.

The Wilcox mansion at 641 Delaware houses the Theodore Roosevelt Inaugural National Historic site, one of three presidents connected to Buffalo—it was also home to Millard Filmore and Grover Cleveland.

Frederick Law Olmsted, the man who designed New York's Central Park, drew the plans for Buffalo's parks and the gracious Victorian Botanical Gardens building. There are twelve greenhouses and everything you tried to grow but never succeeded in are here. Southeast of the city, call 716-828-1040 for directions.

The Museum of Science, 1020 Humbolt Parkway, provides a look at prehistoric times, bugs, birds, jades, and Jupiter. Space shows, earth sciences. 716-896-5200. Still on a roll, the Q.R.S. Piano Roll Factory on Niagara Street, biggest producer ever of perforated piano rolls, is the only player-piano factory left in the world. It's open for free weekday tours. 716-885-4600.

Follow trails in the third oldest zoo in the land where the beast population is up to twenty-two hundred. An African rain forest might get you wet, and the children's zoo is "Neat!" (A direct quote from a six-year-old authority.) In Habicat, the tigers and lions think they are roaming free. Eat your heart out, kids—Buffalo has the only school in the world (grades seven and eight) actually on the grounds of a zoo. 716-837-0738.

North Tonawanda's Herchell Carousel Factory Museum has rides on a 1916 merry-go-round and a chance to watch the wood carvers. Summers. 716-693-1885.

Tour the town on a vintage-style trolley or try a Clipper Boat Cruise around Grand Island, over to Canada (no getting off), and past old Fort Erie with sightseeing or dining-and-entertainment cruises. It's adjacent to Servicemen's Park. 716-856-6696.

There are more than twenty-seven thousand restaurants in Erie County, cooking up French, Polish, German, Mexican, Indian, or Hungarian cuisines. In addition to the original sweet-and-sour chicken wings that were invented here, did you ever hear of beef-on-weck? Beef in a Kummelweck roll is smothered in horseradish. Well...

Crawdaddy's, next to the marina and waterfront, lets you watch the water or skyline and eat lobster as you gape. Lists of restaurants, motels, and bed and breakfasts may be found in the marina information racks. Read up on the events. Greater Buffalo has two big winter carnivals at Ellicottville and Glenwood, the Taste of Buffalo Fest in July, Erie County Fair, and minutes away, the Winter Festival of Lights at Niagara Falls in December.

The Buffalo area's big source of early growth, the Erie Canal, terminates in Tonawanda, just to the north. As Lake Erie is five hundred and seventy-one feet higher than the Hudson River, the project required the hiring of engineers and laborers; most had little or no experience in canal and lock building. The story of its construction is harrowing, but when it was finished and the price of freight from New York to Lake Erie dropped from $100 to $5 a ton, towns and property values in western New York soared, launching an era of canal building all over the Midwest. Today, New York's canal system handles over a hundred and ten thousand pleasure boats each year. Experience the locks with a two-hour narrated tour, going through locks 34 and 35, and getting raised forty-nine and a half feet. For times and directions, call 716-434-7433.

The Greater Buffalo and Niagara region has more than half a dozen ski resorts of varying sizes within a ninety-minute drive of downtown Buffalo. For downhill- and cross-country-skiing information, as well as info on lodges, condos, events, and competitions, call 800-Buffalo. For western New York ski conditions, call 800-367-9691.

For more information:
Greater Buffalo Visitors Bureau, 107 Delaware Avenue, Buffalo, NY 14202. 716-852-0511.

Niagra River

70.

Niagra Falls, New York: Begin At the Edge

It's a terrifying, hypnotic beauty that comes and goes and is always there, a sight to see once or as often as possible. The waters of four inland seas are drawn irrevocably to the Niagara River, which pours over a wondrous brink and a hundred and seventy-five feet down into a broiling, writhing caldron of rock and water, sending up an eternal tower of mist. It's a resource that's poured out, yet is just as constantly replaced. (In truth, not all of the river pours here—much is diverted to pour through tunnels to dynamos that generate power.)

There are higher falls in remote mysterious places, but none in our hemisphere spills a fraction of the volume as Niagara: 202,000 cubic feet per second (5720 cubic meters). The river has been falling for twelve thousand years, wearing the river channel into a deeper and deeper gorge. Once, it fell eleven kilometers (seven miles) downstream from its present position.

One river, one thundering wonder of the world, and at one time there were plans for one large international park. That didn't work out, however, although Niagara Falls, New York, and Niagara Falls, Ontario, are a joint venture in tourism, sharing festivals and bridges and preserving their unmatched blessings along the gorge. Closest to the Falls is Rainbow Bridge, then the Whirlpool Rapids Bridge and, approaching Lake Ontario, the Lewiston/Queenston Bridge, all of them going between the Robert Moses Parkway and the Niagara Parkway.

New York's Niagara Falls City is larger and more industrialized than its Canadian counterpart, but in both places, devotion to tourism spins its biggest wheel. Keep 'em busy while they are dazzled seems to be the creed.

*You can visit Niagra Falls from either
the United States or Canada*

The handsome Wintergarden tropical conservatory, putting seven thousand trees under glass near the Niagara Falls Convention Center and Rainbow Centre Mall, may be a case in point. The tropical setting has become a favorite place for weddings. The

Native American Arts Center (one glance at its ter-
rapin-faced facade explains the nickname "Turtle") has
messages to send through dances, artifacts, galleries,
and its craft shop. 25 Rainbow Road. (As of this writing, the center is having financial troubles. If nothing
is going on, contribute to this important project anyway and look around.)

Points of interest are pretty much in a crescent
around the city and within very easy reach of the
falls. First, there is a bridge to Goat Island at the foot
of First Street, part of the Niagara Reservation State
Park. The isle has parking and hiking room, aside
from its spectacular viewing points. Prospect Point is
a place to board the *Maid of the Mist* sightseeing boat
or go up into the New York State Observation Tower.
Maid passengers don raincoats with hoods while the
boat edges warily into foamy waters. The memory of
seeing that wall of water from surface level (if you
can keep your glasses clear) will rinse out your brain
cells forever. 716-284-8897. Also at this site is the
Schoellkopf Geological Museum with a multimedia
explanation of the falls' four-hundred-and-twenty-
million-year background. Visitors center displays, history, and information.

Driving up the New York side of the river, the
new Aquarium of Niagara Falls overlooks Niagara
Gorge. Electric eels flash off, dolphins leap, sea lions
bark, and gardens bloom. It's a good show, at 701
Whirlpool Street. 716-285-3575.

Tour the Power Project Visitors Center, 5777
Lewiston Road, to understand more about Niagara
power and get another breath-stopping view of the
gorge. While there, stop at the Buscaglia Art Museum.
Up in Lewiston (ambience: ye olde), an Artpark State
Park boasts a twenty-four-hundred-seat theater for all
varieties of performing arts, with artists at work and
art shows. This town loves antiques and bed and

breakfasts with their view of the Niagara Gorge. Moving up the Robert Moses Parkway, Fort Niagara reminds us again that this scenic high ground overlooking both river and Lake Ontario was once a battlefield. Flags of three nations have flown over the gray stone barracks and bastions, where soldiers and ladies in early-nineteenth-century uniforms and dress show how to fire muskets or bake pies.

For more information:

Niagara County Tourism, 800-338-7890 (from northeast states and southern Ontario).

Niagara Frontier State Park & Recreation Region, Prospect Park, 716-278-1770.

71.

Niagra Falls, Ontario

> *"All... descriptions you may read of these*
> *mighty falls can only produce in your mind*
> *the faint glimmer of the glowworm compared with the*
> *overpowering glory of the meridian sun."*
> —John J. Audubon

We shy away from linguistic Victorian overkill, but "overpowering" and "glory" are pretty accurate. Calmer adjectives just don't make it. After all, this is the most-visited scenic attraction in the world and with spell-binding reasons.

From the air, the general contour of the falls is like a question mark, with the straight part on the American side and the horseshoe on the Canadian side of the international line. From Canada, you can see the whole sweep of the cataracts a little better, although the best approach is to view them from both sides as millions of others have done. The falls have also been seen by enough investors to stuff the World

Bank. Every conceivable entertainment, fast-food establishment, oddity collection, fun-o-ride, animal act, and souvenir that has made a nickel anywhere has come to Niagara Falls. One revolving tower inspired another; one wax museum molded the next.

The good news is that even so, meticulously kept parkways, beautiful flower beds, and well-behaved crowds keep the viewing edges pleasant and the back areas from disintegrating into total honky-tonkyness. The city of Niagara Falls, Ontario, and the Ontario Park Commission deserve much credit.

It wasn't always this way. In the mid-1880s, the cliff edge (called the Front) was a genuine mess. Freak shows, gaming houses, and even a garish red pagoda lined the narrow-edge street, all with barkers at their doors competing with noisy buggy drivers and snake oil salesmen. The only exception was the Niagara Falls Museum (still open) and all reformers made note of the museum's decorum. It was a fight to get the money grubbers out of the temple, but what you see today is the result of a hard-fought renewal battle. Beyond the border park, it still gets circuslike; but in blocks beyond the hoopla, municipal Niagara Falls is a friendly little burg with an orderly downtown.

There are basic falls experiences visitors will want to take home:

–The *Maid of the Mist*, already described in the Niagara Falls, New York, section. The Canadian *Maids* leave from the foot of Clifton Street.

–Lunch on the Victoria Restaurant patio or dinner next door at Table Rock House in the second-floor restaurant, both with great views of the falls and of the humanity watching it. Downstairs at Table Rock lies the entrance to the Journey Behind the Falls. You are given slickers for the walk in back of the cascade where the thunder of its roar vibrates right into your toes. Open all year.

215

–The Niagara Falls Museum. On the Parkway, a venerable institution, chock full of rare Egyptian mummies, birds, a display of animal freaks, and the Daredevil Hall of Fame. Muse over the life and times of those desperate ones who bounced in padded barrels to death or fifteen minutes of fame. Seven hundred thousand items, plus view tower. 416-356-2151.

–Skylon and Minolta Towers were built when they seemed to be saying "Anything you can build, we can build higher." Judging which gives the best view is splitting a fine hair, but both have entertainment, dining, and shopping. A third tower is over in Maple Leaf Villages, not many blocks away.

–Niagara Parks Greenhouse and Conservatory, just a short distance south of the falls, is open all year and has a glory of its own. Massed bedding plants, Christmas and seasonal flower shows, and plants from around the globe. Free.

–The Niagara Spanish Areo Car, proven to be one of the safest rides in the world. This bright contraption takes passengers via cables across the gorge and over a swirling whirlpool. Photographers are big fans.

–Niagara Glen, a former channel of the river is entered down a steep flight of steps and paths to the riverbank. Sheltered by high walls, the glen supports plant life uncommon in Ontario and is full of fossil traces of the past. Winding trails, guided tours, or on your own. Lovely, quiet, very special, and free.

Also, on the Niagara River Parkway are the Botanical Gardens, Floral Clock, and Brock Monument at Queen's Park. The top of this simple memorial column offers no dining, only a panoramic view of the river and Lake Ontario.

Meanwhile, back at the falls, visit Marineland with obliging dolphins, whales, and seals, plus rides, game farm, and shops. Of course, there's Tussaud's Wax Museum, Movieland Wax Museum, Lundy's Land Historical Museum, and the Tivoli Miniature

Gardens (Taj Mahal, Vatican, and Eiffel Tower scaled down to eye-level). The visitors centers have volumes of suggestions.

One of them will be to ride the People Movers instead of trying to drive and park everywhere. A loop goes along the Niagara Parkway to Brock's Monument (stop number 12) and is free between stops 1 and 6 all summer.

Stay around for the evening multicolor illumination of the falls. Every night of the year, the Canadian and American falls are lit by twenty-four Xenon gas spotlights, seventy-six centimeters (thirty inches) in diameter each and each producing two hundred and fifty million candlepower watts of light. Add fireworks at 10:00 P.M. on Fridays during summer months. Plus, on Saturday afternoons, there are band concert programs at historic Fort Erie and Queenston Heights Park, then free concerts in Queen Victoria Park during the annual Winter Festival of Lights. Every weekend in the late afternoon and from 7:00 to 8:00 P.M. in the evening, the bells of the Rainbow Carillon can be heard clearly above the sound of tumbling water.

P.S. Go ahead, spend money in the park shops— profits are used to maintain grounds and facilities.

For more information:
**Niagara Falls Table Rock Visitors Information
Centre, 905-356-7944.**
**Regional Niagara Tourist Information,
905-357-7393.**

72.
A Wonder In Winter

When summer and the crowds are long gone, true believers put on their thermal gear and venture to the edge of a fantastic world. Niagara Falls is such a different place in winter that the months of cold become the passage to a separate destination. Mists encase every twig and branch in ice; huge stalactites of crystal dangle from the rocks; floes from the ice-topped river crash over the brink to build up a bridge of solid water that people used to walk across until a couple of lives were lost.

Although the air turns to ice against your cheeks, against the trees, and all over the railings, the river flows on beneath its thickening lid. It's a diamond-studded vision in the morning light; another kind of dazzle is when the colored spotlights go on at night.

In winter, the pace slows down, and the heat goes up. The seasonal outdoor shows stop, but there is jazz to listen to and movies to see. The Botanical Gardens are awash in the colors of a splendid poinsettia show and decorated trees. To underscore the message that Niagara Falls is a year-round destination, the two cities put together a two-months-long Winter Festival of Lights.

From mid-November to mid-January, thousands and thousands of tiny sparkling electric lights are everywhere. There are fireworks extravaganzas, theatrical presentations, candlelight strolls, and pull-the-plug celebrations. On New Year's Eve, the chill melts at a concert in the park, a nonalcoholic free jubilee in Queen Victoria Park, from 8:00 P.M. until midnight.

You might want to pack along your old Christmas tree for a January visit. On the third Sunday of the month (approximately) the Niagara Parks Botanical Gardens turns donated trees into useful mulch, starting at 10:00 A.M. and continuing for the next six hours. One of the better new traditions. There'll be a sign on the parkway just north of the whirlpool.

Although a few shops are closed, the emporiums of British tea cups and Wedgwood dinnerware, Eskimo carvings, native art, maple syrup, Toronto Blue Jay sweatshirts, and plaid tartans keep their lights on. Hotels have winter specials for families and honeymooners, their dining rooms are going full tilt, and their jacuzzis stay cozy. As long as snowplows keep roads clear (or you could come by train), there are warm satisfactions in coming to the falls in winter.

There are many nearby places to remember.

Early in December, Christmas in Jordan has food, carolers, winery tours, and shopkeepers in costume. Main Street, Jordan. QEW, exit 51. 905-687- 9633.

Also early in the month at Niagara-on-the-Lake, a Candlelight Stroll and Christmas Emporium are at the courthouse, plus a Victorian Christmas Wonderland with Father Christmas and special activities for kids. 905-468-4263. The Niagara regions of western New York State have a half dozen major ski areas within ninety minutes of Buffalo, with downhill slopes and cross-country trails. On the Canadian side, excellent skiing is a half-day's drive to Blue Mountain (Collingwood vicinity), near Georgian Bay. There's hockey, curling, or doing the skater's waltz on frozen ponds; bundle up and enjoy them all.

For more information:
Niagara Falls Visitors and Convention Bureau,
905-468-4263.

73.

The Honeymoon Is Far From Over

A s this author went to Niagara Falls on her honeymoon, don't expect me to say its a hokey, has-been idea. Hokey is in the eye of the beholder. However, in those days, there were no heart-shaped tubs or mirrors on the ceiling and no pink satin sheets—only waiters who smiled knowingly.

Today's loving couple can romp through a whole bower of goodies in the honeymoon suite, although you may need to buy your own bubble bath ahead of time. Only the very lucky (or rich) will be able to view the falls from their rooms. But who's looking out the window? Back to the glowing red tub, the circular waterbed, the mirrors.

Different hotels and motels have different ways of treating their honorees (for a tiny extra fee), but you can have champagne and flowers, chocolates and fruit. At no cost in most places is the certificate stating your presence, in flowery French and English. For those who didn't quite get to their own nuptials, things can be arranged in a hotel wedding chapel (such as the one at the Ramada Inn). Store-front chapels seem to have come of age.

Just how the great waterspill became synonymous with honeymoon is not certain, but one legend involves Napoleon Bonaparte's brother Jerome who took his Baltimore bride to Niagara Falls and thus set up the idea for lesser socialites. In the early days, it could be a tough journey, so couples spent weeks, even months. Now the average honeymoon stay is two nights or less.

A party of two could hardly have it better. There's a super-size wonder of nature to gaze at, quick transportation, places to dance the night away, and plenty of garden lanes to stroll arm-and-arm or have a quiet picnic. And don't forget the horse-and-carriage rides around the park, sleigh and hay rides, and moonlight cruises. A top souvenir favorite is a photo showing lovers in a barrel about to go over the falls.

Even if you show up in August, when parents and children on their last days before school seem squeezed into every elevator, there are places to be off by yourselves. From Fort Erie to the edge of the upper falls, the riverside is parklike and quiet, as though no one could stand to be away from the tumbling water. Spread out your blanket, break into the wine and cheese. Just north of the whirlpool is the entrance to Niagara Gorge, where a delightful hike down to the water's rim will find you alone—more than likely—in a mini-Garden of Eden.

Even the short incline lift in back of the falls at Table Rock House ends its short-hill climb in a tree-shrouded park where benches in a semicircle indicate periodic activity, but there hasn't been a soul in sight on my last three visits.

Couples with special interests should take advantage of the festivals. The big Shaw Festival (called one of the "leading festivals in the English-speaking world"), Niagara-on-the-Lake, April through October; the Friendship Festival in which Canada and the States share their patriotic holidays, Buffalo and Fort Erie; the August Royal Canadian Henley Regatta in St. Catharines; the Niagara Wine and Grape Festival in September (for ten days) in St. Catharines; and numerous art fairs, antique shows, and other festive events.

With African safaris beckoning, cruises easy to manage, and bargain plane fares to exotic places, Niagara Falls has lost its appeal to the nabobs. Perhaps it's too much of a cliché. But pay no attention to raised eyebrows—plan a honeymoon (or anniversary) in Niagara Falls because its FUN.

For more information:
Niagara Falls Tourism, 905-468-4263.

Lake Ontario

74.

Niagra-On-the-Lake

The north end of the Niagara Parkway, still beautifully adorned with lawns and flowers, still edging scenic splendors supreme, now turns into Ricardo Street and enters a jewel box called Niagara-on-the-Lake.

It's a real live Victorian village with more houses in town built before 1850 than anywhere else in Ontario, still privately owned and inhabited with persons partial to the queen. The tiny municipal center of growing fame is easily covered on foot, the better to smell geraniums, roses, and fudge kitchens—or the seductive aromas of the Niagara Home Bakery on Queen Street. Take pictures of picket fences, the Prince of Wales Hotel, the gazebo in Queen's Park, the waterfront, or Courthouse Theatre and its clock tower. This scene was not brought to you by Kodak, but it's ready and waiting.

Over two hundred years ago, a few families unsympathetic with the American Revolution came here and established the town of Newark, which became capital of Upper Canada. However, Newark was just too close to the scheming Americans for a capital town to feel safe, so that position went to York (Toronto). When hostilities broke out in 1812, both cities suffered. In an unexplainable move, Americans burned Newark but left the next-door Fort George alone. Burning a village and ignoring a fort was cowardly enough to raise British ire to victorious levels.

Tempers cooled eventually, of course, and Niagara-on-the-Lake gets standing ovations from the whole continent. The enormously successful Shaw Festival started with George Bernard Shaw but

embraces his contemporaries and stars the only professional troupe devoted exclusively to that era. Oscar
Wilde, John Van Druten, Robert Sherwood, and others are featured at the festival, plus there are seminars,
discussions, and reviews. You can spend most of the
day in the Courthouse, Royal George, or Festival The-
atres as the play-going winds its way from April till
the end of October. 800-267-4759 or 905-468-2172.
Meanwhile, there are Festival juried art shows, wine
parties, and all sorts of gala events with theater folks.

Step into the Niagara Apothecary Museum and
imagine you have a tooth ache. How about the pink
stuff in the bell jars? The drugstore has its original
walnut and butternut fixtures and crystal gasoliers,
but no aspirin, and can be found on King Street, half
a block from the Niagara Fire Museum with its collection of antique equipment. In the same neighborhood, McCellands has been in the hand-crafted
furnishing business since 1835, and five generations
of cooks have produced the preserves and other products in Greaves Jams (store).

Opened in 1907 (making it the oldest history
museum in Ontario), the Niagara Historical Society
Museum is full of details on local history—the
biggest and most obvious chunk of which, however,
is Fort George.

Constructed between 1796 and 1799 to replace
Fort Niagara as British headquarters on the Niagara
frontier, Fort George was destroyed and captured by
Americans, then re-occupied by the British. After a
long abandonment, it was restored to the pre-1813
period and made into a National Historic Park. Amid
gates, guardhouses, bastions, officers quarters, and
powder magazine, you expect some military action,
and you get it—soldiers in full uniform fire their muskets and cannons and march briskly to a series of
drum rolls. With the wide, blue lake before you, on a

sunny day it seems like a play, not an echo from a
real and tragic time.

The list of bed-and-breakfast houses challenges
the telephone book. Look in the back pages of the
Shaw Festival brochure. Dining suggestions are there,
too, for times when the Queen's Landing, Moffat Inn,
and Prince have two-hour waits.

It will annoy Californians, perhaps, but the wines
of the Niagara regions are winning prizes in France.
Watch for Wine Route signs for a self-guided tour of
area vineyards and wine-tastings. For exact locations
and wine-fest list, contact the Wine Council of
Ontario. 905-684-8070.

For more information:
Niagara-on-the-Lake Visitors Bureau, 905-468-4263.
Regional Niagara Tourist Council, 800-263-2988.

75.
In the Niagra-Toronto Circuit:
Festival Country

When Loyalists fleeing the American Revolution
needed a place to settle, they headed for upper
Canada and found, on the western shores of Lake
Ontario, a land flowing with the milk, honey, and
hard work. Eventually, they and their descendants
turned this scenic end of the lake into a region of
steel mills, fruit orchards, wine, and wing-dings.
Hamilton, Burlington, and the cities of festival
country (Brantford, Guelph, Kitchner, Waterloo) are
an in-depth meanderer's heaven, close to Niagara
Falls and Toronto.

St. Catharines (briefly described in the Welland
Canal chapter) plays the role of main host to the Niagara Grape and Wine Festival. It was noticed early on
that the Niagara Peninsula was an ideal spot for grow-

ing grapes, but not until 1873 was the first winery established. Now, there are some fifteen wineries in the vicinity. Festival time means ten days of wine gardens, vineyard tours, ethnic concerts, athletic events, dances, and a big parade with floats celebrating an ancient beverage in a new age. Late September. Inniskillin Winery, Newark Wines, Chateau Des Charmes, Jordan and Ste. Michelle, Andres, Barnes, Brights, and Colio Wines are among the big names. The visitors center in St. Catharine's has maps, lists, and fingers to point the way.

A big-steel name in Canada, Hamilton dominates the Golden Horseshoe corner of Lake Ontario and is a study in varying lifestyles. It's blue collar and high tech, traditional carry-ons (how will you have your tea?) and jazz-age change. The city accustomed to big mill stacks not far from fruit farms has updated its downtown and polished its special-attractions list. Headliners: The Royal Botanical Gardens (edging both Hamilton and Burlington) are unplain gorgeous. There are over a thousand hectares (twenty-seven hundred acres) of color, with a wildlife sanctuary, marsh, wooded glens, the world's largest spread of lilacs, and more. Sniff through two acres of roses, a Mediterranean garden, and a greenhouse. Plains Road at Highways 2 and 6; open all year. 416-527-1158.

Dundurn Castle, the nineteenth-century thirty-five-room mansion, hosts visits and special events. There's the impressive Art Gallery of Hamilton, as well as the Canadian Warplane Heritage Museum (all in flying condition), the Children's Museum, the Museum of Steam and Technology, and Military Museum, plus the Canadian Football Hall of Fame, Whitehern (Georgian mansion), and African Lion Safari. Hamilton Place attracts famous stars and is home of the Hamilton Philharmonic Orchestra and

Opera Hamilton. Most attractions turn December into a month-long festival that should warm anyone's toes.

Alexander Graham Bell, inventor of our ear's semi-attachment, placed the world's first long-distance call from his home here in Brantford to Paris, Ontario, eight miles (twelve kilometers) away. Of considerable interest is Her Majesty's Royal Chapel of the Mohawks, oldest Protestant church in Ontario. And there's the Woodland Cultural Centre, where the lives and cultures of the aboriginal people of Eastern Canada are explored.

Kitchner and Waterloo are twin cities with two universities and a common German heritage. You could guess they'd put a large head on any Octoberfest. Twenty festival tents and halls serve beer, saugage, und kraut, then sing around tables with locked-arm Bavarian gusto. Plus, the festival-like farmer's market with old-world charms goes on all summer. Nearby is Doon Heritage Crossroads, a twenty-three-building historic complex of town basics, from school to railway station. Special festivals, concerts, and bright doings fill the warm months. It's only a short run to Stratford, home of the great Shakespearean Festival (see chapter 56).

In Guelph, a city of hills, maple trees, and vintage architecture, spring is greeted with the Guelph Spring (music) Festival. For three weeks in May, halls and churches ring with the sounds of the classics, jazz, and film music and song and dance recitals. Famous names, highly professional programs, a popular event. Check out the Macdonald Stewart Art Centre, Civic Museum, and University of Guelph while you're here, then indulge at Schneider's Reliable Sweets— homemade toffee and Turkish delights (just don't tell Jenny Craig).

For more information:
Ontario Tourism, 800-ONTARIO.

76.

Toronto: Ontario Verve Center

> "Verve...Energy, enthusiasm in
> the expression of ideas, vigor..."
> —*American Heritage Dictionary.*

Toronto did things right. The city has a smooth transportation system, cosmopolitan ambience, and an energy you can feel. This success story on the north shore started as a fur-trading site, grew to a colonial settlement, and became capital of the old Upper Canada. There were set-backs (two wipe-out fires, a cholera epidemic, and the American invasion), but the city continued to grow. Today, it is a financial and merchandising hub, a big, sophisticated provincial capital.

There is more live theater here than in any North American city outside of New York and more movie screens per capita than any place you could name. Numerous performing arts groups (the National Ballet, Toronto Symphony, and Canadian Opera) get top reviews and popular support.

The city's close-packed ethnic diversity has reached legendary status. Waves of refugees and immigrants turned neighborhoods into world minitour opportunities where you can buy a sari, kimono, Greek urn, or Italian pasta. Toronto is farther south than Venice and has the largest population of Italian descent of any city in the U.S. or Canada. The Chinese streets (generations old) have their own mall and restaurants where the food is cooked for Chinese tastes. The second largest Chinese enclave in America centers on Dundas, west of University Avenue. The Portuguese village is on Markham near Queen Street West; Greektown is off Danforth Avenue and Broadview.

East Indians, Greeks, Ukrainians, Hungarians, Germans (these are groups with forty thousand to a hundred thousand family members) and a dozen others put their flags together in a ten-day June extravaganza called Caravan with pavilions of culture, dance, food booths, music, parades, and enormous picnics.

Exploring Toronto means going in every direction including up.

Up is the CN (Canadian National Railroad) Tower, tallest free-standing structure in the world. Zip eleven hundred feet (three thousand meters) upward to a lounge, restaurant, or viewing deck. On a clear day, you can see the mist rising from Niagara Falls, but even in a fog, there's a show called Ecodek that offers an environmental tour of the globe via computer-enhanced telescopes. 419-360-8500. In the tower's base, Spaceport Toronto takes riders through an intergalactic space race.

On or close to the waterfront, Exhibition Place, Sky Dome, Ontario Place, Harbourfront, and the Toronto Islands make a band of concentrated south-side attractions. The annual Canadian National Exhibition works like an out-sized state fair, except that the jams, quilts, and livestock entries come from across the whole country. That's a big late-summer event. In the same block, baseball's Toronto Blue Jays' SkyDome is the only major stadium with a fully retractable roof, one that nests its sections together to let the sky in. Fun to watch. The SkyDome also houses the Argonauts (football) and big concert events and has a hotel within the complex. Just south of Front Street near the CN Tower. 416-341-2770.

Ontario Place mixes indoor-outdoor happenings on artificial islands, rounding up an IMAX theater, exhibits, playgrounds, Childrens' Village, a Naval Museum and more. The sixteen-thousand-seat Molson Amphitheatre showcases bluegrass bands, ballerinas, and big names. 955 Lake Shore West. 416-314-9900 (recorded) or 416-314-9811.

Barely east, Harbourfront Centre fills spaces between the foot of York Street west to Bathurst, a nonprofit cultural group that produces international arts festivals, educational events, and literary galas. It includes York, John, and Maple Leaf Quays. That's ten acres of activities or shops to explore. 416-973-3000. It ties right in with Queen's Quay Terminal, an updated warehouse of stores and multilevel interior courtyards with glass walkways. In Queen's Quay, the Toronto Visitors Centre has all the guides you could ask for, including those to all the free Toronto sights, for wheelchair tourists, bicyclists, and other special interests.

At the foot of Bay Street, catch the ferry for a ten-minute joy ride to the Toronto Islands: Centre, Ward, and Olympic. It's a sweeping big park of lawns and gardens, canals, bike paths, and a bathing beach on the Lake Ontario side. On the city side, the view of the Toronto skyline in the golden rays of a sunset is what foreign visitors write home about. Ferries run every twenty minutes in midsummer.

Yonge Street divides Toronto's east and west sides. Take the Yonge Street subway to Canada's retail giants, the Bay Company (formerly the Hudson's Bay Company), Eaton's, and the three-hundred-shop Eaton's Centre Galleria. Under the Galleria's lofty glass arch, you'll find the Ontario Visitors Information Centre, with Toronto maps of the long underground concourse going to hotels and subway stops. Forget weather.

West of Eaton's is the Nathan Phillips Square in front of Toronto's trend-breaking city hall (halls), a pair of curved buildings that seem a bit like clapping hands. The old Romanesque city hall is in full view across the street. A large rectangular pool takes up much of the square, reflecting buildings and spouting arches of fountains. In winter, it whirls with skating office workers; in summer, the pool is central to bag lunchers, art-in-the-park shows, and political speakers, scheduled or not. A mounted policeman in full Mountie uniform often stands by, camera-ready.

The largest collection of Henry Moore sculptures anywhere, an ancient Chinese tomb, Rembrandt, Picasso, a bat cave—between the Art Gallery of Ontario (AGO) and the Royal Ontario Museum (ROM), you might come away with a "What's left?" feeling. The former is the largest art gallery in Toronto (by far). The latter is the largest public museum in Canada and a rare combination of art, archeology, and science. ROM's auspices include the neighboring McLaughlin Planetarium and Gardiner Museum of Ceramic Art. Even on a tight schedule, these demand visitation rights. AGO: 416-979-6648. ROM: 416-586-5549. So does the Ontario Science Centre deserve a visit. The whys and whats of computers, sound waves, light refraction, and why we can't believe our eyes are captivating displays in a pace-setter among museums of this genre. 416-429-4100.

Toronto's wealthy Sir Henry Pellatt only wanted to live like a king. His gray stone palace, Casa Loma, had all the required turrets, baronial halls, secret passages, mahogany horse stalls, and other regal touches but, when Sir Henry invited real royalty to come on over, they declined. Sir Henry died broke. You can tour one man's truly magnificent dream house at One Austin Terrace. 416-923-1171.

If you're history-minded, try Mackenzie House, home of an 1837 rebellion leader who had a printing business in the back of his dwelling, at 82 Bond Street, two blocks east of Yonge at Dundas. 416-595-1567. Fort York, Toronto's first military post, may have been built in 1793, but it is 1812 when you enter the present stockade gates. The war with the Americans is going full tilt, and the Battle of York is being run on film. Soldiers in the yard engage in periodic artillery drills and musket-firings. It's on Garrison Road near Bathurst and Front Streets. 416-392-6907. On the north city limits, Black Creek Pioneer Village, once a farm with five of the original buildings still on the site, has thirty-five other restored structures, from a schoolhouse to an 1840s mill. Trades, crafts, and costumed guides are at Steeles Avenue and Jane Street. 416-736-1733.

Another Toronto institution is the St. Lawrence Market on Front Street near Jarvis, built in 1844 as Toronto's first municipal hall and now given over to the sale of steaks, salmon, strudels, and zucchini. Closed Sunday and Monday.

Chic Yorkville, just north of West Bloor, is for upscale shoppers, who may be able to find the same items among the bargain shops of Spadina near Queen Street. Bright nightlife, the center of "happening" music, also runs along Queen Street West.

In this heart of a concert-goer's/theater-buff's Valhalla, hear the symphony at the handsome Roy Thompson Hall. Gordon Lightfoot and the great Caruso have both appeared at Massey Hall, an acoustical triumph. O'Keefe Centre features opera and ballet; the Royal Alexandra Theatre puts on London and New York productions.

Naming specific restaurants in cuisine-moxie Toronto is tough, but Ed's Warehouse at 270 King Street West will not be soon forgotten for its lushly flamboyant decor, low prices, and dress code. 416-593-6676. Spinnakers at Harbourfront is for fish, 416-362-3406; for Italian, Trattoria Giancarlo, 416-533-9619; for Chinese, Lee Garden, 416-593-9524; for Greek, Pappas Grill, 416-461-5470. Or look for the splendid deli across the street from the O'Keefe Theatre. Toronto restaurants are a separate book.

In 1995, professional basketball came to Toronto with the Raptors, first NBA franchise outside of the U.S.A. The Blue Jays, Maple Leafs, and Argonauts keep the sports calendar going year round.

Head north from the city to reach Canada's Wonderland theme park stuffed with attractions, ice shows, cliff divers, big-star concerts, and all. It's minutes beyond the north city limits, off Highway 400. 905-832-7000. West on McKenzie Drive from Wonderland to Islington Road, the McMichael Collection of Canadian Art fills a handsome, log-cabin museum. One thousand works of the influential Group of Seven painters and their contemporaries are here, plus art of the west coast, Inuit, and woodland people. 905-893-1121.

Go eastward to the Toronto Zoo (exit Highway 401 at Meadowvale Road) or go to The Beaches by taking the Queen Street trolley to the end of the line. It's a small-townish area with delightful dining and a two-mile boardwalk. If you drive, continue east to see the oddly memorable white cliffs at Bluffers Park.

You may try to leave Toronto, but Toronto won't leave you. And there are still the Parliament buildings, the Canadian National Exhibition, the comedy clubs, dinner theaters, world's largest bookstore, and Thornhill Clock Museum. Returns guaranteed.

For more information:
Toronto Convention and Visitors Bureau, 416-203-2500 or 800-363-1990.

77.

Heritage Highways—East

To those who may be tempted to zip past towns printed on maps with little letters because they think there's probably nothing's there: If this book had a motto, it would have to be, "Something is ALWAYS there."

Oshawa, east of Toronto, doesn't qualify as "little," but there is a Canadian Automotive Museum of great interest to old-car buffs. An 1898 Fisher Electric, an Oshawa product, shows just how far back their display goes. 99 Simcoe Street South. More vehicles are at the Oshawa Aeronautical, Military, and Industrial Museum. The story of the man called "Intrepid," who founded a school for spies, can be delved into here. At the Oshawa Airport, north of Highway 401, exit 416. Three houses, 1835 to 1849, make up the Oshawa Sydenham Museum; the Hutchinson House (he was a nineteenth-century doctor) is another one of high interest. Think rich at the Packwood Estate, the mansion of R.S. McLaughlin, past president of General Motors of Canada. 270 Simcoe Street North.

Out of the fast lane, into Port Hope, Cobourg, Colborne, and Trenton, continuing the Heritage Trail, we come along on the north shore of Lake Erie.

Port Hope, not just another pretty face, was an Indian camp, French mission, and then a trading post. Originally named Smith's Creek, Toronto, it was finally named Port Hope by Loyalists fleeing from the States.

Pretty it is. Streets are lined with grand old trees, mature houses, and stone churches. Like the ancient gear in a firefighters museum, antiques are generally big here, although things go modern at the Thomas Gallery with exhibits of contemporary artists. A river

runs through it (the Ganaraska), and it's a supreme
April rainbow-trout stream.

Cobourg is another case of civic name-changing—
first Amherst, then Hamilton. When England's
Princess Charlotte married Leopold of Saxe-Coburg,
the name was changed again (with a tiny change in
spelling) to honor the pair. Rising with great dignity
over downtown on Albert Street, Victoria Hall was
built when Cobourg thought maybe it had a chance
of becoming provincial capital. Today, the Hall
houses a concert hall and the Art Gallery of
Northumberland, with a select spread of Canadian,
European, American, and Eskimo art. Explore the rest
of the building, especially the courtroom, patterned
after London's Old Bailey.

A cook-inspiring farmer's market is behind the
Hall, and there's a refreshing waterfront park with
lawn bowling, band shell, summer concerts, walkways,
and lots of marina space. The information center is
the house where Marie Dressler (Wallace Beery's
rolling-pin-wielding co-star) was born, an updated little Georgian house at 212 King Street. Inside, information is available on Waterfront Festival and
Highland Games, first weekend in July, bed and
breakfasts, and the route ahead.

Trenton is a water-oriented city on the south
entrance of the Trent-Severn Waterway and is the
western gateway to Quinte's Isle and the Loyalist
Parkway, a scenic route around the Isle and alternate
road to Kingston. Going west by boat? From Trenton,
it's 386 kilometers (240 miles) and 44 locks to Georgian Bay on Lake Huron.

But stay to visit the Royal Canadian Air Force
Memorial Museum, a big, popular show of planes
and related paraphernalia at the Canadian Forces
Base. It's open on weekdays all year; add Saturday
and Sunday during the summer. Or examine the low-

tech military items at Fort Kente, located southwest of town on Kente Portage—the oldest road in Ontario—at Carrying Place. There's also a reconstruction of an 1812 stockade.

Trenton likes to put on festivals: Canada Day blow-out on July 1 (downtown sidewalk sales), Scottish/Irish Fest, Summer Fest (pancake breakfasts, farmer's market, parades, and fireworks), and Winter Games fun in February. There are a lot of factory outlets to explore while waiting for the next parade.

For more information:
Trenton Information Bureau, 613-392-7635.
Cobourg Information Bureau, 905-372-5831.
Port Hope/Oshawa, call Getaway Country,
  800-461-1912.

78.
Belleville, Quinte's Isle

L oyalist territory is where the Union Jack frequently flies next to the Maple Leaf and where you can observe teatime in the proper English manner. Those who approach Quinte from Trenton (there's a bridge over the channel that makes this a real island) and go on to Kingston may miss Belleville; those who go east (or west) through Belleville will miss some Quinte-essential pleasures. So you may want to advance in circles—or stay in Belleville for a while, exploring the territory.

Now that's a good choice. Belleville, home to thirty-seven thousand likes to call itself the "Friendly City," and it's true that if you walk around asking questions, there is much sweetness and quite a lot of light. Halfway between Toronto and Montreal, on the Z-shaped Bay of Quinte and the mouth of the Moira River, Belleville is also between two prime recreation areas: the sandy beaches of Quinte's Isle and the highlands of Hastings (Belleville's county). This is to the north with clear lake retreats and the small-nation-size Algonquin Provincial (wilderness) Park beyond.

This is one of Ontario's finest yacht harbors with abundant repair facilities and restaurants next to marinas. If you are here by boat and planning to go through the Trent-Severn Waterway, pause to have your mast unstepped; last time I looked, there were no commercial facilities for this in Trenton.

Numerous gently aging stone and clapboard buildings, a gray but gracious city hall, plenty of trees and gardens make bustling Belleville appealing. The colorful farmer's market is behind City Hall on Pinnacle Street. Flea markets are open once a month at the Quinte Sports Centre or Ben Blececker Auditorium. There are factory outlets here, too.

Glanmore, a restored 1883 Italianate mansion on Bridge Street, serves as the Hastings County Museum where Victorian furnishings include a large collection of antique lighting equipment. Twenty kilometers (twelve miles) east on Highway 49, there's a place called Native Renaissance II spreading out an array of aboriginal arts and crafts, while in other rooms new works are being created. Close to town, a change of mind-set is found at Shannonville Motor-sport Park, where sounds of varooming cars, trucks, cycles, and even classic autos goes on all summer.

More big fun is in Belleville during the second weekend in July, when seventy floats, ethnic dancers, marching bands, and food stalls bring "friendly" to a new level. Details are at the Log Cabin Tourist Centre, Highway 62 at East Moira Street. 613-962-3911.

Quinte's Isle, an alias for Prince Edward County, was named to honor the father of Queen Victoria. It's an interesting squiggle of off-shore land with twisting roads and scores of inlets, beaches, and scenic vistas. The Loyalists who settled here first were a determined and righteous lot who built churches before schools or roads, were sticklers for law and order, worked fields, mills, and fisheries, and took time out for tea. No one road goes around; to explore, be ready to do a lot of back-tracking. One of the sights you might come across is Birdhouse City on Macaulay Mountain, where dozens of carefully crafted birdhouses reflect the county's historical buildings. Such a project seems logical in a county dotted with whittlers, weavers, and potters who work for their own shops or to fill commissions.

Small historical museums are plentiful. Pick up an area map and find your way to the Ameliasburgh Historical (village type) Museum, the Mariners Park Museum, or the lighthouse on Long Point. Wonderful beaches and dunes are at Sandbanks and North Beach Provincial Parks, and an interesting, scenic spot for a picnic is at Lake on the Mountain Park. (How did that lake get up there? They're not sure.) From here, you can see the little ferry scoot from Glenora on the island to Adolphoustown on the mainland. Picton, deep-water harbor and county seat with a Greek Revival courthouse, copes with increasing traffic on summer weekends, but settles down to total charm in spring and fall. Lots of area bed and breakfasts and resorts such as the Isiah Tubbs place, 800-267-0525, but book ahead. This is a properly popular area.

For more information:
Belleville or Quinte Tourism, 613-962-4597.

79.

Eastern Reaches:
Kingston and the St. Lawrence

The "king's town" didn't get the job it once wanted as Canada's capital, but that was a lucky break for the rest of us. It seems meant for the informal vacationer, the bed-and-breakfast aficionado, and

for tour-taking and serious strolling around. The din
of high politics? Not here.

Situated at the east end of the Great Lakes system, the western reach of the St. Lawrence River, plus
the southern end of the Rideau Canal, boat-conscious
Kingston was invasion-conscious in its early days.
Hence, the massive bulwarks of Fort Henry just across
the Cataraqui River (the Rideau connection), where
the round, self-contained forts called Martello towers
seem to be on guard.

Kingston has several federal prisons (you would
never notice), as well as Queen's University, Lawrence
College, and Canada's Royal Military College (the
equivalent of West Point or Sandhurst). The midtown
waterfront resembles a demure carnival. In a fairly
compact area, one can sit amid flower beds and
strolling families next to the depot/information office
and watch a dancing fountain, children at play
around a retired steam engine, and pleasure boats
coming and going. The depot was a station for the
long-gone Kingston-Pembroke Railway, known locally
as old Kick and Push.

Wearing walls of gray limestone and carved cor-
nices (it's interesting to note the number of buildings with domes), much of the city has an old-world
Victorian ambience. It's big on bookstores, antiques,
and shopping.

The museum list is certainly an eclectic assort-
ment. It includes the Royal Military College Museum,
Pump House Steam Museum, Miller Museum of
Geology and Mineralogy, Maclachlan Woodworking
Museum, International Hockey Hall of Fame and
Museum, Marine Museum, and the Canadian Forces
Communications and Electronic Museum. Add the
Agnes Etherington Art Centre with changing and per-
manent exhibits in seven galleries and Bellevue
House, a handsome Tuscan villa once home to Sir
John A. McDonald, Canada's first prime minister.

Tour trains can take you to all these places as well as to Fort Henry.

Architectural detail, Thousand Islands Park, Alexandria Bay

When you go through the somber sentry tunnel onto the fort parade ground, the year flips back to 1867. In this very complete compound, more than one hundred university and high-school students take over as the Fort Henry Guard, a hand-picked group given historically accurate training in infantry drills, artillery salutes with muzzle-loading cannons, and more. During July and August, a colorful Ceremonial Retreat is a Fort Henry highlight, 7:30 P.M., weather permitting. Visitors are advised to check ahead for this event, as occasionally the Guard goes on tour.

Kingston is an ideal anchor place for exploring in all directions, being less than three hours from Toronto, Ottawa, and Montreal and close to a bridge to New York State. There are frequent ferries to Wolfe Island in the mouth of the St. Lawrence River, to the town of Marysville, with fishing charter boats and inns of country charm, sleigh rides, buggy rides, and camp-grounds, and there's another ferry to New York from early May to late October. Home's Ferry, 613-385-2262. Or press eastward along the river to the Thou-sand Islands National Park. Only a few of the isles are part of the preserve and even if those few were pulled together into one mass, this would still be Canada's smallest national park—and one of the prettiest.

The rocky isles, left smooth and barren by retreat-ing glaciers, could support only lichen at first, but such is the determination of green and growing things that now the stones support miniforests of conifers and hardwoods. There is camping at Mallorytown Landing. Call 613-923-5241. Boldt Castle is a stop on nearly every thousand-isle tour cruise schedule. People have built dream hideaways on these rocky outcrop-pings, but George Boldt's dream was of King Ludwig proportions. Boldt came to America, poor but eager, wound up owning the Waldorf-Astoria Hotel (plus others), and decided his wife needed her own retreat. (Sadly, Mrs. Boldt died before it was completed.) For schedules, call St.Lawrence Cruise Lines, 800-267-7868.

Ask at the information center about other cruises on the river (daily or up to a week), about river towns like Gananoque and Brockville, and about places to watch ocean vessels go through the St. Lawrence Sea-way locks. Another must for those going on to Mon-treal is Upper Canada Village, a pre-1867 town that was saved from rising waters by transporting much of the community farther uphill. There are thirty-five buildings in a beautifully run operation near Mor-risville. Check Chapter 85.

For more information:

**Eastern Ontario Travel Bureau, 613-384-3682 or
    800-567-EAST (ext. 3278).**

**Kingston District Chamber of Commerce,
    613-548-4453.**

Parks of the St. Lawrence, 613-543-3704.

80.

Take a Ride On the Rideau

After the War of 1812 and long after civilians were getting on with their U.S. commerce and peace, military minds decided a canal between Kingston and Ottawa would be useful in case of American attack.

Thus began the Rideau Canal, an idyllic bonus for water-borne travelers.

Seldom has any project had such a sorry history. The great arched dams of the Rideau, with stones weighing nearly a ton apiece, may have taken as many as four thousand lives before the job was done. Today, the work would have been immediately halted to devise safer engineering methods, but the Duke of Wellington (this was mostly his idea) must have decided that workers–like good soldiers–had to keep going. An incredible achievement any way it's looked at, the canal climbs eighty-four meters (two hundred and seventy-five feet) from Ottawa to pass over some of the oldest, hardest rocks on the earth's surface, the Canadian Shield; then it descends forty-nine meters (a hundred and sixty feet) to Lake Ontario. There are forty-seven locks, twenty-four dams, twenty-nine kilometers (eighteen miles) of artificial channels.

The crisis with Americans never came, and the Rideau had no military use, although it helped business for a few years. Today's barges are rigged with cabins and all craft have pleasure goals.

There are small, unhurried treasure towns to visit, with imposing old houses along the banks, and little shops that make their own cheeses, candies, or hand-knit sweaters. It's a mesmerizing trip in fall color, a relaxing one from spring through summer. At both ends, in Kingston and Ottawa, there is much to see and do.

One merry pause would have to be at Perth, named after the city in Scotland. It started out as a military post, and a certain belligerence hung around—the last fatal duel in Canada was fought here. There is a model of the Mammoth Cheese made by eastern Ontario dairy farmers for exhibition at the Chicago 1893 World's Fair. The cheese weighed ten tons (over 9,979 kilograms) and was probably sliced with a sword. After the fair, it was marketed in small pieces to the households of England.

The Perth Museum rings back to olden times in an 1840s Georgian house. At Murphy's Point Provincial Park, there are various places to explore, including an abandoned mine, farmstead, saw-mill ruin, and hiking trails. 613-267-5060

Smith Falls marks the Rideau half-way point. It's a former rail-junction town and a pivotal spot for Rideau Canal travelers. On Highways 43 and 15, if you're driving.

The Hershey Chocolate Company turns out much of its succulent production in a multimillion-dollar Smith Falls plant. You are invited to tour. Non-fattening viewing is at the Rideau Canal Museum, a converted mill with hi-tech displays showing the history and workings of the canal. The Smith Falls Railway Museum puts its rolling stock and artifacts in a former Canadian National Railway station. One more, for lovers of Victoriana is the Heritage House Museum, home of a successful local mill owner. It contains rooms furnished in 1867 fashion.

The Canadian Parks Service and Canadian Government have been working to enhance historic sites along the route.

For more information:
Eastern Ontario Travel Association, 613-384-3682 or 800-567-EAST (ext. 3278).

81.

Ottawa: Capital Gains

It was an unusual way to locate a national capital but it worked. Tired of the squabbling in 1858 about where to put the seat of the Canadian government, Queen Victoria put her royal finger on the map and said, "We have made a decision." The loyal opposition, not amused, is said to have muttered, "At least any Americans who try to capture the capital will get lost in the woods."

Thus, an obscure place called Bytown on the Ottawa River across from Quebec became the city of Ottawa, and an excellent choice it turned out to be.

In a place where two languages swirl about your ears, where there are over fifty galleries and theaters, and where world-consciousness is part of the local business, you are like a true traveler off on a flight. Ottawa sparkles.

Situated on a bluff, the city that grew from a village could start almost from scratch, planning streets, boulevards, and buildings suited to its role. The city fathers erected grandly traditional, Gothic parliament buildings and government structures in chateau forms that today blend with modern glass canopies to make a rich mix. Open spaces downtown are the soul of graciousness, and you can hear debates of world importance in the morning, start a deep-country hike by noon, and have dinner in French-speaking Hull, Quebec, just across the river.

To see Canada's government buildings on Wellington Street, at the point called Parliament Hill, is a subliminal trip to London. The stone grace of the House of Commons, the Senate Chamber, and the Parliamentary Library (a very special beauty) are crowned by the Peace Tower, with a clock and carillon of fifty-three bells, a memorial to World War I dead.

A light burning on top means Parliament is in session. The buildings with their green copper roofs would impress anyone, but when the Guards are parading it's a heart thumper.

Ottawa in winter

A must is to watch the Changing of the Guard, an ancient military rite performed by the Governor General's Footguards and Grenadier Guards on Parliament's front lawn. In scarlet tunics and bearskin busbies (those impossible furry hats), they are so precise in drill that you suspect robots. For thirty minutes, they march and present arms while cameras go into overdrive. Band and drum corps, too—a splendid show. 10:00 A.M., July and August, weather permitting. Tours of the government buildings are conducted all year.

At Wellington and Kent Streets, the Supreme Court of Canada meets in public session. Tours operate from May through August, in other months by reservation only.

The Ottawa/Hull Capital Region (as this close-knit French-English area is called) is home to twenty-nine museums, twelve of them national institutions. History showcases include the Bytown Museum of Ottawa History and the new-era curves and domes of the Canadian Museum of Civilization in Hull on the river. Visitors watch the world's only IMAX-OMNI-MAX combined theater, go to a childrens' museum, dance at an eighteenth-century French Canadian wedding, or walk through an aboriginal village. For really early times, enter the dinosaur halls at the Canadian Museum of Nature. It includes hands-on critter stuff, plants and planets, the whole earth works.

Hitting modern life, visit the Canadian Ski Museum, Canadian War Museum (Canada's largest collection of guns, vehicles, uniforms, and mock-up battles), the National Aviation Museum (aviation eras and planes), the Museum of Science and Technology (make paper, watch chicks hatch, check out Apollo 7), and an Agricultural Museum on a big experimental farm in the middle of the city.

It would be hard to match the National Gallery of Canada, a modern crystal palace, for sheer good looks. On Sussex Drive, this stand-out piece of architecture boasts forty thousand paintings, sculptures, drawings, and photographs in skylit galleries. It houses old masters, impressionists, and the biggest collection of Canadian art anywhere. (If you think the roundish sections on the ends were inspired by the Parliament Library, you're right on.)

The National Arts Centre, on the banks of the

Rideau, is a study in interrelated hexagonal forms, sheltering three theaters, restaurants, the sounds of much music (be it jazz or the N.A.C. Symphony Orchestra), tiptoeing ballerinas, and fantasy puppets.

There are splendid houses around town to see, even though some restrictions on inside tours may be tight—Laurier House (home of two prime ministers), the Mackenzie King Estate, and Rideau Hall, official residence of Queen Elizabeth II's representative. The King estate is located within Gatineau Park, a broad expanse of lakes and wilderness, picnic places and scenic overlooks, and is minutes from Parliament Hill.

Ottawa has all the city fringe benefits like shopping centers, but the downtowner can go from big department store to boutique mall to a farmer's market in one moderate hike. Byward Market has been selling produce and crafts since 1830, and the nearby Rideaux Centre Mall is just a chorus of "Allouette" away from the Sparks Street Mall, where fountains and sidewalk cafes add to the sparkle.

Offers include golf, biking, canoeing, and ice skating, plus NHL hockey and CFL football, as well as the new young-'un need, water parks. The Canadian Tulip Festival is in the spring (four million bulbs are an annual gift from Holland, thanks from the Dutch for Ottawa's care of Dutch Royal Family during World War II). The Central Canada Exhibition is in late August, the Franco-Ontarian Festival is held the third week in June, and Winterlude is a ten-day carnival centered around the frozen Rideau.

For information on river cruises, tours, inns, and dining out, stop at the Visitors Centre, Sparks Street Mall (one block from Wellington and Parliament Hill), and pick up all the guides you'll ever need.

For more information:
Ottawa Tourism Authority, 613-237-5150 or
    800-363-4465.

82.

Rochester: a City In Focus

The roads to Rochester may use up half your film. The environs of the city breathe pleasantness from any direction, but NY 18 is a case in point. Close to but out of sight of the coast of Lake Ontario, the Seaway Trail (marked with green footprint-and-wave signs) runs rather straight-on through fruit orchards and truck farms, flat but easy going. Lake access is limited, although there are lovely openings at state parks and lighthouses on the banks. On this side of Lake Ontario, a sand beach is in shorter supply; the norm is a low, rocky escarpment instead. Fishing along the feeder creeks and out into the deep lake, however, gets rave reviews.

Stop at Golden Creek State Park to walk around Thirty Mile Point's old gray lighthouse, standing high above the water. A sandbar and dangerous shoals at this point caused a half dozen wrecks and loss of life, but the big question is, "What happened to the $15,000 one of the sunken ships (circa 1778) was supposed to have had it its safe?" Divers keep looking. The park gives tours in the summer, has fifty campsites and picnic tables all year. 716-795-3117.

Roughly parallel to the Heritage Road is the route of the Erie Canal, a popular way for pleasure boats to connect from Buffalo to Rochester, Syracuse, Albany, and the Hudson River. A booklet with all the details on locking through the New York canal system (including the Oswego, Champlain, and Cayuga-Seneca Canals) is available by calling 518-457-1187.

Now to Rochester, the city whose best-known citizen once muddled around with chemicals in his tolerant mother's kitchen sink, working on a film and a camera that made photography a snap for everyone.

His name was George Eastman, and to a lot of people, he made Rochester and Kodak synonymous.

Rochester, on the Genesee River, was a thriving mill town, made uniforms during the Civil War, and prospered when the Erie Canal went through. (Canal and river crossed paths, so canal engineers built a viaduct to carry canal traffic over the river.) Escaped slave Frederick Douglass spoke out against slavery with his newspaper *The North Star* in Rochester, and Susan B. Anthony and other reformers lived here. Hiram Sibley, founder of Western Union was a citizen, as were Mitch Miller and Cab Calloway. It's a city with great diversity in its industries, colleges and universities, museums and lively arts, and things to do.

Belted by an outer and inner loop of expressways, the heart of Rochester is easy to reach. Walk around, checking out the cloisterlike atrium of City Hall, looking up at the art-deco *Wings of Progress* (inspired by sea shells) on top of the Times Square Building, studying a statue of Mercury on the Lawyers Publishing Building, and taking in the Midtown Plaza Mall. Across from Manhattan Square Park, where skaters twirl in winter, the Strong Museum will appeal to everyone over the age of two. Five hundred thousand toys, items of furniture, books, and advertising artifacts are here—everyday life in America from the 1820s on. 716-263-2700.

At the Visitors Information Center, 126 Andrews Street, there are directions to avenues of old Victorian houses and notes about the museum trail, where signs with white lettering on brown backgrounds mark routes to various institutions.

Basic Rochester visits include the gracious fifty-room Eastman House, both a museum of film and photography and the historic home and gardens of George E. himself. 716-271-3361. The Memorial Art Gallery at the University of Rochester covers five thousand years of art, from antiquities to Rembrandt, Homer, Monet, and the avant garde. It includes a delightful children's discovery room. 500 University Avenue. 716-473-7720.

Savor the culinary arts at the Rochester Public Market—fresh produce, fish to fry, and chickens to broil, in year-round sales stalls. Off Union Street, two blocks north of East Main Street.

Susan B. Anthony met with Frederick Douglass, Elizabeth Cady Stanton, and other reformers in what's now the Susan B. Anthony House, a museum and where she wrote *The History of Women's Suffrage.* 17 Madison, 716-235-6124. Woodside Mansion, a Greek Revival home with a beautiful spiral staircase, is living a new life as headquarters of the Rochester Historical Society. Filled with paintings, costumes, furnishings, and toys, it's at 485 East Avenue. 716-271-2705. The Victorian Doll Museum, the Landmark Center, and Stone-Tolan House continue the roster of collections. Get more information from the visitors center.

The reputation of the Rochester Philharmonic Orchestra has been enviable for more than seventy years. Hear them again at the Eastman Theater, 716-454-2620. Both the resident theater company at the GeVa Theater, 716-232-GEVA, and the Garth Fagan Dance Company, 716-454-3260, have won recognition for excellence. If it's summer when you come, look for the symphony at the Finger Lakes Performing Arts Center in Canandaigua.

Try a real change from fast-food picnics to gourmet dinners at the post-colonial Clark House, 716-385-3700; the world-class Edwards Restaurant, 13 South Fitzhugh, downtown, 716-423-0140; or the Rio, 282 Alexander, downtown, 716-473-2906. This is another list to get from the visitors center. Cruise on the river, wander through the lively Seneca Park Zoo,

or go back to the big lake via Lighthouse Road off
Lake Road to the historic 1822 light near Ontario
Beach Park. This was once the Coney Island of western New York. The beach has been undergoing reno-
vations, with an updated bathhouse, a new
Performing Arts Center (free summer concerts), a
1905 carousel, and a breezy boardwalk. Catch the
scene on camera.

Three popular annual events: the Lilac Festival in
mid-May shows off more than five hundred varieties
of lilacs, art work, parades, and entertainment; the
Rochester Harbor and Carousel Festival, at Ontario
Beach Lighthouse Park, in mid-June, has more of the
same; then there's the Monroe County Fair. Events
Line: 716-546-6810.

For more information:
Greater Rochester Visitors Association,
   716-546-3070.

83.
Those Beckoning Finger Lakes

Gorges, waterfalls, the low remains of ancient
hills, the greenery of lush farms, and those long,
elegant fingers of water extending like a blue fringe
below Lake Ontario into the heart of New York
State—those are made-to-order getaways for lovers of
manageable adventure (not all of us climb high peaks
or deep dive off coral reefs) and civilized pleasures.

The same glacial forces that carved out the Great
Lakes clawed through the primal earth to form these
lakes. There are several small and six major fingers—
Owasco, Skaneatleles, Cayuga, Seneca, Keuka, and
Canandaigua. The deepest is Seneca at 632 feet
(which is about half the depth of Lake Superior); the
longest is the forty-mile Lake Cayuga.

Until the American Revolution, three Iroquois Nations lived among these waters. After the war, however, and with a generosity that totally ignored Indian rights, grants of land were given to veterans, and white settlements began to appear. Although Syracuse and Rochester are major centers, and there are attractive cities like Ithaca, home of Cornell University, it is the tiny hamlets and crossroads villages that charm the bejabbers out of area visitors.

Touching on the north side of the lakes (for those who come via I 80 or US 20), Geneva, at the top of Lake Seneca, happened to attract a lot of retired ministers and was thus nicknamed the "saint's retreat." It is also in an area called paradise by many fishermen. The town of about fifteen thousand is dotted with handsome old houses, such as the Greek Revival Rose Hill Mansion which may be toured. 315-789-3848. Others can be slept in, as several now serve as bed-and-breakfast stopovers.

The women's rights movement lays historic claim to Seneca Falls where Elizabeth Cady Stanton and Lucretia Mott led the first rights convention in July, 1848. Visit the Women's Hall of Fame, 76 Fall Street, honoring American women of achievement. A grand auto tour, spring or fall, is the one through the Montezuma National Wildlife Refuge, amply supplied with nature trails and observation towers.

Harriet Tubman, the ex-slave who bravely rescued over three hundred others on the Underground Railroad and was called the "Moses of her people," lived at 180 South Street in nearby Auburn on Lake Owasco. Tours by appointment, 315-252-2820. Up the same street stands W. H. Seward's home, the shrewd secretary-of-state who defied opposition to help us buy Alaska. 33 South Street. 315-252-1283.

Auburn is one of the largest cities in the Finger Lakes area and home of the Schweinfurth Art Center,

205 Genesee Street. In the Center's Greek Revival mansion, browse through classical and modern art, folk crafts, and a shop. 315-255-1553. More shops are at the Finger Lakes Mall. Auburn Tourist Information Center, 315-255-1188.

On the south end of the lakes (for those traveling on I 88 or NY 13), Watkins Glen's big gorge can be seen in the middle of town. Waterfalls and rapids, stairways and bridges mark the scenic notches and cataracts of Watkins Glen State Park, an extremely popular place with swimming, camping, and a shuttle bus back to town. 607-535-4511. On the grounds, see "Timespell," a laser-light and panoramic-sound show recreating human history from forty-five million years ago to the present. For reservations, call 607-535-4960.

In Watkins Glen (a name dear to race-car fans) and its immediate area, you'll find at least a dozen bed-and-breakfast choices. The Tudor-style Clarke House on Durland Place, 607-535-7965, or the Rose Window, an elegant home built in 1928 on South Franklin Street, 607-535-4687, are both overnight guest houses in easy reach of restaurants and shops. The racetrack is four miles southwest on County 16. 607-535-2481.

One half mile south of Hammondsport (foot of Lake Keuka), the Curtiss Museum on Route 54 will excite old-plane buffs and antique fans in general. Just a short drive farther south is the Corning Glass Center where visitors watch skilled artists at work and wander through the world's most extensive glass collection. Also, there's the Hall of Science and Industry, the Steuben factory, glass-center shops, and bargain glass. 607-974-8271. The Rockwell Museum's Western Art assemblage (Remington, Russell, and Native American) is also in Corning. 111 Cedar Street. 607-937-5386.

There are scenic winery routes all through this premier wine- producing region, where the life paces back to twenty miles per hour—or per day. You can find out where the tasting rooms are by writing to the New York Grape & Wine Foundation, 350 Elm Street, Penn Yan, NY 14527. Here's a hint for the aficionados: More than half of the wineries are around Lake Seneca, and most of their stock is sold right on the spot, so you could be bringing home a very special gift to the house-sitter.

Local craft and farm markets are special fun. The Windmill Market on Route 14-A in Yates County is open only on Saturdays, but worth a wait. 607-536-3032.

Fishing is good to better, with the Trumansburg area getting the best bets for catching salmon, bass, and trout. Close by, Taughannock Falls State Park can show you the highest (four hundred feet) continuous falls east of the Rockies in a setting sure to use up film. 607-387-6739.

The visitors centers (every town has one) have brochures on excursion trains, summer theater, tucked-away resorts, horse racing, lake cruises, and a world of golf.

For more information:
Finger Lakes Association, 315-536-7488.
Finger Lakes Region Information, 800-KIT-4-FUN.

84.

Syracuse, Oswego

In 1799, not all that long after the American Revolution, neat and friendly Oswego was named the first official freshwater U.S. port by the young federal government. Now a seaway port and mecca for trophy-seeking fishermen, Oswego might have been a major city had not the Erie Canal passed it by.

Like all human history, the Oswego story is told in layers: battles, commerce, and the way inhabitants spent their money. Beginnings on the eastern Lake Ontario site were hostile in the 1700s. British, French, and U.S. troops captured, recaptured, and leveled several forts. One survives. Looking the way it did during the Civil War, Fort Ontario, at the foot of East 7th Street, is a state historic site and shows bits of past military life with demonstrations during the summer. 315-343-4711. Oswego's maritime story gets attention at the Lee White Marine Museum, at the foot of West First Street. Children's collection too. July and August. 315-342-0480.

Few lived like the folks of what's now the Richardson-Bates House Museum, but the lovely Italian villa on the National Register of Historic Places with ninety percent original furnishings has a lot to say about Oswego County history. 135 East Third Street. 315-343-1342.

There are hands-on exhibits at the Energy Center (New York Power Authority) Visitors Center, six miles northeast on Lake Road. There are three nuclear power plants; the displays explain the generating and transmitting process. 315-342-4117. For race-car fans, the Oswego Speedway holds special modified NASCAR meets with free camping for attendees, from mid-May to Labor Day. One block south of Route 104 East. 315-342-0646.

Oswego County, serene and scenic, has fishing hot spots of established legend and is well-stocked with campgrounds, hiking trails, and places to ski.

Informal capital of the Great Lakes/Finger Lakes district, Syracuse is a city of hospitable size. At Syracuse University, they've got the country's sixth-largest domed stadium, plus theater and shows to which the public is invited. The spacious Burnet Park Zoo, performing arts, maple syrup, the Erie Canal, and that great fall fun event, the New York State Fair, are here.

The Landmark Theatre, 1928 "Fantasy Palace" which opens its golden doors for films, concerts, and Broadway pros on tour, is a Loews structure, built in the vaudeville/movie-house days and a show in itself. 315-475-7979. Of another generation (any building by I.M. Pei is always a show in solo), the Syracuse Pei houses the Everson Museum of Art and Syracuse China Center for the Study of American Ceramics, from colonial times to the present—i.e., the nation's biggest cupboardful of dishes. 315-474-6064. Change your tempo at the highly regarded Syracuse Symphony or Opera Company Productions at the Mulray Civic Center. 800-724-3810. September through June, comedy and drama fill the bill at the Salt City (Syracuse nickname) Center for the Performing Arts. 315-474-1122. More: the Onondaga Historical Museum's spread of paintings and manufactured objects and the Rubenstein Museum of Science and Technology which delves into matters of life, atoms, computers, color, and the cosmos. 315-425-9068.

The Erie Canal (which changed the whole pace of life and property values in the counties it went through) looms large in the Syracuse story. At Erie Boulevard and Montgomery Street are the landmark homes of the Syracuse Urban Cultural Park Visitors Center and the Weighlock Building, a restored 1850s canal boat weigh station. Here, you'll find interpretive exhibits, Old Erie Canal State Park, and thirty-five miles of the original canal, still a link to Rome. Canoe launch, biking, and hiking. 315-471-0593.

On Salt City's Lake Onondaga Parkway, a reconstructed salt-factory-turned-museum shakes out facts on our vital condiment. 315-453-6715. Flavors from other realms are at the Cedarvale Maple Syrup Company on Pleasant Valley Road. Follow syrup from trees to sweet treats via holding tanks, evaporation, and on to bottling. Guided tours are by appointment. 315-469-6422.

From Syracuse, try an excursion or camping trip into New York's central Leatherstocking region. The National Baseball Hall of Fame in Cooperstown, 607-547-9983, the Howe Caverns (we've talked boat rides; how about floating down a deep underground river through spectacular caverns?) near Howes Cave, 518-296-8900, or the Americana Village in Hamilton, 315-824-2169.

Two centuries ago, the yellow-and-red maples through these regions were a wonder of color to Europeans unused to such abundance in the old world. They are still a wonder–autumn in this kind of countryside is its own reason for coming.

For more information:

Syracuse Chamber of Commerce, 315-470-1800 or 800-234-4SYR.

Oswego Department of Tourism, 315-349-8322 or 800-248-4386 (U.S.).

85.

From Watertown: a St. Lawrence Circle

The value of a nickel may be lower than a buffalo's ankles these days, but once upon a time (try 1878), it would buy a tea cup or fistful of candy. That was when a young man in Watertown, New York, opened a store with a radical idea: Everything would be priced at five cents or a dime. Frank Woolworth's five-and-ten-cents store made merchandising history, made young Frank rich, and Watertown famous.

Ten miles east of Lake Ontario and twenty miles south of the St. Lawrence, Watertown, situated on the Black River (which whitewaters its way through town for a drop of one hundred feet), has grown to a size of thirty thousand. It is the big shopping center of the Sackets Harbor area and is tuned-in enough to support a fine Sci-Tech Center with hands-on exhibits for children. 315-788-1340.

The Jefferson County Historical Society Museum on Washington Street is in an 1876 Victorian mansion with period rooms, military mementoes, and Indian crafts. More genealogy and local facts are in the neo-classic Flower Memorial Library.

From here, I 81 will deliver you to the Thousand Island doorstep (or across the bridge to Canada) before you finish a burg-n-fries. Described a bit in the chapter on Kingston, there are closer to eighteen hundred of the rocky, scenic isles (some platter-size; others are several miles long) and numerous roadside parks. It makes a great circle tour to go up one side of the river and back on the other side. Just remember to pick up a folder and know the rules as you cross.

Alexandria Bay's preoccupation is getting people to island attractions and back. Uncle Sam Boat Tours, with paddle wheeler, 315-482-2611, or Rockport Boat Lines, 613-659-3402, will take you to Boldt Castle, the humongous dream house that was never lived in by the dreamer. (See Chapter 79.)

In the shadow of the five-span Thousand Islands' International Bridge are three New York State parks: Wellesley Island, DeWolf Point, and Waterson Point (accessible only by boat). More state parks are up the road toward the Quebec boundary, on a delightful scenic river road to Ogdensburg, Messena, and Rooseveltown, across from Cornwall, Ontario's eastern-most city. Ogdensburg's surprise is the Frederick Remington Art Museum, finest single collection of original bronzes, paintings, and sketches by this famed Western artist. 315-393-2425.

Once blocked to deep-draft ocean vessels by the rapids at Montreal and a few difficult stretches between, the St. Lawrence River (Seaway) is now a major highway of the world with ships coming from far distant places to load up with wheat from the North American Midwest or to drop off cargo in Sarnia or Duluth. In Massena, visitors to the Eisenhower Lock view ships going through from a viewing deck or from their picnic tables and are shown videos and models detailing how everything works. May to mid-October. 315-769-2422. Three miles east of town at the Robert Moses State Park (another park has the same name on Long Island), there is a good place to view the Moses-Sanders Power Dam. Visitors' gallery, fishing, swimming, and other summer pleasures.

Cross at Rooseveltown to Cornwall and return on the other side. In Cornwall, Thomas Edison installed his first generating plant for lighting a factory by electricity; today, the city is headquarters for the St. Lawrence Seaway Authority. The Civic Complex next to the river holds hockey games, restaurants, and shopping in the Cornwall Square Mall or in the Pitt Street Promenade. Detour north to Maxville if it's July and you have time for North America's largest gathering of Scots. It's a stirring moment when the whole mass of pipe bands joins in one grand presentation that can probably be heard in Singapore.

Upper Canada Village (see Chapter 79), Morrisburg, is an exceptional presentation; learn about the tricky engineering that managed to save these Loyalist buildings from rising flood waters caused by construction of the St. Lawrence Seaway. In Brockville, you can still have afternoon tea in charming little cafes. The jail and courthouse are the oldest remaining structures of their type in Canada. Gananoque's (Gannon-ock-way) docks are for Thousand Islands tour boats.

For more information:

Thousand Islands-Seaway Region, 800-8-ISLAND or 315-482-2520.

Thousand Islands State Parks, 315-482-2593.
Seaway Trail, 315-646-1000 or 800-SEA-WAY-T.
Ontario Tourism, 800-ONTARIO.
New York State Information, 800-CALL-NYS.

Special Interests

86.
Forts and How To Look at Them

History stands guard. It's hard to picture these Great Lakes as battlefields, but two hundred years ago hostilities were real and forts essential.

The Spanish might be coming up to take the Straits of Mackinac. Native canoes could be hostile. Would the French be back? The Redcoats are coming! Dissatisfied Americans might be up to no good. Being somehow fortified has always been a condition of history and security a part of getting anything done.

Forts encircled the lakes. Some of them, such as Fort Williams on Lake Superior, were basically trading posts, places of business with barricades to keep out meandering bears, bands of thieves, or hostile enemies. Even if a fort's purpose was purely military, its walls gave nearby civilians a place to run to in case of danger.

Compact and orderly, the carefully restored forts of today's Great Lakes give extra lessons in the lifestyles, mind-sets, and ingenuity of life a hundred and fifty to two hundred years ago. From food preparation to musket drills, historical societies and volunteer re-enactment groups have turned these valued relics into unmatched time machines and visitor attractions.

The better to see what you are looking at, here's a very short glossary of fortifying terms:

Banquette: A step running inside the parapet (wall) for troops to stand on while firing.

Barbette: A platform on which guns are placed.

Bastion: A projecting part of the fortification, usually pentagon-shaped and made of earthworks.

Battery: A number of guns placed for combined action and their platforms.

Berm: A narrow level space between the lower part of the foot wall and the ditch.

Blockhouse: Either a detached small fort for controlling strategic points or an edifice of mostly timber, usually two-storied with openings for firing.

Breastwork: A mound of earth, breast-high, to fire over.

Casemate: A vaulted bomb-proof chamber (like a cellar) built into the rampart and provided with gun-ports for defense.

Covered-way: A secure road of communication all around a fortress outside the ditch.

Curtain: The part of the fortress that connects with the bastions.

Ditch: A large, deep trench made around the whole body of works.

Embrasure: Openings for guns made with widening angles from within for sweeping advantage.

Escarp or Scarp: A steep bank below the fort.

Flank: Any fort part designed to defend another part by rifle or artillery fire.

Garrison: Fort personnel.

Glacis: Gently sloping earthwork from fort to country, able to be covered by artillery fire.

Loophole: Narrow, vertical hole for shooting through ("find the loophole").

Magazine: A heavily built building for storing ammunition and extra supplies.

Palisade: Strong, pointed wooden stake, a unit in a fort wall.

Parapet: A defense of earth or stone; the exterior of the rampart.

Rampart: A mound of earth capable of resisting artillery fire. It should be wide enough on the top to allow the passage of troops and guns, and it is surmounted by the parapet.

Redoubt: A small, self-defensive, heavily constructed work without flanking protection.

All forts of the Great Lakes have their own history as well as their mutual causes. Examples:

–Old Fort William, Thunder Bay, Ontario, should be combined with a visit to the enclosure at Grand Portage, Minnesota (very close). Both were established by the same fur company; both have voyaguer-rendezvoux re-enactments. The larger re-enactment, at Fort William, mimics the wild and wooly times when more than a thousand trappers, company agents, and Indians got together to swap for pelts, blankets, alcohol or knives and to sing a little and carouse a lot. Exciting, colorful, and worth making a special trip to see, it begins the second weekend in July. (See Chapter 24)

–Fort Michilamackic, Mackinaw City, Michigan, has its entrance tucked under the south approach to the Mackinac Bridge. One of the oldest continuing archeological digs in North America, the fort with the lengthy name puts on several major re-enactment events a year, plus a continuous program of light and sound effects to make your self-guided tour as realistic as possible. School, barracks, church, quarters for officers' families, and mess hall are within the walls. This fort, built by the French and ceded to the British (who were massacred by Indians), was replaced by the one on Mackinac Island and should be seen in combination with it. 616-436-5563.

–Forts of the Niagara River–Fort Erie, Fort George, and Fort Niagara–make a historic trio extremely close to the falls. The story of the War of 1812 is told behind these ramparts, usually made more dramatic by small squads of marching men in brilliant uniforms. The sorry tales of disease and stupid (to modern thinking) tactics that senselessly cost lives is toned down while the volume is up on everyday life and keeping your powder dry.

–Fort Henry, Kingston, Ontario, has the biggest layout of them all. The gray stone walls of the fort were once the principal stronghold of Upper Canada. With an extensive collection of nineteenth-century military equipment, daily summer military drills are performed by the hundred-and-twenty-five-member Fort Henry Guard. Tour the fort, climb up the walls to look out over Lake Ontario, stay to see the special sunset ceremony on Wednesday and Saturday evening, and don't try to pat the billy-goat mascot. It's a good idea to call ahead, as the Guard is sometimes on tour. 613-543-2951.

And don't forget Fort York in Toronto, Fort Meigs in Toledo, the Military Establishment at Pentang on Georgian Bay, and Fort Malden in Amherstburg–the troops of summer make destinations of their own.

For more information:
Ontario Tourism, 800-ONTARIO.
New York State Tourism, 800-CALL NYS.
Michigan Travel Bureau, 800-5432-YES.
Ohio Tourism, 800-BUCKEYE.

87.

Wilderness Goals In Big-Lake Country

These are areas without settlement, roads, or visible intrusions. You know the air is full of the present–just turn on your pocket radio. But that's profanity in the cathedral. We go to the wilderness to hear birds and windsongs, to unwrap the cocoon, the long strands of propriety, obligation, clock-watching, duty-rendering, and noise.

There are magnificent wilderness parks within easy reach of Great Lakes destinations. The Boundary Waters Canoe Area between Minnesota and Ontario, Algonquin Provincial Park a little east of Georgian Bay, and the softer-toned Adirondacks Park in New York represent a sampling. Killarney and Pukaskwa Provincial Parks, unpaved enclaves on Georgian Bay and Lake Superior, and the back reaches of Michigan's Porcupine Mountains State Park all have sparse to nonexistent human populations.

The basic requirement for a wilderness experience is just that—experience. You must know what you are doing. Real wilderness is something you go into training for, with camping, hiking, and overnights wherever. Tell your plans to someone and carry emergency gear (life jackets are essential); don't expect to live off the land; take nothing but pictures and leave only your footprints. The parks have registers and rules, and local outfitters have a delightful array of gadgets and booklets to help out .

Boundary Waters Canoe Area Wilderness— BWCAW, as it is designated on most maps—is a million-acre network of several thousand pristine lakes and streams, many of them linked only by overland portages. No motors are allowed, and most designated campsites consist of a fire grate and pit toilet. The solitude of BWCAW is maintained by a visitor quota system, with eighty-seven entrance points. Permits are required from May through September 30 and may be obtained from the U.S. Forest Service Gunflint Ranger Station in Grand Marias or from area resorts and outfitters. Full-service outfitters at Ely or along the Gunflint and Sawbill Trails at Gunflint Lake or Seagull River will provide canoes, camping and cooking equipment, and trip routing. Even if this is just a one-day adventure, outfitters will be happy to set you up. Since BWCAW ties in with Quetico Provincial

Park, be sure to have border-crossing info with you. North and west but also with the BWCAW, Voyageurs National Park, on the border, is dominated by thirty lakes, accessible only by boat. There are more than a hundred primitive campsites. However, unlike BWCAW, Voyageurs allows motorboats without size or horsepower restrictions. There are also a great many fully equipped campgrounds on the southern edges of the park. Call 800-622-4014.

Algonquin Provincial Park consists of three thousand square miles (seventy-six hundred square kilometers) of rugged hills and lakes and is crisscrossed with hiking trails and canoe routes. You can enter the park at several places around the perimeter, although there is only one through road, Highway 60, across the southwest corner. A visitors-center film tells the story of the park's wildlife, geology, and history, with exhibits and a bookstore. One of the center's big attractions is its view, a grand sweep of landscape that makes you want to paint. The Algonquin Logging Museum puts its ax into the past with life-size reconstructions, including a "camboose" camp and working log dam and chute. It's open from May until Thanksgiving. There are three lodges, eight campgrounds, picnic spots, and wilderness outfitters, with wonderful isolated distances and plenty of naive fish who think you're bringing dinner. 705-474-6634 or 800-387-0516.

The Adirondacks Park, the least remote of the three, is both a region and a park, where the winter Olympics were held on Lake Placid, and world-class resorts are found at Lake George and Lake Champlain. Yet, six million acres and widely spaced roads make it an almost total getaway; it's dubbed the last great wilderness area of the east.

Get your widest possible lens out for views from the summit of Whiteface Mountain, via an eight-mile toll road, or reach the high meadows on a Whiteface chairlift, running all summer. Near Wilmington.

Along the northern portion of the Ausable River, exits 34 and 35 off I 87, lies Ausable Chasm, a rather awesome and gorgeous gorge. Nearly all the main roads are marked as scenic highways, so the hunt for your particular spot in the wilderness can't be a waste. Adirondacks Park Visitor Interpretive Center, Paul Smiths, 518-327-3000, or Newcomb, 518-582-2000. Adirondack Regional Information, 800-487-6867.

For more information:
New York Tourism Information, 800-CALL NYS.
Ontario Tourism, 800-ONTARIO.
Minnesota Tourism, 800-657-3700.
Michigan Tourism, 800-MICH-YES.

88.
Of Lighthouses and Diving Voyages

> "They (the Great Lakes) are swept by dismasting blasts as direful as any that lash the salted wave; they know what shipwrecks are, for far out of sight of land...they have drowned many a midnight ship with all its shrieking crew."
> —Ishmael, in Herman Melville's *Moby Dick.*

We have come to the varied shores, squinted out over long blue horizons, and touched the fifty-two thousand square miles of surface. Yet no one has really seen the Great Lakes until they have "gone downstairs." Whether or not they are broiling with twelve-foot waves or are placidly mirroring the sky, beneath these enormous expanses lies a still, chilled world of ghosts and phantoms, eerie rooms at rakish angles, silent decks, and lightless cargo holds. There are cups that held the watchman's coffee, anchors that weren't lowered, ropes waving like thin flags in the current.

Anywhere from four thousand to ten thousand shipwrecks lie strewn across the bottom of the Great Lakes—mute witnesses to the wrath of storms or to careless navigation, untended repairs, unheard distress signals, and fog-bound collisions. The saltless water freezes into ice rapidly; captains daring the gales of November had top-heavy masts before they knew it, causing a ship to keel over and flood to its grave.

Without brine to corrode a ship's metal, the wrecks stay in firm shape longer than in the ocean. A plague of zebra mussels is threatening to blanket the bottom of the lakes with a brown tarp, but they are not the problem that barnacles present and can be knocked off ships fairly easily.

There are still a few wooden hulls from the late 1700s, when the United States was in its infancy and hundreds of schooners plied the lakes with cargoes of fur and raw materials. Then came steam over sails and iron hulls over wooden ones. In early days, a compass and experienced captain were the only navigational instruments on board; now, radar, sonar, and fewer ports for the new long ships have reduced the chances of a ship sinking near Keweenaw Point on Lake Superior or Tobermory between Lake Huron and Georgian Bay.

The primary concern for exploring the bottom, of course, is that the diver knows his or her level of skill, has passed certification, has the proper gear, and flies the right flag.

Lake Superior: The three hot areas for diving are around Isle Royale (six major wrecks), the Alger Underwater Preserve near Munising (five), and the waters around Whitefish Point (five), where among others, the *Edmund Fitzgerald* went down. Visit the dandy (but small) Whitefish Point Maritime Museum, concentrating on local disasters.

Lake Michigan and the Straits of Mackinac: This area is full of possibilities, adding up to twenty large ships, five in the Green Bay area, five in the Straits, five in the Manitou Passage Underwater Preserve, and five in Sheboygan, Wisconsin. There are also several ships in the southern waters near Chicago, where the steamer *Eastman* sank with more than eight hundred people out on an excursion for families, shocking the nation in 1913.

Lake Huron: There are three underwater preserves and one park. Five Fathom National Marine Park, at Tobermory, Ontario, is perhaps the most compelling destination, with clear waters and underwater grottos, in a scenic area where hundreds of ships have been lost. Nine wrecks are major sites.

At Alpena, in the Thunder Bay Underwater Preserve, in the waters north of the Thumb, and in the Sanilac Shores Preserve, schooners, freighters, and at least one brig lie quietly about. In November, 1913, the same year the *Eastman* sank, the worst lake storm ever recorded hit with blizzard strength, sinking or wrecking over twenty ships, as well as smashing port facilities forever.

Lake Erie: Here, the Sandusky waters have the biggest pile-up of ships, with others near Cleveland. There are some relics from the War of 1812, but steamers and barges are also among the leftovers.

Lake Ontario: Although some archeological research is going on among the naval leftovers in western Lake Ontario, diving in the lake is most popular at the eastern end. It is said that the whole Thousand Islands area is a mine field for old bottles, dishes, and miscellaneous goodies.

If you are qualified for diving, start with the local visitors center for information or ask a marina operator, at a sporting-goods stores or fishing-gear outlet.

DAN (Divers Alert Network) has hotlines for recompression chambers, evacuation services, and emergency treatment. Call DAN at 919-684-8111.

Below the water is one story; along the shore, there's another—the life-saving lighthouse.

Before harbor bells and deep-throated foghorns, radar, sonar, satellite radio, and devices that nature can still outwit, a ship's safe passage relied on the captain's experience, his compass, and—as darkness fell—a light upon the shore. For countless centuries, this meant a bonfire on a beach or hilltop.

The first steadily tended Great Lakes light was put up in 1781 by the British on a roof of Fort Niagara (it was theirs at the time), and it burned whale oil. Eventually, more than two hundred lighthouses marked the coast. The first lights were dim until French scientist Augustin Fresnel devised a system of prisms that gathered light and refocused it into one concentrated beam. Made in France, the lens came in several sizes and were much sought-after.

For sheer aesthetics, lighthouses are winners. The silhouette of a regal tower with its glass housing and encircling balcony against a red and orange sky has inspired a wealth of paintings and photographs. The keeper's quarters were often quite handsome, built with architectural quality. Enough of them have been turned into museums and are open to make lighthouse tours a real consideration.

The cover girl of all Lakes lights is the sturdy yellow brick tower atop majestic one-hundred-and-seventy-foot Split Rock in Minnesota, near Two Harbors. Although the light is not in operation, on November 10 there is a ritual lighting in remembrance of the

Edmund Fitzgerald, the famed freighter that vanished in a Lake Superior storm. (See Chapter 22.)

The Sodus Point Light at Sodus Point, New York, had its own Paul Revere event in 1813 when an advancing British fleet was spotted on Lake Ontario and a rider was sent to warn the countryside. There's a museum in the restored keeper's house. (See Chapter 84.)

Split Rock Lighthouse on Lake Superior was built in 1905 after a November gale disabled eighteen ships

Marblehead Lighthouse at Bay Point, Ohio (near Sandusky), named by Civil War prisoners held nearby, is the oldest active light tower on the Great Lakes. It's open four times a summer, and the keeper's house/museum is nearby. (See Chapter 62.)

The light at Whitefish Point, Lake Superior, went temporarily out in the storm that sank the *Edmund Fitzgerald*. There's a small top-class museum, and the video tells the story of this and other ships. It's near a wide sandy beach. (See Chapter 30.)

Unusually short and boxy, the Michigan City, Indiana, lighthouse (it looks more like a local library) is an easy-to-reach source of lake lore. Close to Chicago and Detroit expressways. (See Chapter 19.)

There are lights on the Apostle Islands and Isle Royal (Lake Superior), on the Manitous and in Door County (Lake Michigan), on Manitoulin and Presque Isle (Lake Huron) and Presque Isle, Pennsylvania; additional lights are at the ends of piers or on little islands of their own. Meet a few of these silent sentinels. Listen to the wind whistling around the tower or the buoy bell sounding. A lighthouse is almost a sacred place.

For more information:

Great Lakes Lighthouse Keepers Association, P.O. Box 580, Allen Park, MI 48101.

Great Lakes Historical Society, 480 Main Street, Vermilion, OH 44089.

National Park Service, Maritime Initiative (with a database containing much information about U.S. lighthouses), P.O. Box 37127, Washington, D.C. 20013-7127. 202-343-9508.

Addendum

Crossing the Border

Visitors to Canada can claim a refund for some of the tax paid on accommodations as long as it was less than a one-month stay. Certain goods are also eligible for tax refunds.

Goods and Services Tax = 7 percent.

Manitoba Sales Tax = 7 percent.

Quebec Sales Tax = 6.5 percent.

You qualify for a refund if you are not a resident of Canada, if you stay at least forty-eight hours and have the original receipts, and if you spend at least $400 (Canadian) or more on accommodations and/or eligible goods for each tax you are claiming. All three conditions must be met. The authorities do not accept photocopies of receipts.

Goods qualify for a refund if:

You paid a tax on the goods,

You bought the goods to use outside of Canada,

You remove the goods from Canada within sixty days of purchase.

If you buy a vehicle, you must provide the original bill of sale along with a copy of the vehicle's registration in your own country.

There is no refund for the tax paid on:

Meals and beverages,

Wine, liquor, beer, or other alcoholic beverages,

Tobacco products,

Transportation, such as train, planes, bus, or car rentals,

Services such as dry cleaning, shoe repairs, auto repairs, and hair care,

Entertainment and movies,

Rentals of campsites, tents, houseboats, travel trailers, or recreational vehicles,

Cruise-ship cabins or train berths,

Automotive fuel,

Any goods consumed or left in Canada.

A booklet explaining the details (it includes a form to be used for mailing in your request for a refund) is available at the border in duty-free shops.

You must be on your way out of Canada to receive a refund, be able to provide photo identification, have your purchases ready for the shop staff to examine, and provide proof of export if the goods are not in your possession.

The maximum you can claim at a participating duty-free shop is $500 (Canadian).

For more information, call toll-free from anywhere in Canada: 800-66VISIT.

From outside Canada, call: 613-991-3346.

Index

A

B

G

Q

W